Dodge Challenger AND Charger

2006–Present

HOW TO BUILD AND MODIFY

Randy Bolig

CarTech®

CarTech®

CarTech®, Inc.
838 Lake Street South
Forest Lake, MN 55025
Phone: 651-277-1200 or 800-551-4754
Fax: 651-277-1203
www.cartechbooks.com

© 2016 by Randy Bolig

All rights reserved. No part of this publication may be reproduced or used in any form or by any means, electronic or mechanical, including photocopying, recording, or by any information storage and retrieval system, without prior permission from the Publisher. All text, photographs, and artwork are the property of the Author unless otherwise noted or credited.

The information in this work is true and complete to the best of our knowledge. However, all information is presented without any guarantee on the part of the Author or Publisher, who also disclaim any liability incurred in connection with the use of the information and any implied warranties of merchantability or fitness for a particular purpose. Readers are responsible for taking suitable and appropriate safety measures when performing any of the operations or activities described in this work.

All trademarks, trade names, model names and numbers, and other product designations referred to herein are the property of their respective owners and are used solely for identification purposes. This work is a publication of CarTech, Inc., and has not been licensed, approved, sponsored, or endorsed by any other person or entity. The Publisher is not associated with any product, service, or vendor mentioned in this book, and does not endorse the products or services of any vendor mentioned in this book.

Edit by Paul Johnson
Layout by Monica Seiberlich

ISBN 978-1-61325-550-6
Item No. SA340P

Library of Congress Cataloging-in-Publication Data
Names: Bolig, Randy, author.
Title: Dodge Challenger & Charger : how to build & modify 2006 to present / Randy Bolig.
Other titles: Dodge Challenger & Charger
Description: Forest Lake, MN : CarTech, [2016]
Identifiers: LCCN 2015016423 | ISBN 9781613252154
Subjects: LCSH: Challenger automobile--Customizing. | Challenger automobile--Motors--Modification. | Dodge Charger automobile--Customizing.
 | Dodge Charger automobile--Motors--Modification.
Classification: LCC TL215.C44 B65 2016 | DDC 629.28/722--dc23
LC record available at http://lccn.loc.gov/2015016423

Written, edited, and designed in the U.S.A.
Printed in the U.S.A.
10 9 8 7 6 5 4 3 2

Title Page:
Although the grille of the 2011 Charger featured Dodge's distinctive "cross hair," it was slightly revamped. The grille became a double-bar design. This grille continued until the next redesign in 2015.

Back Cover Photos

Top:
The Chrysler LX lineup of cars is truly impressive. From left to right are the Chrysler 300, Dodge Charger, Magnum, and Challenger.

Middle:
A heavy-duty clutch should be part of a high-performance engine build when you're using a manual transmission.

Bottom:
A non-stock camshaft is necessary when you alter the powerband of the engine. The Hemi engine in your Challenger, Charger, 300C, and Magnum wagon is known to respond well to engine-upgrade modifications. I've seen as much as a 27-hp increase just by swapping the camshaft in a 5.7-liter engine.

CONTENTS

About the Author 4
Acknowledgments 4
Preface 5
Introduction 6

Chapter 1: Choose Your Ride 8
   Dodge Charger 2006–2010 9
   Dodge Charger 2011–2014 14
   Dodge Challenger 2008–2014 18
   Chrysler 300 2005–2014 23
   Dodge Magnum 2005–2008 27

Chapter 2: Basic Engine Identification 30
   5.7-Liter Hemi 2003–2008 31
   5.7-Liter Hemi 2009–2014 33
   6.1-Liter Hemi 2005–2010 36
   6.4-Liter Hemi (392) 2011–2014 38
   Engine Accessories 40
   Intake Manifolds 41
   Transmissions 42
   Rear Ends 44
   Hemi Engine Technology 46
   Variable Camshaft Timing 47

Chapter 3: Bolt-On Performance 49
   Programmable Tuners 49
   Custom Tuning 52
   Project: DiabloSport I-1000 Installation 53
   Cold-Air Intakes 57
   Project: Cold-Air Kit Installation 61
   Headers 65
   Stock Exhaust System 68
   Performance Exhaust Systems 71
   Performance System Types 72
   Project: TTi Full Exhaust Installation 75
   Nitrous Oxide 80
   Throttle Body 85
   Clutch Assembly 89
   Project: Ram Clutches Performance Clutch
      Installation 91

Chapter 4: Modifying Your Engine 95
   Supercharger and Turbocharger Design 96
   Project: ProCharger Supercharger Installation 101
   Fuel Selection 109
   Intercooler 110
   Built-In Durability 111
   Pistons 111
   Connecting Rods 114
   Crankshaft Dampener 116
   Harmonic Balancer 117
   Cylinder Heads 118
   Camshaft 122
   Stroker Engines 126
   Valvetrain 129

Chapter 5: Custom-Built Engine Packages 132
   Buy or Rebuild 132
   Cost Considerations 135
   Quality and Reliability Factors 135

Chapter 6: Suspension, Brakes and Chassis 140
   Front Suspension 140
   Rear Suspension 141
   Tires 141
   Springs and Shocks 141
   Noise Isolation 142
   Step-Out 142
   Bushing Basics 142
   Frame Details 144
   Project: Hotchkis Suspension Installation 145
   Racing Considerations 152
   Strut Bracing 154
   Body Bridging 156
   Roll Bar or Roll Cage 157
   Suspension Upgrades 159
   Aftermarket Brake Upgrades 164
   Performance Brake Kits 167
   Wheel Alignment 173

Source Guide 175

DEDICATION

To my wife and social activities coordinator, Paula, and "the kids," Jason, Misty, Cortney, and Kaylyn. Were it not for their understanding and support when I took a chance at this career, I would have never accepted the challenge and life change that got me to this point. I would probably still be driving a truck and shoveling coal!

ABOUT THE AUTHOR

Randy Bolig has been working on cars and involved in the car hobby since he bought his first car at age 14. Buying the car before he could drive it gave him the opportunity to work on it, learn about the ins and outs of auto mechanics, and build the car the way he wanted. He had two years to build the car so that it was ready to go when he could finally, and legally, drive it.

His passion for cars caught the attention of many locals, and he began to help them with their cars. Eventually, his automotive knowledge and persistence helped him land a job as an automotive magazine editor in 2001. Not only was he the editor of *Mopar Muscle* magazine, he also edited several issues of *Muscle Car Review* and launched the all-late-model Hemi performance magazine *Mopar Now*. Randy's technical knowledge allowed him to work on the cars he was photographing and writing about, combining the talents of a mechanic, writer, and photographer.

In 2014, Randy was fortunate to be able to start his own company and work with many of the manufacturers that he had dealt with in the past, only this time on a more personal level without corporate "directives." These days, Randy lives in Lakeland, Florida, and remains involved in the industry. You can find several of his bylines in places such as *Mopar Collector's Guide*, *Cars & Parts*, and various automotive websites.

ACKNOWLEDGMENTS

When Chrysler first introduced the late-model Hemi cars in 2005, I was editor of *Mopar Muscle* magazine. I knew at the time that these 21st-century muscle cars were going to be a big thing. Little did I realize how right I was. The Magnum, Charger, 300, and Challenger were the cars that breathed new life into Dodge's muscle car history. Until then, Dodge was basing its muscle persona on . . . who are we kidding? Before the third-generation Hemi came along, no real "muscle" had been built since the mid-1970s.

When I began writing this book, I knew that I could not do it alone. I had a lot of material to gather and images to take and supply. I knew that I needed help, and a lot of it.

Therefore, I would like to acknowledge some of the people and companies that made this possible. First, I need to thank my wife, Paula. Without her support, I would have never been able to pull this off. I was traveling often and had to leave the family at home; she didn't complain too often and the locks were never changed, so all went well.

Next, I need to thank Dave Weber of Modern Muscle, Ken Jones of ProCharger, and Eric Hruza of shopHemi.com. If it weren't for those guys allowing me to invade their shops and get most of the images and information that I needed, this book definitely would not have materialized.

Finally, I want to thank you. If you had no interest in this subject, there would have been no reason to compile all of this information. I just hope that you find some, if not most, of the material, worthwhile reading.

PREFACE

Before I began to compile the information required to write this book, I was asked why. Why would I want to take the time to compile all of this information about late-model Hemi-powered cars? The answer was easy: I wanted to do something that might help people.

From 2001 to 2014, when I was the editor of *Mopar Muscle* and *Mopar Now* magazines, I noticed a huge shift in the Mopar hobby. Many people were coming to the hobby because they had discovered the 2006 and later Dodge/Chrysler cars. This included the Charger, Challenger, Magnum, and 300 cars. It didn't matter what car show or cruise night I went to, these cars were prevalent.

Despite the popularity these cars were gaining, it seemed that no one in the publishing world was paying attention. The magazine industry was not developing articles that pertained to these vehicles. If a late-model-Hemi owner wanted to upgrade his or her ride, they were on their own to search the Internet and hope they could find reputable information. It was at this time that I launched a late-model-Hemi performance magazine to cater to these enthusiasts. The magazine seemed to be a hit with readers, but for some reason, the corporate machine did not feel it was viable and shuttered the project. That was in early 2014, and I knew that enthusiasts needed help. Enter the decision to create this book.

When I was the editor of *Mopar Muscle*, I tried to develop each month's issue with an emphasis on helping people. Sure, the magazine was easy to do because I enjoyed what I did, so it wasn't really like work, but ultimately, if an issue went out the door without content that could help someone, I would have called it quits.

So, this book is my way of helping people. Gathering this information and compiling it in this book is a way I can direct enthusiasts when they decide that it's time to modify their car. I could have taken the easy route, simply showed how to bolt on a few simple parts, and called it done, but who does that really help? There's so much more to these cars than just bolting a few parts to them.

With that said, let's get to it. Let me and the people who helped me show you what it takes to modify your late-model Hemi-powered car with everything from some simple bolt-ons to getting "in deep" and really modifying things to make your car be the best it can be.

And thanks for letting me help.

INTRODUCTION

When you review the history of the muscle car, not many vehicles are as iconic as the Dodge Charger. Let's face it, when it came to the movie *Bullitt* and the television show *Dukes of Hazzard*, it was a Charger that the movie industry called upon to be the hero car. For many car enthusiasts, the reign of the Charger ended in 1974. Gone was the two-door conveyance with a big engine. Or was it?

In 2005 Chrysler introduced the latest generation of the Dodge Charger, the LX. Because the name was synonymous with muscle cars during the 1960s, it seemed like a natural fit, even if the name *Charger* wasn't the first choice of Dodge designers. The then-all-new 2006 Charger was successfully marketed as contemporary, with provocative styling and substance, and all of the convenience of a modern sedan.

Not only was there once again a rear-wheel-drive Charger, but Chrysler was also building a 300 (touring sedan) and a Magnum wagon. All were designed as rear-wheel-drive vehicles with an available Hemi V-8 engine! It was official: Chrysler was once again building rear-wheel-drive "muscle" cars. Immediately, though, controversy ensued. Many purists cried foul when Chrysler decided to use the iconic Charger name on the new four-door sedan. That's right: The LX Charger was delivered with four doors instead of a history-repeating two.

According to Craig Love, vice president of Rear-Wheel-Drive Product Team, Chrysler Group, "With proven rear-wheel-drive technologies and the legendary Hemi engine, we are able to produce a modern muscle car with everyday functionality. The all-new Dodge Charger offers an exceptional blend of performance, safety, and flexibility that today's market demands." Although the purists were scoffing the name, Chargers, 300s, and Magnums were flying off the showroom floors. The American public loved the car for its good looks and dependability (even with four doors), and performance enthusiasts found it to be a great platform to accept upgrades.

Some fans, however, did not embrace the LX cars because these Dodge fans wanted something to compete with Ford's new Mustang. Many felt that the four-door Charger didn't fit the bill. But according to some at Chrysler, the redesigned Charger was never intended to compete with the new Mustang. Performance enthusiasts were taken aback at Chrysler's thought process. How could Chrysler not answer the challenge that Ford had thrown down!

Despite criticism, initial Charger sales topped 30,000 units by November of its inaugural year, 2005. The new Charger was an immediate success despite having those two extra doors. At first I must admit, I, too, was a bit confused by a four-door sedan receiving the Charger name. I was initially one of the guys screaming "What the . . ." but then I finally drove one. I was sold: I knew that car was here to stay.

The success of the new Dodge Charger could only mean one thing: Another iconic car would probably be making an introduction. Retro was hot, but whatever Chrysler came out with next had to be a car that could go head to head with the Mustang. This meant that it could have only two doors. In 2008 that introduction occurred with the new SRT Challenger.

Finally Chrysler fans had a rear-wheel-driven car with a V-8, and *two doors*! The limited production run of 2008 cars immediately sold out, and Chrysler scrambled to make sure that in the following year enough cars were built to supply anyone who wanted one.

With the immediate popularity of the new Charger, 300C, Magnum wagon, and then the Challenger, it was just a matter of time until the aftermarket started making performance-enhancing parts for enthusiasts. Unfortunately, there was really no "gathered" information to let enthusiasts know what was available and what worked, until now.

During my stint as editor of *Mopar Muscle* magazine, I felt that these new muscle cars from Chrysler were going to be the cars that literally saved Chrysler's performance heritage. Unfortunately, it was tough to convince the powers that be that we needed to expose these cars for what they were, performance cars. After a few years of adding an

INTRODUCTION

occasional article to the pages of *Mopar Muscle,* I finally convinced the bean counters that a magazine dedicated to late-model Hemi performance was needed. Unfortunately, after four issues they canceled the all-late-model magazine and left enthusiasts without any place to find compiled information. That is why I came up with the idea for this book.

What you have in your hands is what I feel can help you accomplish your performance goals with your Magnum, 300, Charger, or Challenger. Maybe you want to find out how you can add some power and reliability to your car using a few simple bolt-on items. I test several primary bolt-on performance adders and tell you if they work. There is no need for you to guess at what you need; this book has the answers. Maybe you want to add some serious power to your car by adding a supercharger. I explain how they work and show you how to install one. If you're in the market for an upgrade suspension, again, congratulations, you're on the right path.

How To Build & Modify the Dodge Challenger and Charger: 2006–Present is not simply a guide to bolt-on accessories for your Charger, Challenger, 300, and Magnum. This book is an in-depth look into what you can do to modify, upgrade, and improve every aspect of your car's performance.

The LX/LD and LC/LY platforms underwent many changes over the nine years that are covered in this book, so I wanted to make sure to help you figure out what options and changes pertain to the year car that you have. This way, you know exactly what you need to acquire to make your car exactly the way you want it.

CHAPTER 1

CHOOSE YOUR RIDE

From 2005 to 2014 Chrysler Corporation built some great cars. When the Charger, 300C, and Magnum were introduced as 2006 models, fans of Chrysler/Dodge automobiles once again had a V-8–powered, rear-wheel-drive car. It was built on what Chrysler called the LX platform, and the Charger, 300C, and Magnum shared a lot of very similar suspension characteristics, which allowed interchangeability of many parts.

The full-size LX platform was developed in the United States and built in Brampton, Ontario, Canada. It replaced the previous LH platform, which was designed for use in front-wheel-drive cars. This new platform design allowed the cars to be easily changed to rear- and all-wheel-drive configurations.

Because Mercedes-Benz was involved, a lot of that company's ideas are built into it, including the S-Class Mercedes-Benz front and E-class rear suspensions. Even the design of the firewall and floorpan is derived from Mercedes-Benz. Even though Chrysler had already chosen to build a rear-wheel-drive platform for production before the merger took place, hooking up with Mercedes-Benz allowed the use of existing technologies, including the A580 5-speed electronic automatic transmission, rear differential/suspension, as well as stability control and steering.

The Mercedes-Benz–derived independent rear suspension and differential is contained within a module that is mounted in a cradle and isolated from the body. The LX platform was the first Chrysler vehicle to receive an independent rear suspension (IRS). The cradle attaches to the car as a unit and can be removed from the car as a complete assembly. The front suspension/engine mounting is also via a cradle mount.

In 2006, if you were looking for the quickest sedan in the Dodge lineup, you wanted the SRT Charger. It came from the factory with a tire-frying 6.1-liter Hemi packing 425 hp. The SRT package gave owners a car that was performance oriented, complete with race-bred handling and world-class stopping power. In testing, the SRT Charger showed 0-60 mph times in the low-5-second range, a 0-100-0 mph in the mid-16-second range, and braking capability from 60 to 0 mph in approximately 110 feet. The car also featured an SRT-exclusive hood scoop. (Photo Courtesy Fiat Chrysler Automobiles US LLC)

In 2008, Dodge introduced the Challenger. Once again, Chrysler was building a V-8–powered rear-wheel-drive muscle car. The platform used was to be the LX, but the shorter wheelbase that was actually developed was called the LC platform. The LC is virtually the same as the LX, except that it was approximately 4 inches shorter to support the Challenger's wheelbase.

Dodge Charger 2006–2010

The 2006–2010 Dodge Charger is based on Chrysler's LX platform. This platform is also the base for the 300C, and with slight modifications was used for the Challenger as well. For this reason, many chassis parts interchange. Equipped with the Hemi V-8, the Charger could reach 60 mph in around 6 seconds. Although the initial base engine was a 3.5-liter V-6, the 2.7-liter V-6 was added to the option list in mid-2007. When dealers saw the car for the first time, they were asked to choose from the name choices Intrepid, Magnum, and Enforcer. The dealers actually wrote in the name Charger. Ralph Gilles of Mopar confirmed, "It was never supposed to be called a Charger."

2006

In 2006 the Charger was available in one of two trim levels: the base SE and the sportier R/T.

Engine choices were designated by trim level. The SE came with a 3.5-liter V-6 with 250 hp. If you wanted more, the R/T had a 5.7-liter Hemi V-8 with output rated at 340 hp and 390 ft-lbs of torque. Chargers that were equipped with the optional Road & Track Performance Group or Daytona R/T package gave an extra 10 hp with stiffer suspension and bigger

Although considered a performance car, the 2005 and later Dodge Charger has never received a manual transmission. Even though this has been a bone of contention for many Mopar enthusiasts, Chrysler maintains that the Challenger is the "muscle" of the group. (Photo Courtesy Fiat Chrysler Automobiles US LLC)

Have you ever seen a station wagon in hot pursuit? Dodge has long been known for making top-performing police vehicles, but when the Magnum wagon got the nod, police personnel received it only half-heartedly. Although the Magnum wagon is a great wagon for the family, some of the driving maneuvers that police encounter really stretch its handling capabilities (Photo Courtesy Fiat Chrysler Automobiles US LLC)

CHAPTER 1

The 2006 Dodge Charger is a full-size, four-door performance sedan that shares many of its mechanical components with the Chrysler 300 and Dodge Magnum. The angular headlights and large cross-hair grille definitely give the car an "in-your-face" appearance. The distinctive body character line that begins at the rear flanks adds some styling flair to the aggressive look. Based on the same Mercedes-Benz–derived suspension platform that carries the Chrysler 300 and Dodge Magnum, the Dodge Charger offers a very roomy interior and an exceptionally smooth ride. The interior of the Charger looks almost identical to that of the Magnum, and even the engine choices are very similar. Dodge called this the LX body style until 2011, when a redesign occurred. (Photo Courtesy Fiat Chrysler Automobiles US LLC)

The Dodge Charger SRT8 Super Bee became available in 2007. The new Super Bee was the first special-edition LX Charger released from Chrysler's SRT group. The car featured a special Detonator Yellow paint scheme with a blacked-out hood and deck-lid face. The sides of the car were adorned with Super Bee logos on the front and rear fenders.

Inside, the car featured contrasting yellow stitching on the seats, steering wheel, and even the shift knob. The Super Bee option was designed for the enthusiast that wanted to own an SRT Charger, but didn't feel the need for some of the extra bells and whistles (such as navigation) that the SRT8 delivered.

Like other SRT vehicles, this car was powered by the 6.1-liter Hemi V-8 with 425 hp and 420 ft-lbs of torque. It delivered an additional 85 hp over its R/T brother. That's 25-percent more than the 5.7-liter Hemi. (Photo Courtesy Fiat Chrysler Automobiles US LLC)

brakes. A 5-speed manually-shiftable automatic transmission came standard on all models.

An SRT8 version of the Charger debuted at the 2005 New York International Auto Show. A 425-hp 6.1-liter Hemi powered this new high-performance version. It also featured upgraded Brembo brakes and interior and exterior updates. The 6.1-liter Hemi was the only engine available in the SRT8 Charger. Upgrades such as retuned shocks, firmer spring rates and bushings, and stiffer anti-sway bars gave it a 1/2-inch-lower ride height and also helped create a better handling package.

2007

Because it was only one year old, the Charger received only minor changes in 2007. A base-level 2.7-liter V-6 engine joined the lineup, and all-wheel-drive variants were available at all trim levels, except the high-performance SRT8. Bigger powerplants than the 2.7 V-6 were also available: the 3.5-liter V-6 and the 5.7-liter Hemi V-8 with 340 hp. The Hemi also acquired a multi-displacement system (MDS). This new technology shuts down four of the eight cylinders when full power is not needed. This system improved fuel economy slightly. The high-performance SRT8 was again available and came with a 6.1-liter Hemi V-8, again with 425 hp.

The 2007 Charger came in three main trim levels: SE (base), R/T, and SRT8. The Charger R/T generally had the same equipment as the lower-trim models, but added the 340-hp 5.7-liter Hemi V-8. The Enhanced R/T Performance Group was reported to add 10 hp to the V-8. The Daytona Package added to the

Enhanced R/T Performance Group by offering unique decals, paint colors, and instrument panel customization.

The SRT8 once again came standard with the larger 425-hp 6.1-liter Hemi V-8, a sport-tuned suspension, 20-inch forged wheels, and more powerful brakes. This was the first year of the new SRT8 Super Bee Special Edition package. The Super Bee option added unique graphics and a black/yellow color theme.

2008

When the 2008 Dodge Charger was released, it came in four trim levels: SE (base), SXT, R/T, and SRT8. All but the SRT8 were offered with the optional all-wheel drive. Although the R/T was similarly equipped as the SXT, an upgrade to the R/T again added the 340-hp 5.7-liter Hemi V-8 with dual exhaust and an enhanced Auto Stick transmission. The Daytona Edition and Road & Track performance packages added a sport-tuned suspension and steering, and a special exhaust system that reportedly added 10 hp to the V-8.

The SRT8 once again came standard with special hardware and trim that distinguished it as the top performance model. Some of these items still included the larger 425-hp 6.1-liter Hemi V-8 and a specially tuned and lowered suspension. A Super Bee Special Edition package (for the SRT8 only) came with unique graphics over special blue exterior paint.

When the Charger was first introduced in 2005, one of the key design elements that grabbed enthusiasts' attention was the headlight cluster. The sharp edges and distinctive design let no one be confused about what car it was.

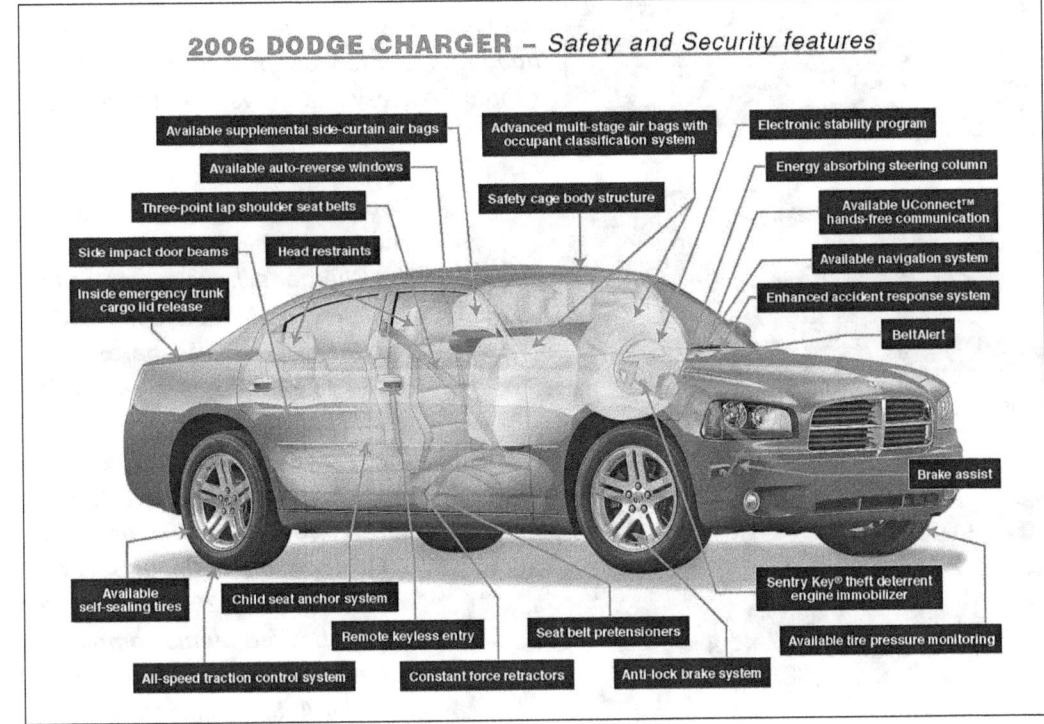

As illustrated by Chrysler, the new Dodge Charger included many safety features. (Photo Courtesy Fiat Chrysler Automobiles US LLC)

CHAPTER 1

When the Charger was first introduced, the largest engine available was the 5.7 Hemi. The Gen III Hemi featured 340 hp. Engineers changed conventional small-block design by first raising the camshaft's location within the block. This change allowed them to shorten the pushrods. The use of shorter pushrods reduces valvetrain flex and inertia, and allows the simplification of the rocker arm design. The Hemi has a deck height of 9.25 inches, and it has a cylinder bore of 3.92 inches. (Photo Courtesy Fiat Chrysler Automobiles US LLC)

When the LX Charger was first introduced, it was available in SE, SXT, and R/T models. The top of the performance heap was the R/T, equipped with a 5-speed automatic transmission and the 5.7-liter Hemi producing 350 hp. The R/T also received an upgraded suspension and tires. Visual additions included a special front fascia with a chin spoiler and a black rear spoiler. As retro touches, the Daytona R/T featured black "Hemi" decals on the hood and rear fender and high-impact colors. (Photo Courtesy Fiat Chrysler Automobiles US LLC)

Dodge introduced its re-entry into NASCAR in 2005 based on the Charger silhouette, replacing the Intrepid. Unlike the Intrepid, the Charger actually shares rear-wheel drive and a V-8 engine with its NASCAR counterparts. The Dodge Charger race car made its NASCAR Nextel Cup Series debut at the Daytona 500 at Daytona International Speedway on February 20. Four Dodge factory-backed teams competed in the race. (Photo Courtesy Fiat Chrysler Automobiles US LLC)

CHOOSE YOUR RIDE

The 2006 Dodge Charger Daytona R/T model was distinguishable by the addition of special exterior paint colors, an exclusive front fascia with a chin spoiler, a black honeycomb grille, unique black "Daytona" and "HEMI" decals, R/T badging, and a black rear trunk lid spoiler. The Daytona model also included large, bright dual-exhaust tips, and 18-inch polished wheels with low-gloss jet-black painted insets. The powerful Hemi engine featured a color-coordinated engine cover.

The interior of the 2006 Dodge Charger Daytona R/T featured performance front seats with suede inserts and embroidered "Daytona" logos on the front headrests. Body-color accent stitching appeared on the front and rear seats as well as on the leather-wrapped steering wheel. The center stack featured a matching body-colored bezel, and finally, a "Daytona Limited Edition" display with a sequentially numbered limited edition Daytona badge on the instrument panel completed the unique interior. (Photo Courtesy Fiat Chrysler Automobiles US LLC)

2009

For 2009, styling of the Charger went virtually unchanged. The 5.7-liter Hemi now made 368 hp, but the new, variable valve timing and multi-displacement technology allowed the Hemi to nearly match the fuel economy of the 3.5-liter V-6. The 2009 Charger was again available in SE, SXT, R/T, and SRT8 trim. Although rear-wheel drive was standard, the SXT and R/T were available with all-wheel drive.

The Charger R/T included the SXT's popular items as standard and added the 368-hp 5.7-liter V-8. The Road & Track performance package included a sport-tuned suspension and steering. The Daytona package is identical to the Road & Track package, but it adds a more performance-oriented exhaust, a unique exterior paint color, and "Daytona" graphics.

The SRT8 was equipped much like the R/T with the Road & Track

The 6.1-liter Hemi was designed to be an SRT-exclusive engine and a big brother to the 5.7-liter Hemi. The 6.1-liter is a heavy breather, with the use of new high-flow cylinder heads, a specially designed intake manifold, and tube-style exhaust manifolds that closely resemble headers. The exhaust manifolds have individual primary tubes that are encased in a stainless steel shell. Also unique to the 2005 6.1-liter Hemi engine are larger-diameter valves and reshaped cylinder ports. These design improvements in the heads allow for maximized airflow. The intake manifold was designed with large-diameter runners for high-RPM tuning capabilities. (Photo Courtesy Fiat Chrysler Automobiles US LLC)

package, but again added the bigger 425-hp 6.1-liter Hemi V-8, high-performance brakes, hood scoop, limited-slip differential, and different exterior trim. The SRT8 Super Bee package added bright Detonator Yellow or Hemi Orange paint and Super Bee graphics.

2010

The last year of this body design was 2010; not many changes were made. The 2010 Charger was available in base, 3.5, Rallye, R/T, and SRT8 trim. All-wheel drive was optional on all but the base and SRT8 models. The R/T package added to the Rallye package with a 5.7-liter Hemi V-8 engine with 368 hp. You could also get the Road & Track package that included a sport-tuned suspension and steering, and a rear spoiler. The Super Track Pak added performance tires, a steeper rear-axle ratio, and upgraded brakes and shock absorbers.

The SRT8 was equipped much like the R/T with the Road & Track package, but again added the bigger 425-hp 6.1-liter Hemi V-8, high-performance brakes, a hood scoop, and a limited-slip rear differential.

Dodge Charger 2011–2014

In 2011, the Charger saw a major style and platform change. The platform (now designated LD) supported an all-new body design that added styling cues from the late-1960s Charger. These cues included the scalloped doors and hood. The redesign not only looked good, it gave the Charger better aerodynamics with a lower hood line, leaned-back windshield, headlights that were blended into the body line, wheel openings that are closer to the wheels, lower sills, and a smoother underbody. All of these design features were instrumental in helping to increase the fuel mileage rating.

2011

The 2011 Charger was available in SE, SXT, R/T, SRT8, and SRT8 Super Bee (limited) trim packages. The Blacktop package was new for this year and is the same as the R/T, with the exception of painted wheels and a special blacked-out grille.

The R/T received a 5.7-liter Hemi V-8 that was now good for 370 hp and 395 ft-lbs of torque. A 5-speed automatic transmission and rear-wheel drive were standard, but all-wheel drive was again optional on all but the SRT version. An all-new 6.4-liter Hemi V-8 making 470 hp and 470 ft-lbs of torque powered the SRT8. A 5-speed automatic transmission and rear-wheel drive were standard.

2012

The 2012 Charger was available in SE, SXT, R/T, SRT8, and SRT8 Super Bee trim. The R/T again received a 370-hp 5.7 Hemi V-8 engine. The Super Track Pak added 20-inch wheels, a sport-tuned suspension, performance steering, upgraded brakes, and an adjustable stability control system.

The 2012 SRT8 featured a bigger 6.4-liter Hemi V-8 engine with 470 hp, an adaptive high-performance suspension, 20-inch wheels, adjustable stability control, upgraded brakes, a rear spoiler, and special styling. The SRT8 Super Bee was essentially a more affordable version of

In 2011, the face of the Charger received a complete redesign. Not only did the car look entirely different, it also received a number of significant upgrades. The most noticeable change was the new exterior styling. This new Charger sported what many consider an even more aggressive looking front-end design. On the sides and hood of the car, defined scallops harkened back to the late 1960s and early 1970s Charger. The rear of the car featured a new, futuristic taillight treatment. The taillight has been compared to a racetrack around the car's rear end. The SRT8 model was dropped for this year. (Photo Courtesy Fiat Chrysler Automobiles US LLC)

CHOOSE YOUR RIDE

the SRT8, with some of the luxury bells and whistles eliminated. It also did not have the adaptive suspension. The Super Bee still had its own personality, via the Stinger Yellow or Pitch Black paint, accented with Super Bee emblems and graphics, a unique grille and hood treatments, and special cabin features including striped cloth seats with embroidered Super Bee logos on the front headrests.

The 2011 redesign created what was widely believed to be the most aggressive looking Charger ever. It was an instant hit and performance enthusiasts flocked to it. This 2012 SRT8 model was powered by a 6.4-liter Hemi V-8 that made 470 hp and 470 ft-lbs of torque. A 5-speed automatic transmission was standard. Screams from passengers were also optional. (Photo Courtesy Fiat Chrysler Automobiles US LLC)

The most striking change that occurred with the 2011 redesign was probably the taillights. They featured a whopping 164 LEDs that are arranged in a distinctive "racetrack" pattern around the rear of the car. (Photo Courtesy Fiat Chrysler Automobiles US LLC)

2013

The 2013 Charger was available in five trim packages, SE, SXT, R/T, SRT8, and SRT8 Super Bee trim. The R/T added a 5.7 Hemi V-8 engine, again with 370 hp and 395 ft-lbs of torque. The Road & Track package added to the R/T Plus with a black grille, 20-inch alloy wheels, and a performance calibration for the engine and transmission.

The Super Track Pak option, which was only available on the Charger with the Road & Track package, added a sport-tuned suspension, performance steering, upgraded brakes, and the adjustable stability control system.

The SRT8 featured the bigger 6.4-liter Hemi V-8 making 470 hp and 470 ft-lbs of torque. A 5-speed automatic and rear-wheel drive were standard. The SRT8 Super Bee was, again, a less luxurious, more affordable version of the SRT8.

2014

The Charger for 2014 received no significant changes. With a redesign slated for 2015, the 2014 style was a simple carry over. The 2014 Charger was offered in SE, SXT, R/T, SRT8, and SRT8 Super Bee trim. The R/T added the 370-hp 5.7 Hemi V-8 with a 5-speed transmission. The Road & Track package added a black grille, 20-inch wheels, a rear deck lid spoiler, upgraded brakes, a Sport mode setting for the transmission, and steering wheel mounted paddle shifters. The Super Track Pak tacked on a performance-oriented stability control system, performance brakes, sportier/firmer steering, and an even firmer suspension.

The SRT8 model added the bigger 470-hp 6.4-liter Hemi V-8 engine, a sport suspension, 20-inch wheels,

DODGE CHALLENGER AND CHARGER: HOW TO BUILD AND MODIFY

CHAPTER 1

The Charger saw a major redesign in 2011 that included the interior. The plastic used for the dashboard construction included leather-like graining, the seat fabrics improved, and the roof pillars were covered in headliner fabric in place of exposed plastic. Real aluminum trim embellished the dashboard, and the introduction of soft surfaces was a welcome addition. A new, smaller-diameter steering wheel, wrapped in soft leather, hosted buttons for radio tuning, volume, cruise control, and trip computer. (Photo Courtesy Fiat Chrysler Automobiles US LLC)

The redesign even afforded the Charger-distinct headlights a small revamp. Although the angular cut was definitely reminiscent of the previous Charger, new projector-beam headlights were used. (Photo Courtesy Fiat Chrysler Automobiles US LLC)

CHOOSE YOUR RIDE

In 2011, the 5.7-liter Hemi carried over from the previous year with 370 hp. Although the Hemi was the big-dog engine, the V-6 wasn't relegated to the rental-fleet cars any more. The Hemi was once again backed by a 5-speed automatic transmission, but featured updated shift programming. (Photo Courtesy Fiat Chrysler Automobiles US LLC)

Although the grille of the 2011 Charger featured Dodge's distinctive "cross hair," it was slightly revamped. The grille became a double-bar design. This grille continued until the next redesign in 2015. (Photo Courtesy Fiat Chrysler Automobiles US LLC)

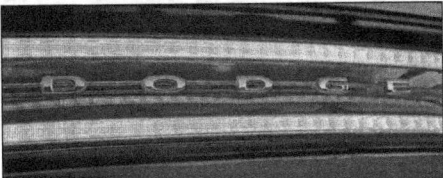

It takes 164 LEDs to create the racetrack-style taillight treatment that was introduced on the 2011 Charger. This was the first year that an American automotive manufacturer was able to design and implement such a taillight assembly. (Photo Courtesy Fiat Chrysler Automobiles US LLC)

Universal Pictures liked the newly redesigned Charger so much that they teamed up with Dodge in the action-thriller Fast Five (shown here are actors Vin Diesel, left, and Paul Walker, right). Dodge supplied multiple 2010 and 2011 Dodge Charger vehicles that were used in chase scenes throughout the movie. (Photo Courtesy Fiat Chrysler Automobiles US LLC)

DODGE CHALLENGER AND CHARGER: HOW TO BUILD AND MODIFY

the stability control system, launch control, upgraded brakes with red Brembo calipers, a rear spoiler, and other race-inspired styling features. The SRT8 Super Bee might have had fewer bells and whistles, but that just made it a more affordable version of the SRT8. It started by including most of the base R/T's equipment, but added the bigger 6.4-liter Hemi V-8, 20-inch wheels, unique exterior Super Bee graphics, black Brembo calipers, yellow and silver cloth upholstery with Super Bee logos on the front headrests, and heated rear seats.

Well, there you have the breakdown of the Charger offerings, but what if you are looking for something a little sportier? Maybe a four-door car just isn't what you had in mind. Enter the Challenger.

Dodge Challenger 2008–2014

If you're looking for a late-model Challenger, production actually started in 2008. The 2008 Challenger was a limited-production SRT model with only 6,400 U.S. models built. In a stroke of marketing genius, all were sold before they were even built. In addition, 500 Challengers were built for sale in Canada, and another 100 or so were built for sale in Mexico. Each 2008 Challenger has a limited edition numbered dash plaque.

The Challenger was loosely based on Chrysler's LX platform, but is slightly shorter than the 300 and the Charger. The LC-designated Challenger standard features included 20-inch alloy wheels with 245/45 high-performance tires, a sport suspension, and a rear spoiler. Options included a sunroof, navigation and music server system, and ultra-performance summer tires.

2008

The 2008 Challenger SRT8 had only one engine choice: a 6.1-liter Hemi V-8 with 425 hp and 420 ft-lbs of torque. The transmission was a 5-speed automatic, and no manual transmission was available for this inaugural year. The limited edition 2008 Challenger was available in three colors: Hemi Orange, Bright Silver Metallic, and Brilliant Black Crystal Pearl Coat. At the 2008 Barrett-Jackson Auction in Scottsdale, Arizona, Chrysler offered two 2008 SRT8s for charity. One was the very first car built, which sold for $400,000, and the other one was a B5 Blue car, the 43rd car built, which received a winning bid of $228,143.43.

The return of the Dodge Challenger in 2008 brought tire-smoking performance packaged in a head-turning design. Dodge offered the Challenger SRT only as a limited edition in 2008, and it was available in just three colors: Hemi Orange, Bright Silver Metallic, and Brilliant Black Crystal Pearl Coat. No manual transmission was available on the inaugural model. (Photo Courtesy Fiat Chrysler Automobiles US LLC)

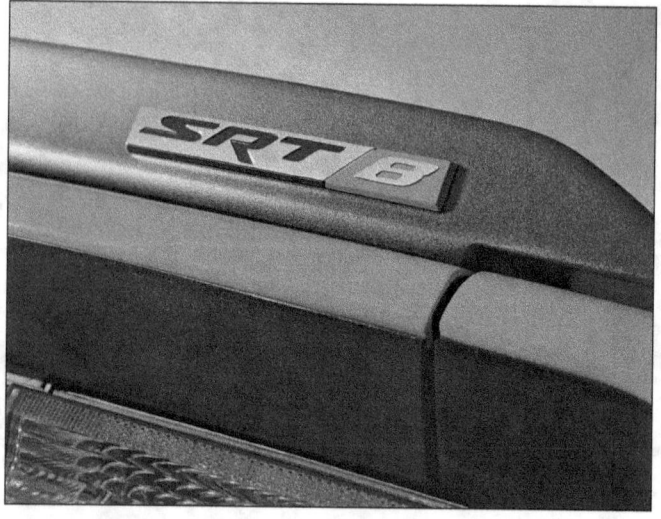

Dodge introduced and released the Dodge Challenger in 2008 as a limited-production SRT-only option. (Photo Courtesy Fiat Chrysler Automobiles US LLC)

CHOOSE YOUR RIDE

The grille in the new Challenger is an updated design, made to mimic the 1970 Challenger. (Photo Courtesy Fiat Chrysler Automobiles US LLC)

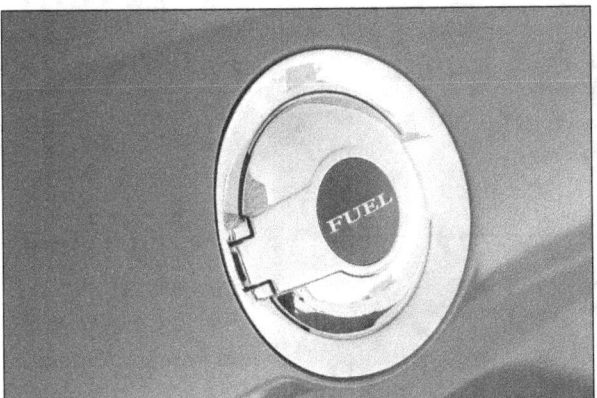

As iconic as the Challenger itself, the flip-open fuel filler door, reminiscent of Challengers past, was an element Dodge considered essential. This styling cue has remained with Challenger throughout the production run. (Photo Courtesy Fiat Chrysler Automobiles US LLC)

The biggest downfall in the release of the Challenger in 2008 was probably the unavailability of a manually-shifted transmission. (Photo Courtesy Fiat Chrysler Automobiles US LLC)

Exclusive to SRT8 cars, the front seats are well bolstered and fitted with suede-like inserts. These help keep you in place during aggressive maneuvers, yet are comfortable enough for daily driving. (Photos Courtesy Fiat Chrysler Automobiles US LLC)

DODGE CHALLENGER AND CHARGER: HOW TO BUILD AND MODIFY

2009

When the 2009 models were released, Dodge expanded the Challenger's available options with a couple of alternatives less intimidating than the SRT. This made the retro-styled Challenger more accessible. They started with a new base SE Challenger and fitted it with a V-6 engine and a 4-speed automatic transmission. If the base Challenger wasn't to your liking, the vehicle between the base Challenger and the SRT8 model was considered by many to be the best pick: the new R/T Challenger. It came with a 370-hp 5.7-liter Hemi V-8.

The year 2009 also brought back another iconic Mopar option, the Pistol Grip shifter. If you ordered the R/T, you could also get the Track Pak option, which featured a 6-speed manual gearbox, a limited-slip differential, Hill Start Assist (prevented rolling backward when starting on hills with the manual transmission), and a recalibrated, performance-oriented steering system. Challenger R/Ts with a manually-shifted transmission came with a retro shifter poking through the console. When equipped with the 6-speed gearbox, the 5.7-liter Hemi delivered an additional 5 hp.

At the top of the option packages was the SRT8. It came with an even more powerful 425-hp 6.1-liter Hemi V-8, black hood stripes, 20-inch alloy wheels, an even sportier suspension and steering than the R/T, a limited-slip rear, and Brembo brakes.

2010

The 2010 Challenger didn't receive any changes from the previous year. Trim levels were still arranged in line with the three engine choices. The base SE had a V-6, the

Finally, in 2009, the Challenger was fitted with a manual transmission. The Tremec TR-6060 6-speed gearbox, which is also used in the Viper, is connected to Challenger's Pistol Grip–esque shifter. (Photo Courtesy Fiat Chrysler Automobiles US LLC)

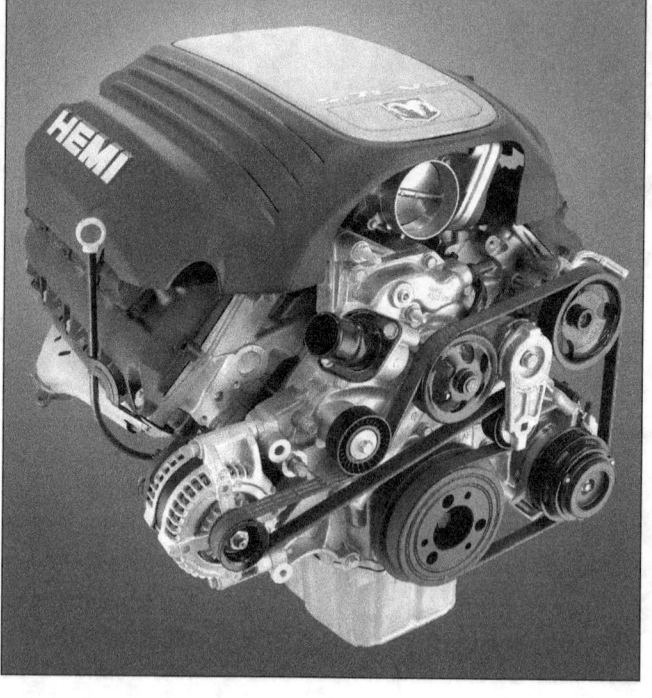

The 2009 5.7-liter Hemi was the first to receive MDS; it was standard on 2009 and later automatic-equipped Hemi cars. (Photo Courtesy Fiat Chrysler Automobiles US LLC)

R/T had the 372-hp and 400 ft-lbs of torque 5.7-liter Hemi V-8. The maximum-performance SRT8 came with a 6.1-liter Hemi V-8, still packing 425 hp and 420 ft-lbs of torque.

Again this year, if you purchased the R/T you could also order the Track Pak option, which featured the 6-speed manual transmission, a limited-slip rear differential, the Hill Start Assist, and a recalibrated performance steering system. A late-availability Super Track Pak included the regular Track Pak's equipment, plus ultra-high-performance tires, a larger rear stabilizer bar, performance brake pads, and a revised stability control calibration with an "ESP off" function. The 5.7-liter Hemi was paired with a 5-speed automatic transmission as standard equipment, but a 6-speed manual was also available as an option. If you chose the R/T's manual transmission, you increased power output to 376 hp and 410 ft-lbs of torque.

The SRT8 added dual scoops and black stripes to the hood, 20-inch alloy wheels, a suspension and steering arrangement that was more oriented to performance than the R/T, a limited-slip rear differential, and Brembo brakes. The SRT8 came with a 6.1-liter Hemi V-8, with either the automatic or manual transmission that was also found in the R/T.

2011

For 2011, the Challenger received a host of upgrades. Benefiting from many changes made to the suspension, brakes, and steering, the 2011 Challenger became even more capable of keeping up with its rivals when the road took some twisty turns. The new Pentastar 3.6-liter V-6 delivered a significant improvement in both power (up to 305 hp) and fuel economy. This was also the year that Dodge added the 392 Hemi V-8 to the SRT8 model. The 392-inch (6.4-liter) Hemi was now the top Hemi engine.

The 2011 Challenger again came in SE, R/T, and SRT8. The R/T once again had a 5.7-liter Hemi V-8, which was good for 372 hp and 400 ft-lbs of torque when connected to the standard 5-speed automatic transmission. Add the 6-speed manual transmission that was available when ordering the Super Track Pak group, and you increased output to 376 hp and 410 ft-lbs of torque. For 2011, the 5.7 Hemi (when equipped with the automatic transmission) included new fuel-saving cylinder-deactivation technology.

The SRT8 received all of the R/T's basic equipment, but the Track Pak added the 6-speed manual transmission. The SRT8 with the 392 Hemi Inaugural Edition received special blue or white paint, full body stripes, and other special exterior trim. Inside, you found two-tone white-and-blue leather upholstery and interior trim plus special 392 monogramming on the front seat headrests. The all-new 392-inch Hemi V-8 produced 470 hp and 470 ft-lbs of torque. The 5-speed automatic was standard, and a 6-speed manual was available with the Track Pak.

2012

Once again, there weren't many changes to the Challenger for 2012. You could still get the three basic packages, but now the SXT replaced the SE.

Just as in 2011, the R/T had the 5.7-liter Hemi V-8. When connected to the 6-speed manual transmission, the 5.7 delivered 376 hp and 410 ft-lbs of torque. When it was hooked to the available 5-speed automatic transmission, output dropped to 372 hp and 400 ft-lbs of torque. The R/T Classic

The 2011 Challenger was the recipient of a more powerful Hemi V-8 engine. The 5.7 Hemi's power was increased to 372 hp and the SRT version received the new 392 (6.4-liter) Hemi with 470 hp. All Challengers benefited from many changes and upgrades to the suspension, steering, and brakes. (Photo Courtesy Fiat Chrysler Automobiles US LLC)

CHAPTER 1

In 2011, Dodge completely overhauled the interior (including slight visibility improvements), and added sound insulation for a more subdued cabin experience. Many of the materials used in previous cars were replaced by better-quality materials. For instance, the dash featured a soft-touch material. (Photo Courtesy Fiat Chrysler Automobiles US LLC)

package included the R/T Plus items as well as 20-inch "heritage-style" wheels, black body-side stripes, and functional hood scoops. The Super Track Pak included even-higher-performance-oriented steering, brakes, shocks, tires, and stability control programming.

The SRT8 again had the 392 Hemi V-8 with 470 hp and 470 ft-lbs of torque; it also received all the R/T's basic equipment. The 5-speed automatic transmission was standard, and a 6-speed manual transmission was available with the Track Pak.

2013

For 2013, no significant changes were made to the Challenger lineup. The 2013 Challenger was available in three trim levels: SXT, R/T, and SRT8.

The R/T's 5.7-liter Hemi V-8 delivered 376 hp and 410 ft-lbs of torque when connected to the 6-speed manual transmission. When hooked up to the available 5-speed automatic transmission output dropped to 372 hp and 400 ft-lbs of torque. The R/T Classic package included the R/T Plus items as well as 20-inch heritage-style five-spoke wheels, black side stripes, and functional hood scoops. The Super Track Pak option included high-performance suspension/steering/brakes and revised stability control programming.

The SRT8 benefited from the R/T's basic equipment but added the larger 6.4-liter Hemi V-8. The 392-inch 6.4-liter Hemi V-8 produced 470 hp and 470 ft-lbs of torque. A 6-speed manual was standard, and the 5-speed automatic transmission was optional.

2014

The last year prior to a major redesign was 2014. The only real change for the 2014 model year was the edition of the SRT8 Core package. This year the Challenger was offered in four main trim levels: SXT, R/T, SRT8, and SRT8 Core.

The R/T received a 5.7-liter Hemi V-8 with a standard 6-speed manual transmission. In this configuration, you had 376 hp and 410 ft-lbs of torque. When connected to the available 5-speed automatic transmission, the 5.7-liter Hemi's output dropped to 372 hp and 400 ft-lbs of torque. The R/T Classic package included the R/T Plus items and 20-inch heritage-style wheels, black side stripes, functional hood scoops, and Xenon headlights.

The R/T Super Track Pak included a high performance suspension/steering and brakes, with performance-oriented stability control programming. The R/T Blacktop edition came with the Super Track Pak and added black 20-inch wheels, black exterior trim including the ordinarily silver fuel door, and a matte graphite-colored body stripe with red edges. The R/T Redline edition was available with or without the Super Track Pak package, and it featured 20-inch black wheels with red trim, a body stripe similar to the Blacktop's stripe, a body-color grille surround, metal pedals, and the T-handle shifter (available with automatic transmission only).

The SRT8 392 started with the R/T Plus' equipment and added the 6.4-liter Hemi V-8, launch control, performance-oriented stability control programming, high-performance brakes and steering, and adaptive suspension dampeners. The SRT8 Core was a new package for 2014. It was meant to be a stripped-down, more affordable SRT8. This meant no frills; it lost standard luxuries. In fact, the Core's interior is closer to the base SXT's equipment level. It even came with the entry-level six-speaker audio system.

The oomph on both SRT8 models (392 and Core) came from a 6.4-liter Hemi V-8 that produced 470 hp and 470 ft-lbs of torque. A 6-speed manual transmission was standard, and the 5-speed automatic was optional.

Chrysler 300 2005–2014

The 2005 Chrysler 300 was an all-new, rear-wheel-drive flagship sedan that replaced the Concorde and 300M. This redesign was a clear departure from the previous years' cab-forward design theme that Chrysler followed in the 1990s. The 300 represented the company's new direction and incorporated much Mercedes-Benz technology.

The Chrysler 300 was a well-equipped, elegantly styled vehicle that came in four trim levels: 300, 300 Touring, 300 Limited, and 300C.

The Chrysler 300C is the only level that had the available 5.7-liter Hemi V-8 engine (340 hp), which was the same engine found in the Challenger and Charger. It was mated to an electronically controlled 5-speed automatic transmission.

In 2005, the Chrysler 300 was introduced as an all-new, rear-wheel-drive "luxury" sedan. It replaced the Concorde and 300M. The 300 represented the company's new direction and made use of Mercedes-Benz technology, which was newly available to Chrysler. Available features of the 300C included the 5.7 Hemi V-8, stability control, and during mid-year production, all-wheel drive. (Photo Courtesy Fiat Chrysler Automobiles US LLC)

2005

In 2005, the Chrysler 300C was the first modern production vehicle in North America to feature cylinder deactivation when it went on sale in the spring of 2004. The MDS turned off the fuel consumption in four of the eight cylinders of the engine when V-8 power was not needed.

2006

When the 2006 models hit the showroom floor, it was difficult to tell the difference between them and the 2005 models; there were no significant changes.

2007

The 2007 Chrysler 300 was again available in four trim levels: 300, 300 Touring, 300C, and SRT8. Step up to the 300C and you had the venerable 5.7-liter Hemi V-8 that knocked out 340 hp and 390 ft-lbs of torque. The 5.7 again used the MDS, which selectively deactivated four of the engine's cylinders to save fuel in cruising situations. The beefy 6.1-liter Hemi V-8 that delivered tire smoke–inducing 425 hp and 420 ft-lbs of torque powered the performance-oriented SRT8.

The high-performance SRT8 model featured a more powerful Hemi, and also came with a rear spoiler, sport-tuned suspension, a stability control system that allowed more aggressive driving, 20-inch alloy wheels, and Brembo disc brakes with four-piston calipers.

The W. P. Chrysler Executive Series Package (available on Touring and 300C models) was an uncommon and not well-known option. It added 6 inches to the car's wheelbase and provided more space for rear-seat passengers.

The Chrysler 300C was introduced as an LX-platform car in 2005 and pays homage to the 300 letter-series lineage that was created 50 years before. All 300C models feature dual exhaust tips, large performance disc brakes, and unique chrome exterior trim. The 2005 300C was the first modern production vehicle in North America to successfully feature the Multi-Displacement System (MDS, or cylinder deactivation) when it went on sale in the spring of 2004. (Photo Courtesy Fiat Chrysler Automobiles US LLC)

Designed to be Chrysler's flagship luxury car, the 2005 300 models included an eight-way power-assisted driver's seat, manual tilt/telescoping steering column, and a premium cloth interior. This was also the year that the first Original Equipment Manufacturer application of Boston Acoustic Premium Sound System was initiated. If you opted for the 300C, you received upgraded features such as patented tortoise shell interior highlights, power tilt/telescoping steering wheel, rain-sensing wipers, adjustable pedals, Boston Acoustics six-speaker 288-watt digital amplifier sound system, seven-speaker 380-watt digital amplifier, and finally, GPS navigation. (Photo Courtesy Fiat Chrysler Automobiles US LLC)

According to Bob Lee, vice president of the Powertrain Product Team, "The MDS was part of the engine's original design. This resulted in a cylinder-deactivation system that is simple and completely integrated into the engine design. The benefits are fewer parts, maximum reliability, and lower cost."

The first-generation 5.7-liter Hemi could transition from running on eight cylinders to running on four cylinders in 0.04 seconds. This was done by keeping the valves in four opposing cylinders closed.

Although some energy is lost through the compression created, none of it is lost by pumping air through the valves. The system was able to increase fuel economy by roughly 10 percent. (Photo Courtesy Fiat Chrysler Automobiles US LLC)

CHOOSE YOUR RIDE

The new 2005 300C was an instant success. In the January 2005 issue of Motor Trend, the 300C was awarded Car of the Year honors, and editors heralded the car as "the rejuvenation of the great American full-size sedan." The Chrysler 300, they said, "evokes the vibrant American sedans of yesteryear, and steals the show in a highly competitive Car of the Year field." (Photo Courtesy Fiat Chrysler Automobiles US LLC)

As successful as the Chrysler 300 was after it debuted in 2004, the company was backed into a corner. How could they improve the car? Trying to redesign a car, especially while working through a bankruptcy issue, was a daunting task. For that reason, the 300 received only a cosmetic upgrade, rather than a complete redesign.

The sheet metal wrapping the 2011 300 features a beltline body line that is more pronounced, and is above the door handles rather than through them. The 300's new corporate grille and badge were designed to appear smaller to make the car look more streamlined. (Photo Courtesy Fiat Chrysler Automobiles US LLC)

2008

For 2008, the 300 was available in five trim levels: 300 LX, 300 Touring, 300 Limited, 300C, and SRT8. The 5.7-liter Hemi V-8 engine generating 340 hp and 390 ft-lbs of torque powered the 300C. The 300C was also available in all-wheel drive. The high-performance 300C SRT8 model was equipped relatively the same as the standard 300C, but came with the even more powerful 6.1-liter Hemi V-8 that cranked out 425 hp and 420 ft-lbs of torque. That helped this luxury cruiser boast 0-60-mph runs in the low-5-second range. The SRT8 also came with a sport-tuned suspension, 20-inch alloy wheels, Brembo brakes, special stability control calibration, and a rear spoiler.

If you opted for all-wheel drive or selected either of the 300C models, you received a 5-speed automatic transmission.

2009

The 2009 Chrysler 300 was available in LX, Touring, Limited, 300C, and SRT8 trim levels. All but the LX and SRT8 were available in an all-wheel-drive version.

The 300C had the new-and-improved 5.7-liter Hemi V-8 with 359 hp and 389 ft-lbs of torque. The 5.7-liter Hemi now featured variable valve timing that increased horsepower and torque for better performance. All-wheel-drive models received a new active transfer case that disconnected the front axle for better fuel efficiency and performance under normal driving conditions.

A comfort-tuned suspension debuted for those seeking a softer ride. Driving enthusiasts surely appreciated the new Chrysler 300C Heritage that featured the same sport-tuned steering and suspension as the Charger R/T Daytona.

The 300 SRT8's 6.1-liter V-8 cranked out 425 hp and 420 ft-lbs of torque. A 5-speed automatic transmission was standard.

2010

The 2010 Chrysler 300 is a full-size sedan that was available in Touring, Touring Plus, Walter P. Chrysler Signature Series, Limited, 300C, 300S, and

CHAPTER 1

The reshaped lighting included LED running lamps and optional Xenon bulbs. These upgraded features brought the 300C up to date with current lighting trends. (Photo Courtesy Fiat Chrysler Automobiles US LLC)

The redesign gave the rear of the car some attention that resulted in a much cleaner appearance, with exhaust finishers integrated into the valance and a chrome bar connecting the taillights. (Photo Courtesy Fiat Chrysler Automobiles US LLC)

SRT8 trim levels. Gone was the base LX.

Going with the 300C gave you the 5.7-liter Hemi V-8 engine with 359 hp and 389 ft-lbs of torque. It was also available in rear-wheel and all-wheel drive. A 5-speed automatic transmission was standard. The 300S added 20-inch wheels, and performance suspension, tires, and steering.

The 300 SRT8 started with the same equipment as the 300C, but added the even more powerful 6.1-liter Hemi V-8 with 425 hp and 420 ft-lbs of torque through a 5-speed automatic transmission. It also wore 20-inch wheels, Brembo brakes, special stability control calibration, a performance-oriented rear differential, and a rear spoiler.

2011

The Chrysler 300 had received an overhaul by the time the 2011 models hit the showrooms. Although the structure and exterior appearance remained relatively the same, almost every component had been revised or redesigned.

The 2011 Chrysler 300 was available in base, Limited, 300C, and SRT trim levels.

The 300C came with a 5.7-liter Hemi V-8 that was good for 363 hp and 394 ft-lbs of torque. It came in either rear-wheel drive with the 5-speed automatic transmission standard or all-wheel-drive. Although an SRT8 version powered by a 6.4-liter 392 Hemi V-8 with 470 hp was unveiled at the 2011 New York International Auto Show, it was not available this year.

The year 2011 saw changes to the 300's styling and structure. Styling changes were slight and the 300 retained a familiar look. But changes to the structure added strength, and a recalibrated suspension delivered an even better ride quality and handling. The 300C was powered by the 5.7-liter Hemi V-8 that was good for 363 hp and 394 ft-lbs of torque. Although rear-wheel drive and the 5-speed automatic transmission were standard, it could also be had with all-wheel drive. (Photo Courtesy Fiat Chrysler Automobiles US LLC)

2012

Despite a complete overhaul the previous year, the Chrysler 300 for 2012 received more changes and enhancements. Now, the new 8-speed automatic transmission was available with the V-6 engine, which could be paired with all-wheel drive. The three new/returning models for 2012 included the uniquely styled 300S, the high-luxury 300 Luxury Series, and the high-performance SRT8.

The 2012 Chrysler 300 was available in seven trim levels: base, Limited, 300S V-6, 300C, 300S V-8, 300C Luxury Series, and SRT8.

The 300C added the 5.7-liter Hemi V-8 engine. Since its inception in 2003, the Hemi's power has continually increased. This year, it was good for 363 hp and 394 ft-lbs of torque. The 300C and 300S V-8 not only received the 5.7-liter Hemi, but a 5-speed automatic transmission and rear-wheel drive were standard; all-wheel drive was optional.

Returning after a one-year hiatus, the SRT8 with the 6.4-liter Hemi V-8 was good for 470 hp and 470 ft-lbs of torque. Rear-wheel drive and a 5-speed automatic transmission were standard.

2013

For 2013, the 300's lineup was revised. All but the SRT8 versions came with the 3.6-liter Pentastar V-6 as the standard engine. However, the 5.7-liter Hemi V-8 was still available on the S and C trim levels. The SRT8 version came with launch control and an expanded range for its adaptive suspension, which offered three modes. Like the Challenger for this year, there was a new, more affordable version of the SRT8 called Core.

The 2013 Chrysler 300 was available in six trim levels: 300, 300S, 300C, 300C Luxury Series, 300C John Varvatos Collection, and SRT8. The 3.6-liter Pentastar V-6, which was available in all but the SRT version, produced 292 hp and 260 ft-lbs of torque. The 300S version of that engine came with minor tweaks (including a sport-tuned exhaust) that bump output to 300 hp. An 8-speed automatic was standard, as was rear-wheel drive. All-wheel drive was optional.

Optional on all but the base 300 was the 5.7-liter Hemi V-8, pumping 363 hp and 394 ft-lbs of torque. A 5-speed automatic and rear-wheel drive were standard, but all-wheel drive was optional.

The SRT8 received (in addition to most of the luxury features of the 300C) special styling and interior trim plus the high-performance 6.4-liter Hemi V-8 with 470 hp and 470 ft-lbs of torque. It also received special 20-inch wheels, high-performance tires, Brembo brakes, launch control, an adjustable sport suspension, and sport-tuned steering.

The Core version of the SRT8 included most of the high-performance hardware but did without the adjustable suspension and other "niceties." Both SRT8 versions boasted rear-wheel drive and a 5-speed automatic with paddle shifters standard.

2014

For 2014, the Chrysler 300 was available in the same six trim levels as in 2013: 300, 300S, 300C, 300C John Varvatos Luxury Edition, SRT8 Core, and SRT8. Other than just a few minor trim-level adjustments, the 300 was unchanged for 2014.

Dodge Magnum 2005–2008

The March 1, 2004, press release announcing the all-new 2005 Dodge Magnum touted among its virtues the benefits of a sport-utility vehicle (thanks to its available all-wheel drive) and towing capacity of up to 3,800 pounds. And it could do so while delivering the ride and handling of a sports sedan.

Power, load capacity, and good looks. In 2005, the Magnum R/T received the then-new 340 hp 5.7-liter Hemi V-8. An SRT8 model was available from 2006 until the car's demise, and it came with the 425-hp 6.1-liter Hemi engine. The all-wheel-drive version became an option in mid-year 2005 on SXT and R/T models. The Magnum wagon was on Car and Driver's Ten Best list for 2005. (Photo Courtesy Fiat Chrysler Automobiles US LLC)

CHAPTER 1

Unfortunately, despite the popularity of the "station wagon" and its sizable audience, on November 1, 2007, Chrysler announced that the Dodge Magnum would be one of four models discontinued after the 2008 model year. On March 28, 2008, production ceased. Ralph Gilles, then Chrysler Group Design Chief and head of the SRT division (and former head of Dodge Division), told the *New York Times* that Chrysler might revive the Magnum. As of this writing, it has not happened.

2005

The 2005 Dodge Magnum was available in three trim levels: SE, SXT, and R/T. The R/T was the introduction to V-8 power. The available 5.7-liter Hemi V-8, delivered a conservative 340 hp and 390 ft-lbs of torque. All Magnum wagons were rear-wheel drive, unless you specified all-wheel drive as an option (available mid-year). A 4-speed automatic transmission came standard with V-6 models, and the R/T and all-wheel-drive SXTs upgraded to a 5-speed automatic.

2006

Not much changed for 2006; the Magnum was still available in the SE, SXT, and R/T trim levels. The R/T still used the Hemi. All Magnum wagons were still rear-wheel drive, unless you specified all-wheel drive as an option. Mid-year, the 4-speed automatic transmission was replaced with the 5-speed automatic.

2007

In 2007, and SRT version entered the lineup. This year, you could get one of four main trim levels: SE, SXT, R/T, or SRT8. The R/T added the 5.7-liter Hemi V-8 with the MDS that was still good for 340 hp and 390 ft-lbs of torque. The R/T also received 18-inch wheels (19-inchers with all-wheel drive) and a slightly firmer suspension. A new R/T Performance Group package was also available for the Magnum R/T this year, and added 10 hp. The high-performance SRT8 was equipped similarly to the R/T but added the 6.1-liter Hemi V-8 that produced 425 hp and 420 ft-lbs of torque, 20-inch alloy wheels, upgraded brakes, a stiffer suspension, and special interior and exterior trim details.

SXT and R/T models could be ordered in either rear-wheel- or all-wheel-drive configurations. All others were rear-drive only. The SE came with a 4-speed automatic; all others came with a 5-speed automatic.

2008

Not much changed for 2008, except for a little more aggressive styling, as the Magnum's good looks were updated with a revised front fascia, newly sculpted hood, and a reshaped grille. Exclusive to this year's SRT8 model was a functional hood scoop. The 2008 Magnum was still available in four trim levels: SE, SXT, R/T, and SRT8. Engine and transmission options were the same as in 2007.

The SRT versions of the Charger and Magnum received a fresh-air scoop in the hood. Although the scoop was not directly connected to the air filtration system, it was still a sinister-looking setup. (Photo Courtesy Fiat Chrysler Automobiles US LLC)

Just like the Charger and the 300, the Magnum wagon was never offered with a manually-shifted transmission. (Photo Courtesy Fiat Chrysler Automobiles US LLC)

CHOOSE YOUR RIDE

The major selling point of the Magnum wagon was its hauling capacity. When the tow package was added, which consisted of a larger radiator and special leveling rear shocks, the Magnum R/T was rated to tow 3,800 pounds. The SRT is a performance version of the Magnum and is therefore not actually tow rated. With all of the seats in place, the interior boasted 27.2 cubic feet of carrying capacity. (Photo Courtesy Fiat Chrysler Automobiles US LLC)

Even during the Magnum's short-lived production run, the 5.7-liter Hemi was the engine of choice with most Magnum owners. The same engine (ratings and all) that powered the Charger, Challenger, and 300C, also powered the Magnum. That makes all car engines interchangeable by year specification. (Photo Courtesy Fiat Chrysler Automobiles US LLC)

The design layout of the Magnum was almost unchanged during its production run. (Photo Courtesy Fiat Chrysler Automobiles US LLC)

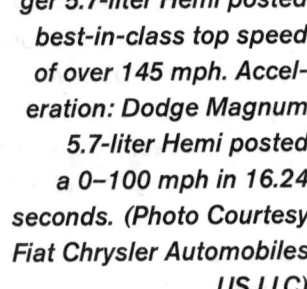

Like the Charger, the Magnum was available to law enforcement. When tested by the Michigan State Police, the September 2005 evaluation program included the following preliminary results: Top Speed: Dodge Charger 5.7-liter Hemi posted best-in-class top speed of over 145 mph. Acceleration: Dodge Magnum 5.7-liter Hemi posted a 0–100 mph in 16.24 seconds. (Photo Courtesy Fiat Chrysler Automobiles US LLC)

DODGE CHALLENGER AND CHARGER: HOW TO BUILD AND MODIFY

CHAPTER 2

BASIC ENGINE IDENTIFICATION

In the 1950s and 1960s, if you mentioned to someone that your car had a Hemi engine you immediately gained respect. The Hemi was known as a powerhouse, and in automotive circles, it was tough to beat. Sadly, the cost to build the Hemi and strangling insurance regulations led to the demise of the legend in 1972.

With the introduction of the 2003 model year, the legendary engine made a return. However, production of the engine actually began in June 2002 at the Saltillo plant in Mexico. In 2003, Chrysler showed a Hemi engine with a supercharger to the public. Using the 5.7 Hemi engine and a Whipple supercharger, that engine made 430 hp and 480 ft-lbs of torque. That doesn't sound like a lot, but for a completely new engine design, it was a start. The engine initially found its way into Dodge trucks.

For this, its third, generation of design, Chrysler incorporated some new build processes and design features. The block, for instance, is precision cast and the connecting rods are powder metal.

The Gen III Hemi was designed with two spark plugs per cylinder. One coil pack was over each spark plug, and a plug wire also connected from that coil pack to a spark plug on another cylinder (each cylinder shares a coil pack with another cylinder). This means that a separate coil fires each of the two plugs on a given cylinder. One spark plug fires during the power stroke to begin the combustion process and the second spark plug fires during the down stroke of the piston to help burn any residual fuel and hydrocarbons that didn't burn during combustion.

The 5.7-liter Hemi V-8 found in the new 2006 Charger Daytona featured 350 hp and 390 ft-lbs of torque. That's 10 horses over the previous year's 5.7-liter Hemi that came in the R/T Charger. Engineers at Chrysler say that the horsepower increase was accomplished by using a less restrictive intake system, and by moving to a straight-through muffler design instead of the previous years' three-pass muffler. A styling enhancement meant that the Daytona also received a color-matched engine cover. (Photo Courtesy Fiat Chrysler Automobiles US LLC)

BASIC ENGINE IDENTIFICATION

Over the years, the third-generation Hemi has undergone many revisions, and when looking for an engine, some of these revisions can affect choices in aftermarket parts. Do you have an idea of how you want to build your Hemi? Are you looking for a max-performance monster, or do you want to just add some bolt-on parts to increase the performance? Either way, you need to know which late-model Hemi you actually have.

5.7-Liter Hemi 2003–2008

The 5.7-liter Hemi engine made its 2003 debut in the Dodge Ram as the standard engine. That first generation was capable of producing 330 hp at 4,800 rpm, and 375 ft-lbs of torque at 4,200 rpm. The 5.7-liter Hemi engine was also available in the Dodge Durango.

By the time the 2005 model year cars were introduced, the 5.7-liter Hemi had become a proven performer, so it was a natural fit to make its way under the hood of the new LX-platform cars, including the 300 and the Magnum (eventually the Charger, in 2006). The Hemi was smaller and cheaper to build than the older LA-series small-block that it replaced, but produced more power and torque.

When building the engine, designers incorporated a very strong deep-skirt design into the block. The deep-skirted block made it possible to create a stronger, four-bolt support system for the crankshaft. This means that supporting the crankshaft are four bolts at each main bearing (two that mount vertically through the bearing cap, and two that mount horizontally through the block into the bearing cap). The new Hemi block is precision cast, and this allows it to be much lighter than other engines of the same relative size.

The pistons are made using a cast eutectic alloy, and are relatively light (413 grams). It's believed that using a relatively small cylinder bore and a long stroke can aid in reducing emissions, so the cylinder bores of the 5.7-liter Hemi were designed at 3.197 inches, and the crankshaft stroke comes in at 3.578 inches.

The connecting rod was also designed to minimize weight but keep some much-needed strength. The connecting rod is built using a powder metallurgy. This is the process

The 5.7 Hemi used in cars from 2003 through 2008 used short blocks that interchange between car and truck engines. The difference is that all cars since 2005 are MDS equipped with the solenoids and lifters. In 2007 the Ram and Durango also benefited from the addition of MDS. With the exception of a few minor sensor changes these short blocks are identical. (Photo Courtesy Fiat Chrysler Automobiles US LLC)

The 2003–2008 5.7-liter Ram with a 5.7-liter DR (truck) engine used a seven-rib front accessory drive; the front cover, water pump, and accessories do not interchange. This setup mounts the accessories high in front of the intake, prohibiting the use of car intake manifolds. (Photo Courtesy Fiat Chrysler Automobiles US LLC)

CHAPTER 2

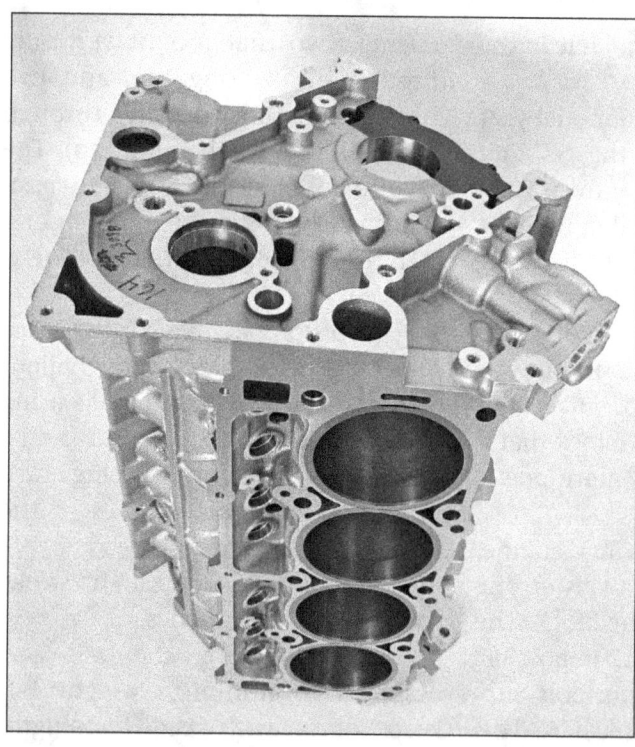

The cylinder block of the new Hemi is precision cast. This process of making the block allows it to be lighter than other 5.7-liter engines. This is accomplished even though it has a taller deck height than GM's equivalent V-8.

The Gen III Hemi uses a block with Siamese bores. Siamese cylinder bores are generally more stable than cylinder bores that are cast as part of the engine block. Siamese bores are often used with aluminum blocks because the steel cylinder inserts of the Siamese bores add rigidity.

of blending fine-powdered materials, and then compressing them into a desired shape or form. Once this "compacting" is complete, the connecting rod is then heated in a controlled atmosphere (called sintering) to bond the material/powder into the desired product.

The use of powder-metal technology eliminates the need to manufacture the product by traditional forging and metal removal processes (casting and machining), thereby reducing costs. Also, instead of using a through-bolt with a nut, as with previous engine designs, Chrysler employed a cap bolt. The result is a 6.24-inch connecting rod that is more than sufficient in stock applications.

The crankshaft has large inner counterweights but doesn't result in an unnecessarily heavy crankshaft. The crankshaft features radius leading-edge counterweights and is definitely performance oriented. The factory 5.7- and 6.1-liter Hemi V-8 crankshafts do interchange, but the reluctor wheel on the 5.7-liter uses three mounting bolts whereas the 6.1-liter uses four bolts.

The new Hemi also features a camshaft that is located considerably higher within the block than on previous V-8 designs to minimize the pushrod length required to operate the rocker arms. Shorter rocker arms

All 2008 and earlier 5.7- and all 6.1-liter engines have a 32-tooth reluctor wheel. All 2009 and later 5.7-liter engines have a 58-tooth reluctor wheel.

The stock rocker arms in your Hemi engine are a cast design. Although they perform well in your production engine and are interchangeable from 5.7 and 6.1, they can be considered a weak link when valvespring pressures are increased.

32   DODGE CHALLENGER AND CHARGER: HOW TO BUILD AND MODIFY

BASIC ENGINE IDENTIFICATION

You can identify a block that has the MDS by looking under the intake manifold. Four round solenoids are mounted in the block (one for each group of lifters); they receive electrical connectors from the harness. If you remove the MDS function, round nylon pieces, each with a retainer, are used to plug the holes.

deflect less, creating a more stable valvetrain. To help keep the weight down, the cam is a hollow-core billet piece. The stock 5.7-liter Hemi camshaft measures .477/.462–inch lift, and 255/236–degrees duration. As built, the stock valvetrain is good to around 6,200 rpm.

This first version of the 5.7-liter cylinder head is found on all Dodge trucks and passenger cars (not SRT). That usage makes it the most common head in the family. The intake runner is 161 cc, and typically flows around 250 to 260 cfm at .600-inch lift. The exhaust port is unusually small at 50 cc, and again, the exhaust port flows around 155 to 165 cfm at .600-inch lift.

In 2004, Chrysler introduced MDS on 5.7 Hemi engines installed in cars; it was added to Hemi-powered trucks later. The MDS turns off the fuel in four opposing cylinders when power is not needed. Chrysler estimated that the MDS saved nearly 100 million gallons of gasoline between 2005 and 2009.

The MDS is designed to selectively deactivate cylinders 1, 4, 6, and 7 to improve the fuel economy of a Hemi engine. All deactivated cylinders have unique hydraulic lifters that collapse when the MDS is activated, to prevent the valves from opening. Pressurized engine oil is used to activate and deactivate the valves. The oil is delivered through special oil passages that are drilled into the cylinder block, and the MDS solenoid valves control the flow. When activated, pressurized oil pushes a latching pin on each MDS lifter, which then becomes a lost-motion link. This means that the base of the MDS lifter follows the camshaft while the top remains stationary. The MDS lifter is held in place against the pushrod by an internal light-pressure spring, but it is unable to move because of the much higher force of the valvespring.

5.7-Liter Hemi 2009–2014

When 2009 arrived, the 5.7-liter Hemi (now designated Eagle) was modified to increase both power and fuel mileage. These changes included a higher compression ratio (from 9.6:1 to 10.5:1), better-flowing heads, intake and exhaust, and the all-new Active Intake Manifold. This manifold incorporated new-for-the-time technology. This design allows the intake to switch between using long or short intake runners by simply moving a flapper door. The ability to switch runner length can create better torque at low RPM and higher horsepower as the RPM increases. The intake manifold integrates the manifold absolute pressure (MAP) sensor, fuel rails, and electronic throttle control.

Also new in 2009 was the variable valve timing (VVT) system. The camshaft and timing sprocket used with the VVT system is completely different from that used on earlier engines. The VVT system is operated by hydraulic pressure via the engine's pressurized oil to actuate cam phasing. The hydraulic-roller camshaft has oil passages machined in the front that direct the oil to "move" the cam phasing sprocket, and either advance or retard the engine's timing as required.

The 5.7-liter Hemi has an oil control valve (OCV) that is mounted behind the timing cover. The OCV is an electro-hydraulic pulse-width-modulated solenoid that controls oil pressure to the camshaft phaser sprocket by taking engine oil and routing it to the two oil passages inside the valve. The newly designed camshaft phaser replaced the standard camshaft timing chain sprocket, and is attached to the camshaft by

CHAPTER 2

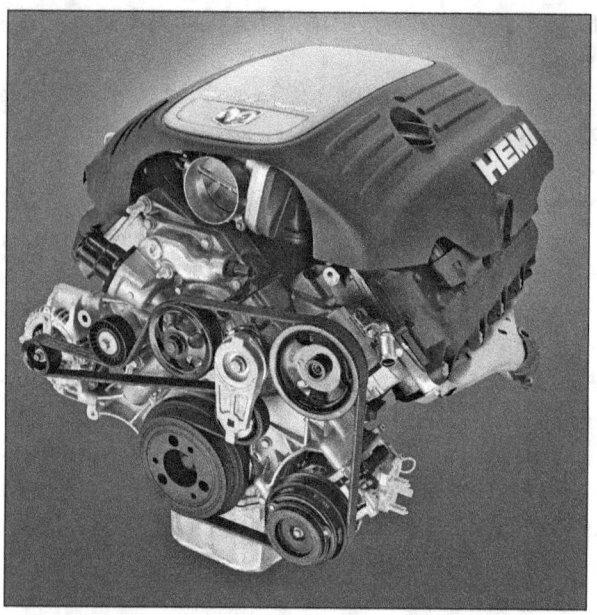

When the engineers started to make improvements to the 5.7-liter Hemi for 2009, they began by increasing the engine's ability to breathe. One way to accomplish this was to incorporate a new technology, variable cam timing (VCT). The job of VCT is to boost power and torque levels throughout the entire engine RPM range. Other mechanical upgrades included structural upgrades to the crankshaft, inclusion of a dual-mass crankshaft dampener, and finally, the addition of floating wrist pins. The combination resulted in a rating of 380 hp and 404 ft-lbs of torque. That's an increase of 10 and 8 percent, respectively, over the previous 5.7-liter Hemi. (Photo Courtesy Fiat Chrysler Automobiles US LLC)

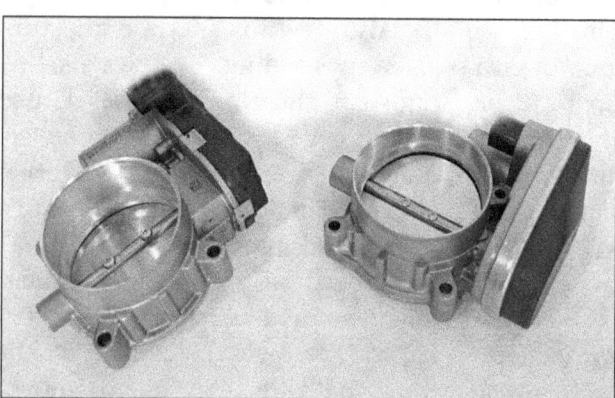

Another big change in 2009 was with the Hemi's throttle body. Until this time, a Continental Corporation VDO-design throttle body was used. In 2009, Mopar started using the Magnetti-Marelli throttle body on all of their Hemi cars.

a single bolt. The phaser itself has internal vanes, and the OCV regulates the oil flow to either side of the vanes.

This oil flow to either side causes the phaser to rotate right or left and thus change the position of the camshaft's orientation. One oil gallery supplies oil to the OCV and two separate oil galleries supply oil to the number-1 camshaft bearing for advancing and retarding timing via the camshaft phaser.

A newly redesigned piston-and-rod assembly this year allowed the pistons to use thinner walls with a stronger-alloy wrist pin that was now a floating-style pin. The crankshaft was also stronger, and the oil pump featured a higher flow capacity to help with the VVT system.

The use of the VVT system also meant that a new, deeper timing chain cover and water pump were used. The timing cover from 2008 and older engines does not fit on 2009 and later engines with the VVT.

The cylinder heads featured a few revisions, too. The intake and exhaust ports were redesigned with the exhaust-port floor raised and larger intake valves (2-mm larger) used. The Eagle cylinder head is found on 2009

The Hemi's new VVT system improves fuel economy in two ways. First, it reduces the engine's pumping effort by closing the intake valve later during the combustion cycle. Second, it increases the expansion process of the combustion event. This expansion allows more work to be transferred to the crankshaft instead of being released out of the exhaust port as wasted heat. Essentially, VVT improves engine breathing, which improves engine efficiency and power.

The VVT system does not keep the valves open longer; instead, it opens them later in the combustion cycle, and also closes them later in the cycle. This is done by oil pressure rotating the camshaft forward a few degrees. If the intake valves normally open at 10 degrees before top dead center (TDC) and close at 190 degrees after TDC, the total duration is 200 degrees. The opening and closing times can be shifted using the hydraulic mechanism that rotates the timing of the camshaft ahead a little as it spins. So the valve might open at 10 degrees after TDC and close at 210 degrees after TDC.

DODGE CHALLENGER AND CHARGER: HOW TO BUILD AND MODIFY

BASIC ENGINE IDENTIFICATION

In 2009 the 5.7-liter Hemi received an all-new piston and connecting rod assembly design. The new pistons were built with thinner walls to reduce weight, and the piston's wrist pin was now a "floating" style instead of a press fit. You can see that the wrist pin on this assembly (upper left) has a different look to it. When a wrist pin is "floating" the fit of the piston to the wrist pin is not a press fit; the piston is able to move on the wrist pin. (Photo Courtesy Fiat Chrysler Automobiles US LLC)

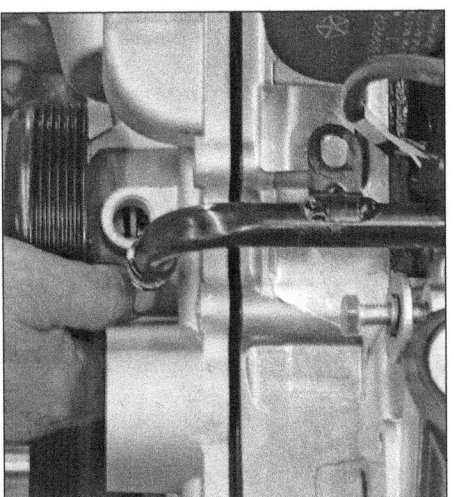

The water pumps also changed for 2009 and later engines. The face of the pulley on 2008 and earlier engines is flat, and the impeller fits in a recess in the timing chain cover. On 2009 and later models, the pulley is beveled, and the impeller is flush with the water pump housing, because the timing chain cover does not have a recess for water flow.

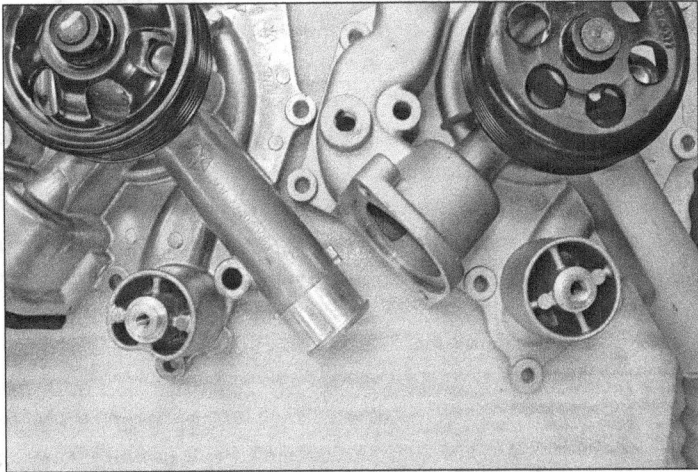

Another small difference between 2008 and earlier water pumps (right) and 2009 and later units (left) is the boss that supports the belt tensioner pulley.

The oil pump in your third-generation Hemi differs significantly from the previous small-block (LA) design. The oil pump itself is driven by the crankshaft timing gear rather than by an intermediate shaft as on V-8s of the past. Notice the grooves in the center of the pump; these grooves mesh with the crankshaft timing gear.

DODGE CHALLENGER AND CHARGER: HOW TO BUILD AND MODIFY

and later non-SRT passenger cars and trucks with VVT. The intake manifold has been changed on all applications and is model specific.

Note that 2009–2012 5.7-liter Hemi engines with the 6-speed manual transmission do not have MDS.

6.1-Liter Hemi 2005–2010

In 2005, engineers at SRT (Chrysler's performance division) set out to create their own version of the third-generation Hemi. They developed a 6.1-liter version of the Hemi engine. They increased displacement by boring the 5.7-liter Hemi's cylinders 3.5 mm larger.

The SRT group mandated that the engine must make more power than the standard 5.7-liter Hemi to be considered a success. They accomplished their goal with an increase of 25-percent more power (an additional 85 hp and 30 ft-lbs of torque).

The result of their work was a 425-hp Hemi with the highest specific output of any V-8 engine ever offered by Chrysler. Would you believe it developed 69.8 hp per liter? You should, because it does.

To meet their goal and also make the engine durable, SRT engineers modified and/or upgraded numerous standard 5.7-liter Hemi engine parts. The 6.1-liter Hemi and the 5.7-liter Hemi both have the same dimensional stroke (3.58 inches). The crankshaft dampener on the 6.1-liter was re-tuned to handle the higher engine speeds that the engine was designed to reach. The large-diameter

A comparison between 2008 and earlier cylinder heads and those used for the 2009 5.7-liter Hemi engines reveals big differences. The size and shape of the intake port are different, plus the 2009 cylinder head (bottom) uses 2.05-inch intake and 1.55-inch exhaust valves that are larger and have longer stems. The rocker arm support pedestals are taller, and the valveguide boss sits higher on the top side of the cylinder head, moving it out of the intake port. The 2009 head also has a "closed" combustion chamber (notice the circular ring around the chamber in the top head but not in the bottom head). (Photo Courtesy Fiat Chrysler Automobiles US LLC)

In 2012, Chrysler issued a recall for 5.7-liter Hemi-equipped Challengers, Chargers, and Chrysler 300C models that were built between 2009 and 2012. All cars recalled had the MDS feature with automatic transmission (MDS was not available with manual shift). A timing chain issue occurred whereby the car could realize sudden and catastrophic engine damage while in MDS mode if the timing chain broke.

For some reason, the timing chain on 5.7-liter Hemi cars suddenly failed without warning while driving at normal highway speed. This occurred while the engine was in 4-cylinder fuel-saving mode.

Technicians at the dealerships were authorized to perform only the recall service work to the timing chain. In other words, they were required to replace the chain, reassemble the car's engine, and attempt to start it. If engine damage was confirmed when the engine was started, the technician could then tear the engine apart (again) to repair the more significant damage that had occurred.

BASIC ENGINE IDENTIFICATION

The SRT group designed the 6.1-liter Hemi, introduced in 2005, to be the big brother to the 5.7-liter Hemi. The engine's increased ability to breathe was achieved with the use of new high-flow cylinder heads, a specially designed intake manifold, and tube-style exhaust manifolds that closely resemble headers.

Also unique to the 2005 6.1-liter Hemi engine are larger-diameter valves and reshaped cylinder ports. These design improvements in the heads allow for maximized airflow. The intake manifold was designed with larger-diameter runners for higher-RPM tuning capabilities.

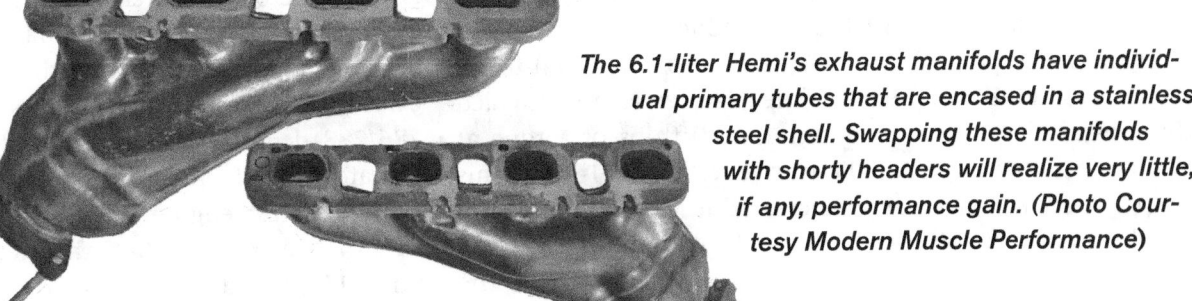

The 6.1-liter Hemi's exhaust manifolds have individual primary tubes that are encased in a stainless steel shell. Swapping these manifolds with shorty headers will realize very little, if any, performance gain. (Photo Courtesy Modern Muscle Performance)

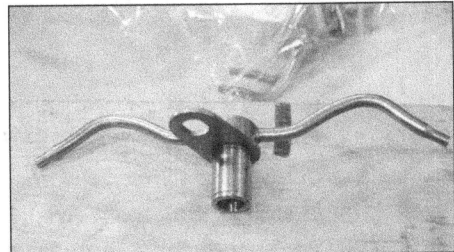

All 6.1-liter Hemi engines came with these oil squirters, which were located under the pistons. They connected to the underside of the cam, and oil was sprayed from them to help keep the pistons cooler, thereby helping decrease detonation. These were later adapted to other Hemi engines. When installing a stroker crankshaft these squirters need to be modified if retained (the tubes must be shortened).

flat-top pistons, which were rotated by the new forged-steel crankshaft, created higher-pressure loads. The deep-skirted engine block structure was redesigned with reinforced bulkheads to handle these higher-stress loads.

The 6.1-liter Hemi was built with a higher compression ratio, which was increased from the 5.7-liter Hemi's 9.6:1 to 10.3:1. The 6.125-inch connecting rod's redesign used higher-strength powder-metal material. New floating wrist pins were used.

Oil squirters aimed at the underside of each piston were added to aid piston cooling for increased engine durability. A special oil pump pressure-relief valve was added to accommodate the pressure loss that was created for squirter oil flow.

Even the oil pan and windage tray were modified to manage oil return to the oil pan sump at high engine speeds for improved power.

The 6.1-liter Hemi cylinder head ports were designed with a larger cross-sectional area. This allowed for an 11-percent increase in flow for the intake ports and a 13-percent increase in flow for the exhaust ports. The camshaft featured more overlap and lift to help increase performance.

The 6.1 Hemi head is found only on SRT-equipped vehicles. The intake port measures around 185 cc, and depending on the flow bench, flows 310 to 320 cfm at .600-inch lift (using a 2.08-inch valve). The exhaust port is D-shaped and measures 57 cc in testing; again, depending on the flow bench, it flows 185 to 195 cfm at .600-inch lift with a 1.650-inch exhaust valve. The beehive-style spring that is used on the 6.1-liter head has proven to handle up to .580-inch cam lift. With its 74 cc, the open chamber is smaller than that of the 5.7-liter.

Although the valves are larger (2.00/1.55 inches to 2.08/1.650 inches), the 6.1-liter Hemi uses the same 1.65-ratio shaft-mounted rocker system and valve orientation as the 5.7-liter head. The 6.1-liter camshaft has .547/.541–inch lift and 283/286–degrees of duration.

6.4-Liter Hemi (392) 2011–2014

Although introduced in 2007 as a "crate engine," the 392-inch 6.4-liter Hemi did not replace the 6.1-liter in production vehicles until 2011. With 470 hp and 470 ft-lbs of torque, the 6.4-liter Hemi provided an additional 90 ft-lbs of torque at 2,900 rpm over the 6.1-liter. This engine created just over 73 hp from each liter of displacement.

The block was made with the same high-strength iron and featured an increased bore of 4.06 inches. As with all Gen III Hemis, five main-bearing supports provide a rigid structure for the crankshaft, and each of the main-bearing caps is attached with four bolts (two vertical and two horizontal).

The forged-steel crankshaft with a stroke of 3.795 inches provides the basis for an extremely strong rotating and reciprocating assembly. The crankshaft is once again connected to powder-metal forged connecting rods, but now they measure 6.2 inches long.

The 6.4-liter Hemi still used cast pistons, but they have been optimized to reduce friction and noise under both hot and cold operating conditions. With the compression ratio of the 6.4-liter Hemi at 10.9:1, premium fuel with an octane rating of 93 is highly recommended. The camshaft has .577/.537–inch lift and 286/288–degrees duration, and again actuates by variable cam timing.

This latest engine is designated the Apache. You can find this head on 2011–present (as of this writing) SRT 6.4-liter Hemi Challengers, Chargers, and Grand Cherokee Jeeps. The combustion chamber volume is 73.4 cc and valve angles are 18 degrees on the intake and 16.5 degrees on the

In 2011, the 392/6.4–liter Hemi came standard in the new Challenger and Charger SRT8s. When delivered, and in stock form, many owners have experienced impressive 12-second quarter-mile times at the dragstrip. Not bad for a car that weighs more than 4,000 pounds and has air conditioning and a sound system. The new 6.4-liter engine is a bored and stroked version of SRT's 6.1-liter Hemi. As found in the 2011 Challenger, the 6.4-liter Hemi delivered 470 hp at 6,000 rpm and 470 ft-lbs of torque at 4,200. (Photo Courtesy Fiat Chrysler Automobiles US LLC)

BASIC ENGINE IDENTIFICATION

Supporting the rotating assembly of the Hemi engine is an impressively strong block and main cap structure. All five main caps are a four-bolt cross-bolted design. Cross-bolting the main cap has two distinct advantages. First, it connects the two sides of the engine block together, making it stiffer overall and less prone to flexing. Second, it helps to hold the bearing cap against the downward force created from the combustion process and the movement of the piston.

This 6.4-liter Hemi from an SRT8 Jeep Grand Cherokee uses a six-rib belt to drive the accessories. The power steering uses an attached reservoir and mounts to the cylinder head. The alternator on a Jeep fits tight to the engine and bolts in from the side with three bolts. (Photo Courtesy Fiat Chrysler Automobiles US LLC)

exhaust side. The Apache cylinder head uses the same rockers and bolt pattern as the 6.1-liter Hemi but the head uses larger 2.14-inch intake and 1.65-inch exhaust valves.

The intake ports are almost a perfectly square 2 x 2 inches, and the flow is in the 340-cfm range. To accommodate the larger valves and improved port design, the valveguide was moved. This means that the heads only fit a 6.4-liter Hemi engine or a head with at least a 4.06-inch bore and custom pistons.

The 6.4-liter Hemi engine is fitted with a cast-aluminum oil pan that is designed to provide better oil management characteristics and additional structural rigidity to the engine than previous designs. The pan was designed with special channels, baffles, and scrapers to help funnel engine oil back into the bottom of the pan and away from the crankshaft. Externally, strengthening ribs were cast into the oil pan. This improved oil pan fits all current Gen III Hemi engines and makes a good upgrade for earlier engines.

The 6.4-liter Hemi uses an integral gasket and windage tray design that is fitted between the pan and engine block to reduce the amount of oil that comes in contact with the crankshaft. This helps prevent the possi-

In 2014, the 6.4-liter Hemi became available in Ram Trucks. The new 6.4-liter Hemi V-8 produced 410 hp at 5,600 rpm with 429 ft-lbs of torque. It also carried VVT and MDS fuel-saver cylinder deactivation. (Photo Courtesy Fiat Chrysler Automobiles US LLC)

bility of horsepower loss because of engine oil aeration or sloshing.

Once again an Active Intake Manifold is used. The active intake system is designed to harness the pressure waves that exist in the intake runners to improve the volumetric efficiency of the engine. Depending on engine speed, the intake manifold switches between short and long runners. This allows greater tuning capabilities over a wider RPM range than a fixed runner intake.

CHAPTER 2

A major change to the engine in the 2014 Ram was that the new 6.4-liter's throttle body was moved forward and angled to the passenger's side of the vehicle. *(Photo Courtesy Fiat Chrysler Automobiles US LLC)*

After 2007, the coil is segregated by cylinder, and the multiple sparks required are controlled individually on each cylinder.

Note that 2011 and 2012 engines with the 6-speed manual transmission do not have MDS.

Engine Accessories

Maybe you're looking for an engine that you can build for your car but don't want to use the one that's already under the hood. That's not a problem; many owners do that so they can keep the original engine. When looking at an engine that is out of a car a few clues will help identify what engine you are actually looking at.

Below is a short list of some of the most notable differences that you can use to identify an engine.

LX is the standard car setup found on 300s, Chargers, Magnums, and Challengers.

DR is the standard truck setup found on all Dodge trucks equipped with a Hemi.

5.7-Liter Hemi (Truck) 2003–2008

DR engines use a seven-rib front accessory drive, and the front cover, water pump, and accessories do not interchange with other models. This setup mounts the accessories (alternator and air conditioner pump) high in front of the intake; this prohibits the use of stock passenger car intake manifolds. The front cover assembly/

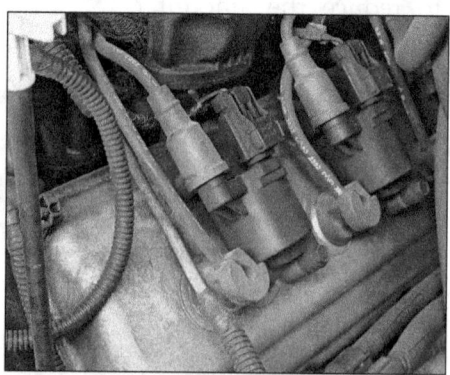

Hemi truck engines up to 2008 have a coil and plug wire for each cylinder. This is to accomplish the multiple sparks required for emissions.

accessory drive can be changed to a car unit.

5.7- and 6.1-Liter Car and Jeep Hemi 2005–2008

These front covers interchange; the only difference is the location of the alternator and power steering pump. These are all six-rib belt units.

The car-style power steering uses a remote reservoir and mounts to the cylinder head. The Jeep unit attaches the same way but has an attached reservoir.

The car alternator bolts to the engine from the side, utilizing three bolts. The Jeep alternator mounts the same, but fits a little tighter to the engine.

5.7-Liter Hemi (Truck) 2009–2012

With the introduction of the Eagle engine, the front cover was redesigned to accept the VCT and new block. Although these do not interchange with earlier Dodge Rams, they also use a seven-rib serpentine drive system. Mounting of the air conditioner compressor and alternator is the same as on previous Ram trucks: up high.

BASIC ENGINE IDENTIFICATION

Truck engines like this one from a 2009 Ram feature an intake system that is entirely different from both the car and Jeep Hemi engines. The truck intake features a throttle body that points upward from the front of the intake. (Photo Courtesy Fiat Chrysler Automobiles US LLC)

Earlier truck engines featured a small engine cover that was positioned over the throttle body. The throttle body on these engines also pointed upward (and a little forward) but was located at the center of the intake. (Photo Courtesy Fiat Chrysler Automobiles US LLC)

5.7-Liter Eagle 2009–2012 and 6.4-Liter Apache 2011–2012

These engines share the same front cover, which does not interchange with earlier models. The alternator and power steering fit earlier engines, but care should be taken to ensure correct interchange as there are concerns other than physical fitment, such as electrical.

Intake Manifolds

Until the 1990s, most automotive intake manifolds were made of cast iron or aluminum. Manufacturers eventually made them of a composite or plastic material that was durable enough to survive engine use. The benefits of both lower weight and cost made them popular.

5.7-Liter Hemi (Truck/Durango) 2003–2008

These intake manifolds are made of a composite material and place the throttle body in the middle of the engine facing forward. They fit correctly only on pre-2009 5.7-liter heads. The MAP sensor is located at the front of the intake.

5.7-Liter Hemi (Car and Jeep) 2005–2008

This intake manifold is also composite but places the throttle body directly above the front accessory cover, parallel to the ground. This intake fits only pre–2009 5.7-liter heads. The MAP sensor is located at the rear of the intake.

5.7-Liter (Truck) 2009–2012

As with previous versions, this intake manifold is composite. It fits all square-port heads. Unlike previous truck intakes, this one places the throttle body at the front of the intake, at a 90-degree angle (facing upward).

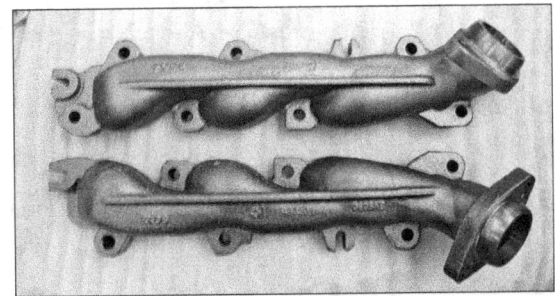

These stock 5.7 car manifolds are barely adequate for a stock Charger, Challenger, Magnum, or 300, but you can add aftermarket bolt-on goodies, and forget it.

DODGE CHALLENGER AND CHARGER: HOW TO BUILD AND MODIFY

CHAPTER 2

All Gen III Hemi intakes (except for the 6.1-liter) are of a composite design. This reduces weight and helps reduce intake-charge heat. This intake is for a 2008 or earlier passenger car. The passenger car intake varies from the truck intake, which typically has the throttle body in a different location and pointed upward.

5.7-Liter (Car and Jeep) 2009–2012

This intake is composite but looks and performs like that of the 6.1-liter intake manifold. The throttle body is located horizontally at the front of the intake, above the timing cover. This intake fits all square-port intake heads and the MAP sensor is located at the rear of the intake.

6.1-Liter Hemi 2005–2010

All applications use this aluminum intake. It is designed for square-port heads. It is a two-piece design with a removable plenum cover. This removable cover makes porting and polishing easy. The throttle body is located horizontally at the front of the intake above the accessory drive cover. This intake fits both 5.7- and 6.1-liter blocks, making it a great choice.

6.4-Liter Hemi 2011–2012

In all applications, this intake is composite. It features a variable-length runner design that is RPM controlled. The throttle body is located horizontally at the front of the engine, above the accessory drive cover, but is angled toward the driver's side of the car. This intake fits all square-port heads, but may require the use of spacers.

Transmissions

Many companies offer transmissions for Hemi-powered cars. The following are the most popular among Hemi car owners.

NAG1/A580 2005–2014

With the merger of Chrysler and Daimler/Benz, it wasn't long before some of the Benz parts began to appear in Chrysler vehicles. Enter the NAG1 automatic transmission. The NAG1/A580 transmission had advantages over existing Chrysler automatic transmissions. For example, it was more efficient than the previous 4-speed automatic that was used with less-powerful LX cars. Compared with the 545RFE 5-speed automatic transmission that Chrysler was using

---

MAP Sensor

A 1-BAR MAP sensor reports barometric pressure, which is approximately 14.7 psi or 30 in Hg (inches of Mercury). As an example, a typical three-wire MAP sensor has 5 volts and ground to power the circuit. The signal circuit, or return voltage to the computer, is about 4.5 volts at a barometric pressure of 14.7 psi; this measurement is taken at key on, engine off. The sensor can withstand about 1.5 BAR of pressure, but the return voltage peaks at about 4.8 volts.

This type of sensor is designed for a normally aspirated engine to read a negative pressure, or vacuum, at a typical barometric pressure. A reading of 2 or 3 BAR simply means two or three times above barometric pressure.

Common MAP sensor readings are:

- 1 BAR is for a normally aspirated engine
- 2 BAR handles a forced induction up to 14.5 psi of boost
- 3 BAR handles a forced induction up to 29.0 psi of boost

A MAP sensor measures both vacuum and pressure. (Photo Courtesy Fiat Chrysler Automobiles US LLC)

BASIC ENGINE IDENTIFICATION

If you ordered an automatic-equipped Hemi car, your shifting duties were handled by the Mercedes-Benz–derived NAG1 transmission. The NAG is an electronically-controlled 5-speed transmission that has a lock-up clutch inside the torque converter. A large 13-pin electronic connector located on the passenger's side of the transmission (just above the fluid pan near the bellhousing area) identifies the transmission.

Gear Ratios

Gear	NAG1/A580	545RFE
1	3.59	3.00
2	2.19	1.67
3	1.41	1.00
4	1.00	0.75
5	0.83	0.67

All rear-wheel-drive LX cars from 2005 to 2012 use an aluminum oil pan with a front sump. All 2003–2012 two-wheel-drive Ram trucks use a stamped steel rear sump pan (shown). Jeeps use a unique cast-aluminum rear sump oil pan.

in their trucks, the NAG1/A580 had a wider gear range, was considerably smaller, and weighed less.

The NAG1/A580 automatic transmission is an electronically-controlled 5-speed transmission that uses a lock-up clutch encased inside the torque converter. Fifth gear is an overdrive with a high-speed ratio, and the different ratios are actually selected by three planetary-gear sets.

The NAG1/WA580 was used in different cars, starting with the 2005 Chrysler 300 and Dodge Magnum with Hemi V-8 engines. Later, it was put into service in the Jeep Liberty, Grand Cherokee, Charger, Challenger, and eventually, the Ram truck. The NAG1/WA580 was built at Chrysler's Transmission Plant II, in Kokomo, Indiana. Plant I built the 45RFE and 545RFE electronically-controlled transmissions starting in 1998.

Visually, the NAG1/A580 transmission can be identified by the round 13-pin connector located on the passenger's side of the transmission near the front corner of the transmission's oil pan.

The torque converter and transmission housings are made from a light alloy and are sealed and bolted together with a coated intermediate plate. The fluid pump and the outer disc carrier are then bolted to the torque converter housing. The stator shaft is pressed into the housing and is positioned with splines, which prevent it from rotating. The electronic control unit is bolted underneath the oil pan.

On early models (2003–2005), some owners experienced transmission "shudder." At that time, Technical Service Bulletin 21-011-05 was issued; it was later superseded by 21-003-06. This bulletin applied to LX and LE vehicles equipped with an NAG1 transmission (sales code DGJ) built prior to December 2005 with a transmission build date of July 8, 2005.

The shudder condition may have been because of the torque converter clutch continually sticking and slipping because of contaminated transmission fluid. The transmission fluid contamination was thought to be caused by water getting past the transmission filler-tube (dipstick

CHAPTER 2

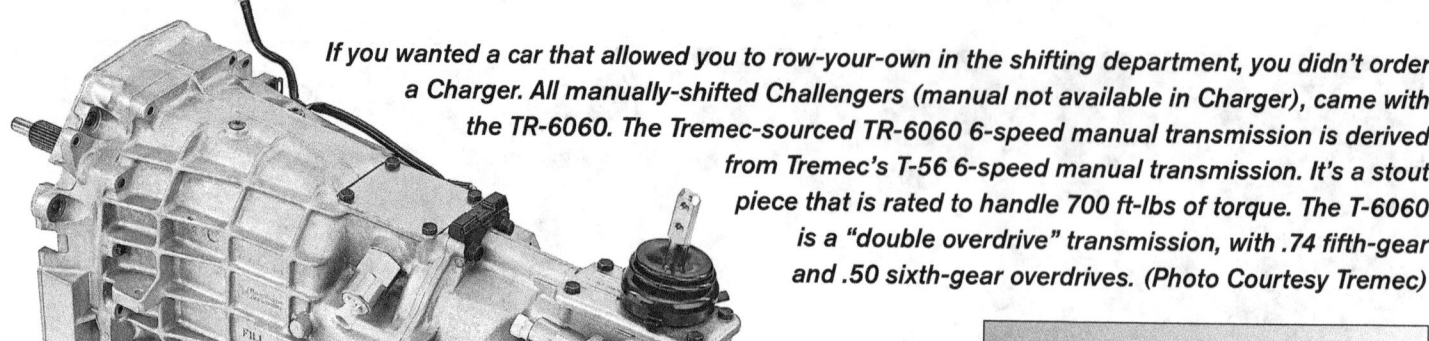

If you wanted a car that allowed you to row-your-own in the shifting department, you didn't order a Charger. All manually-shifted Challengers (manual not available in Charger), came with the TR-6060. The Tremec-sourced TR-6060 6-speed manual transmission is derived from Tremec's T-56 6-speed manual transmission. It's a stout piece that is rated to handle 700 ft-lbs of torque. The T-6060 is a "double overdrive" transmission, with .74 fifth-gear and .50 sixth-gear overdrives. (Photo Courtesy Tremec)

TR-6060 Gear Ratios

Gear	Ratio (:1)
1	2.97
2	2.10
3	1.46
4	1.00
5	0.74
6	0.50

tube) seal. Depending on the amount of water in the transmission oil, car owners experienced a transmission shudder or vibration and/or an audible high-frequency buzz-like sound.

The shudder/vibration or buzz-like sound was most noticeable during light driving (cruising) in 3rd, 4th, or 5th gear. The fix was to flush the transmission thoroughly (Chrysler recommended three times) and install a new filler-tube seal. Some owners flushed the transmission and simply applied RTV to the seal area.

A popular and simple modification to the NAG1 is to replace the OEM-supplied brown-top solenoids with AMG blue-top solenoids as on the stock valve body. The blue-top solenoids have larger ports and provide firmer and faster shifts over the OEM brown-top units. If you are looking for even firmer shifts, a shift improver kit is also available but requires a little more work to install.

Tremec TR-6060 2008–2014

The 6-speed Tremec TR-6060 manual transmission was derived from its predecessor, the T-56. Dimensionally, they fit within the same location, but the T-56 was never used in the Challenger.

Upgrades from the T-56 include reduced friction while shifting, thanks to a new cam and anti-friction plunger to control the side loading of the shift detents. The forward and rearward shift-detent grooves are broached on the front of the main-shaft with a spring-loaded anti-friction roller. This gives a more positive shift feel. In addition, anti-friction ball struts, sintered hubs, and fine-pitch splines on all synchronizers also help reduce friction between the components. The two-piece gears are wider and have machined teeth for more precise gear engagement and reduced potential for gear block-outs and missed shifts.

To use a manually-shifted transmission in the Challenger, Dodge looked to the already proven TR-6060 that was used in the Viper. Internally, the TR-6060 comes with triple cone synchronizers for first and second gears, and then twin cone synchronizers for third through sixth gears. These multi-cone synchronizers greatly reduce shifting effort.

The clutch chosen for use in the Challenger was also sourced from the Viper. It is a 250-mm twin-disc design that is capable of delivering great torque-handling capacity and clutch life. The TR-6060 features a first- through fourth-gear skip-shift property, reverse inhibit solenoids, and a 5:1–ratio shifter.

As usual, the helical-cut forward gears are synchronized, but the reverse gear operates through a fully synchronized constant-mesh system. The TR-6060 contains removable wear pads on the shift forks and uses an aluminum alloy for the main case, extension housing, and clutch housing. In stock form it is rated for 600 ft-lbs of torque.

Rear Ends

When the LX cars were released in 2005 (and the Challenger in 2008), Chrysler needed to find a rear end that would hold up to the performance demands of the new Hemi but still deliver uncompromising ride quality. For years before the introduction of the LX cars, a solid, or "live," axle was used. A live axle is a rigid rear end that connects the two rear wheels. The axle shafts are within tubes that are connected to the differential housing.

BASIC ENGINE IDENTIFICATION

The rear suspension and differential on Chargers and Challengers is one complete module that is isolated from the body via bushings. It was initially designed to be compatible with parts from Mercedes-Benz. The five-link rear suspension offers a better ride quality than a traditional solid or live rear axle. The multiple suspension links maintain independent control of each rear wheel's camber and toe angle during suspension movement. The entire rear suspension module is mounted to the body with bushings and can be removed as a complete unit.

Because this type of axle is solid, when making a turn under severe cornering the wheel on the inside of the corner tends to lift. At the very least, the tire's angle to the asphalt changes, minimizing the tire's contact patch with the road surface. Also, when a wheel on the passenger's side of the vehicle hits a bump, it channels that energy to the wheel on the other side of the vehicle.

The differential on an IRS is rigidly mounted to the body, and the axles are connected to the differential and wheels via constant velocity (CV) joints. With the differential rigidly mounted and the wheels "suspended" individually they can move independently of one another. So, when energy is created as one wheel hits a bump, it is isolated only to the wheel that has to travel over the bump. Suspension travel of an independent suspension system also allows the tire to remain perpendicular to the road surface, maximizing tire contact with the road during hard cornering.

Although the Charger and Challenger use IRS, solid-axle suspension systems aren't all bad. They are significantly less expensive to build than an independent suspension because they're less complex. By design, they require fewer moving parts. Depending on what you use your vehicle for, a solid axle might work just fine.

For example, if you drive a pickup truck and want to carry heavy loads, a solid axle can do that job with ease. A solid axle can even work in some performance situations. In drag racing, for example, when cornering isn't part of the performance picture, an IRS doesn't offer an advantage.

If you decide to build a corner-handling monster, you will recognize the benefits of an IRS as soon as you hit the first corner. With an IRS, the inside rear wheel remains firmly planted on the road surface, and acceleration out of the corner is a lot better when the inside rear wheel doesn't want to leave the ground spinning.

Getrag Differential 2005–2014

The R/T has 2.82 (rear-wheel-drive) and 3.07 (all-wheel-drive) rears; the SRT has a 3.07:1 gear.

When looking at the rear end of your Charger, Magnum, Challenger, or 300, keep in mind that there were actually three different rear ends available. To decide which one is in your car or what you might be looking at in a salvage yard, you need to understand the metric system. The late-model Mopar rear ends are denoted by the size of the rear end's ring gear in millimeters.

Automatic-equipped R/Ts were given the 215-mm Mercedes-Benz–sourced open rear end: No limited-slip differential (LSD) was available. SRT8s came with the 226-mm Getrag rear, with the exception of the 2008 model. In 2008 they had a 215-mm rear. Automatic SRTs have a 3.06:1 gear ratio; manually-shifted cars received 3.91s. Manual-transmission R/Ts also had the 226-mm rear, and cars with 18-inch tires had 3.73 gears; those with 20-inch tires had 3.91 gears.

In 2009 a limited-slip differential was available with 6-speed cars. In 2012 R/T cars with an automatic transmission were available with an optional limited-slip 226 Getrag rear if you ordered the Super Track Pac option.

A popular R/T upgrade is to replace the stock rubber/Kevlar coupler that is between the differential and the driveshaft with an SRT 392 coupler. The coupler that is used in stock R/T applications does not completely seat into the machined depressions that are found in the yoke and driveshaft. This poor fit can cause a condition whereby the driveshaft and differential yoke contact each other and cause damage.

Hemi Engine Technology

Any engine referred to as a Hemi is one that has hemispherical (bowl-shaped) combustion chambers that position the valves of a two-valves-per-cylinder engine facing each other from across the chamber, rather than being positioned side-by-side as with a wedge-style head. This layout allows the use of larger valves and straightens the airflow passages through the cylinder head. This creates a cross-flow chamber design; the intake charge flows directly across the chamber from the intake to the exhaust valve that is located directly opposite it. This feature can significantly improve the engine's airflow capability, which can result in relatively high power output from a given piston displacement.

The Active Intake Manifold that was first used on 2009 Hemi engines was designed to harness the pressure waves of intake airflow, which exist in the intake runners. The intake manifold works via a built-in "flapper," or door, that rotates, varying the intake-runner length to either shorten or lengthen it, depending on engine speed. This runner-design variability allows a more complete tuning advantage over a wider RPM range than is capable with a fixed-length runner intake.

Constructed of thermoplastic, the intake provides near-identical distribution of the air/fuel charge across all eight cylinders. The thermoplastic construction also contributes to a cooler intake charge because heat is not transferred as it is with an aluminum intake and cylinder head.

Another piece of technology that Chrysler installed in 2004 on the 5.7-liter Hemi V-8 is the MDS. This system helps increase overall fuel efficiency ratings. The MDS deactivates four of the engine's eight cylinders when the throttle is closed or when the car is at non–engine-loading speeds (cruising).

The 5.7-liter Hemi system uses a "latching" lifter. When the control system signals for a particular cylinder to deactivate, an electronic signal is sent to a solenoid that then opens. The opened solenoid allows pressurized engine oil to travel through a control gallery in the engine block. This pressurized oil goes into the appropriate lifter and acts on a pin in the lifter to "unlatch" it.

Inside the latching lifter is an extra spring called a lost-motion spring that retains pressure on the pushrod when the pressure in the lifter's piston is released. The purpose of this spring is to keep the lifter in contact with the cam and the pushrod while allowing the lifter's internals to remain motionless. When in MDS mode, the lifter

The Active Intake Manifold on 2009 Hemi engines shortens or lengthens the airflow pressure waves in the runners to maximize power production. (Photo Courtesy Fiat Chrysler Automobiles US LLC)

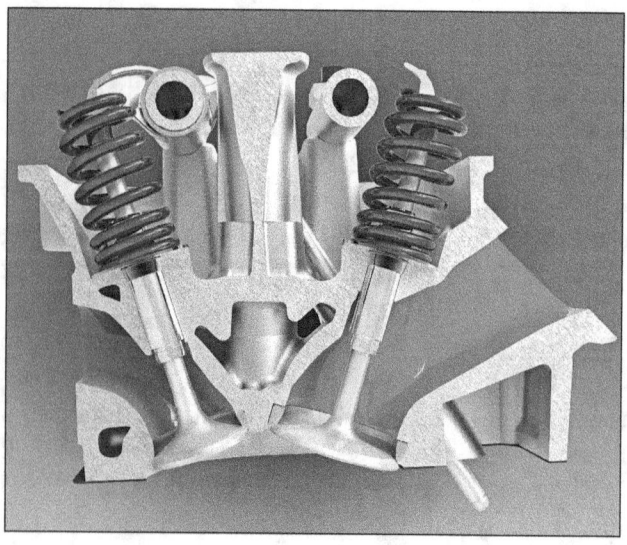

The Hemi head is larger (wider) than standard "wedge" designs because it needs to make room for the intake and exhaust valves that point in different directions. This style of cylinder head also requires a complex rocker arm system with multiple rocker shafts. (Photo Courtesy Fiat Chrysler Automobiles US LLC)

BASIC ENGINE IDENTIFICATION

In an effort to increase overall fuel efficiency ratings, Chrysler introduced its MDS in 2004 on the 5.7-liter Hemi V-8. The function of the system is to deactivate four of the engine's eight cylinders when the throttle is closed, or when the car is at non–engine-loading speeds (cruising).

The lost-motion spring keeps the lifter in contact with the cam and the pushrod while allowing the lifter's internals to remain motionless. When in MDS mode, the lifter is allowed to compress as the camshaft rotates, while not moving the pushrod. (Photo Courtesy Fiat Chrysler Automobiles US LLC)

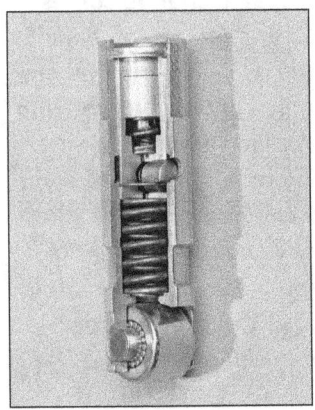

The camshaft lifter that is used with the MDS in the Hemi is unlike any other lifter. The system in the 5.7-liter Hemi uses a "latching lifter." The ECU signals for a cylinder to become deactivated and a solenoid opens and sends high-pressure engine oil through a control gallery in the block. This pressurized oil acts on a pin in the lifter to "unlatch" the lifter. Inside this special lifter is an extra spring called a lost-motion spring. It keeps the roller tip of the lifter in contact with the cam and the pushrod in contact with the rocker arm.

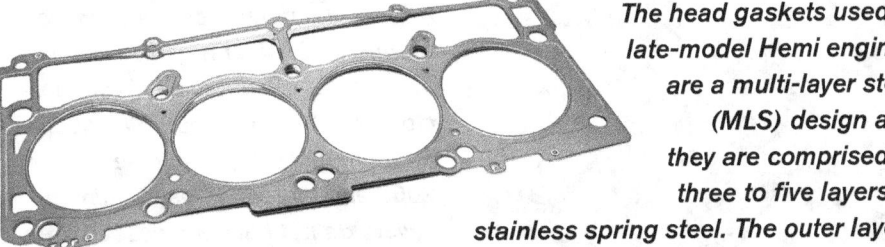

The head gaskets used in late-model Hemi engines are a multi-layer steel (MLS) design and they are comprised of three to five layers of stainless spring steel. The outer layers are an embossed Viton-coated stainless steel, providing a superior seal with excellent rebound characteristics and corrosion resistance. MLS head gaskets reduce bore distortion and withstand extreme cylinder pressures. The MLS design is used in exhaust manifold gaskets as well.

compresses as the camshaft rotates without moving the pushrod.

Variable Camshaft Timing

The variable cam timing camshaft and sprocket used by Chrysler works by advancing and retarding the actual camshaft timing. This changes the intake and exhaust valves' opening and closing points during the combustion process. Advancing the camshaft opens the valve earlier in the engine's cycle, whereas retarding the camshaft does the opposite. Advancing the camshaft gives the Hemi more bottom-end power, higher engine vacuum, and better idle characteristics. Retarding the camshaft helps with top-end power. Because the lobes are part of the camshaft, a movable phaser (sprocket) is needed to achieve this change in timing.

To make the system work, pressurized engine oil is diverted from the camshaft bores into the hollow camshaft. From there the oil travels forward and into the cam gear (phaser). The hydraulically actuated phaser directs the oil to different passages within the phaser body to either advance or retard the camshaft as needed, depending on driving conditions.

The function of advancing or retarding the camshaft is initiated by the electronic control unit (ECU), which sends an electronic signal to a solenoid that is mounted in the timing cover. The solenoid applies pressure to the oil control valve (OCV) that is bolted to the front of the camshaft. The control valve re-routes pressurized engine oil. The pressurized oil is then directed to flow in one of two directions in the phaser, thereby advancing or retarding camshaft timing.

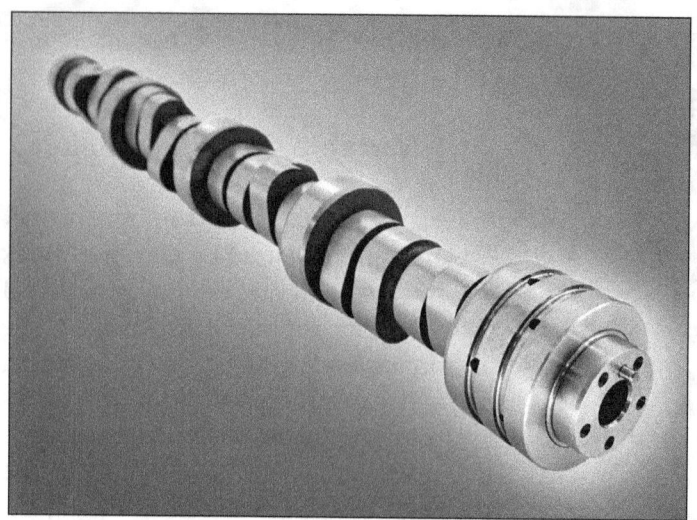

In 2009, the late-model Hemi engine acquired variable valve timing (VVT). A camshaft phaser is mounted to the front of the camshaft within the timing-chain gear. VVT changes the timing of the engine valves' opening and closing. Pressurized engine oil is sent through an oil control valve that changes the relative position of the camshaft within the phaser assembly. (Photos Courtesy Fiat Chrysler Automobiles US LLC)

A not-so-noticeable change comes with the 2009 and later Hemi engines. These engines use a different timing cover from those of previous years to allow room for the variable camshaft timing. Timing covers from 2008 and earlier Hemi engines do not fit 2009 and later Hemi engines. The entire cover is deeper, to cover the variable valve timing (VVT) system (larger camshaft gear with phaser).

The difference in timing covers reflects the difference between water pumps on 2008 and earlier Hemis; they do not interchange. If you look closely at the water pump location on the timing cover, you can see that on 2009 and later engines, the timing covers do not have a recessed area for the water pump impeller and water flow. The impeller on 2008 and earlier engine is thicker than that of 2009 and later engines.

CHAPTER 3

BOLT-ON PERFORMANCE

When your Charger, Challenger, 300C, or Magnum was built (unless you purchased a Drag Pack Challenger), it was designed within a set of constraints dictated by the need for reliability and the highest efficiency possible. Mopar did its best to make sure that the cars ride comfortably, are reliable, and as of late, deliver the highest fuel mileage they can. There's nothing wrong with that; owning a 400- to 500-hp car that gets 20 mpg used to be unheard of. But, this set of constraints could leave some performance on the table. Some of the high-performance bolt-on parts can and do make a positive difference, but you're probably not aware that there are trade-offs when installing aftermarket parts, or that they may actually decrease power if not chosen carefully.

In this chapter I touch on several of the most popular bolt-on items, focusing on handheld tuners, cold-air kits, exhaust upgrades, throttle bodies, and nitrous oxide.

Programmable Tuners

Bolt-on performance parts used to be the simplest of parts purchases for the weekend mechanic, but in today's age of advanced engine controllers and computer control systems, you don't even need to pick up a wrench to increase a car's performance. Today's high-tech Hemi-powered cars are almost entirely controlled by computers. Modifying the parameters that the OEM has programmed into your Hemi's ECU can yield very rewarding gains, especially if added to a collection of other performance parts. When adding multiple performance parts, however, keep in mind that manufacturers usually design their part to work on an

The installation of a performance tune from a handheld controller, such as this inTune from DiabloSport, is a simple task. It is as easy as plugging it in to the OBD-II port that is located under the dash of your car, usually on the driver's side, and following the instructions that come across the screen of the controller.

The inTune programmer is the latest programmer from DiabloSport. It replaces the Predator handheld tuner that has been the standard for years. The DiabloSport inTune has all of the famous preloaded tunes and available adjustments as the Predator, in a smaller, more advanced, and easier-to-use device.

DODGE CHALLENGER AND CHARGER: HOW TO BUILD AND MODIFY

unmodified vehicle. Results vary when multiple parts are installed.

Even if you own a stock or near-stock LX car, I'm sure that you have at least heard of handheld tuners/programmers. These little computerized devices install (or flash) a performance tune into the car's ECU, altering the factory's settings and replacing them with tuning that is more suitable for high performance.

When considering a handheld performance tuner, your only choices for the LX cars are from DiabloSport or SCT Performance. Programmers have been around for years and have developed from simple devices consisting of just a tune and not much more to a comprehensive "computer."

The DiabloSport and SCT tuners are designed to increase the performance of your Hemi by altering the parameters the computer uses to make the engine run. For instance, because your Hemi responds very well to an increase in timing a tuner can tell the computer that more timing is needed during a particular engine running scenario.

Not only do the DiabloSport and SCT tuners increase the Hemi engine's performance, the parameters controlling the transmission can also be altered. Most automatic-equipped LX cars are shipped from the factory with very conservative shift points. The tuners enable you to raise those shift points to a more performance-enhancing level.

Finally, both tuners enable you to diagnose trouble codes if you see a check engine light, and include a myriad of other options, such as live engine data logging, engine functions monitoring, and even drag racing without going to the track.

HP Tuners offers more complex, laptop-based tuning capabilities, and they require at least some specialized training if an authorized installer does not perform the computer programming.

Hemi engines are notorious for using more fuel to run than is required. Not only does this rich running condition hurt fuel mileage, but power is sacrificed as well.

Many Challenger, Charger, 300C, and Magnum owners have noted a significant increase in fuel efficiency with the install of a handheld tuner (typically 3 to 5 mpg). Both DiabloSport's inTune and Trinity programmers feature tunes that are based on minimum octane-use ratings. So, your options in the tuning menu for increasing performance are a 93- or 91-octane performance tune.

Finally, whatever modifications you make to your car, unless you are building a car for maximum power, what's important to focus on is not only the peak horsepower and torque gains but also the amount of power gained throughout the RPM range. Let's face it, how often does your car really spend time at 6,000 rpm?

Many companies offer programmable tuners for Hemi-powered cars. The following are the most popular among Hemi car owners.

DiabloSport

The DiabloSport inTune adds horsepower and torque to your Challenger, Charger, 300C, or Magnum using preloaded tunes supplied by DiabloSport. A preloaded (canned) tune is one that is developed by the manufacturer to fit a certain set of parameters for a car, and is supplied with the programmer. These tunes work great whether installed on a stock vehicle or in conjunction with a mildly modified car (such as one with a cat-back exhaust and cold-air intake). When you plug the inTune into your car, before it downloads the new tune it saves a copy of the vehicle's factory tune in its memory. With the factory tune saved, the car can be returned to stock in a matter of minutes by just plugging in the tuner and reinstalling the stock tune.

The tunes already installed and delivered in the inTune start with a 93-octane tune. This tune has the potential to give a 15- to 40-hp increase in power, improve drivability, and even improve fuel economy. If 93-octane fuel is not available to you, the 91-octane performance tune gives you a performance increase (typically 10 to 35 hp) but only requires 91-octane fuel.

DiabloSport also developed an 87-octane tune that can increase power from 12 to 30 hp.

Finally, the inTune can also calibrate your speedometer (needed after a gear or tire-size change) and remove the top-speed limiter.

The inTune has the ability to store up to five custom tunes. A custom tune is a tune that is specifically engineered for a given vehicle. Generally, vehicles needing a custom tune have additional modifications on them, such as a blower, or have received a head or camshaft swap. Many aftermarket modifications available today require custom tuning in order to work properly. Two ways are available for you to get a custom tune for your DiabloSport inTune. The first is to contact an authorized DiabloSport dealer. The dealer can run your car on the dyno and tune it accordingly.

You can also receive a tune via e-mail. This is a little more complicated for the do-it-yourselfer, as you first need to read your vehicle's stock tune with the inTune programmer

DiabloSport's Trinity handheld tuner adds horsepower and torque to your vehicle by using DiabloSport's dyno-tested performance tunes. The DiabloSport tunes are preloaded into each Trinity and are specifically designed to increase your Hemi engine's power, economy, and even drivability. The tunes are compatible whether being used on a stock vehicle or even a mildly modified (such as a cat-back exhaust and cold-air intake) car. (Photo Courtesy DiabloSport)

and then transfer the tune onto your home computer or laptop using DiabloSport's Windows-based PC interface. Next, you email the factory tune to a DiabloSport-supported shop/tuner. The tuner then builds a modified tune from your factory tune, per your specification. Finally, the shop/tuner emails the custom tune back to you so you can reprogram your vehicle.

The "canned" tunes supplied in the DiabloSport tuners are a good start for achieving a performance increase in your Hemi engine. If you have installed other performance-enhancing items, such as headers, full exhaust, or even a supercharger, you might want to check into a special tune for your particular Challenger, Charger, 300C, or Magnum.

A DiabloSport tuner always saves a copy of the vehicle's factory tune in its memory; that way, in case your car needs to be serviced at the dealership at some point in the future, you can reinstall the factory tune.

So you always have a copy of your vehicle tune on your tuner, and once it's restored, there is no trace of the aftermarket tune in the vehicle's computer.

If you are looking just to increase the fuel mileage of your Hemi, both the inTune and Trinity programmers also have a "mileage booster" tune, which optimizes fuel efficiency for daily use. With the mileage booster tune, horsepower gains are minimal, but mileage typically improves; again, typically by 3 to 5 mpg. When using the performance tunes, horsepower increases of 15 to 25 are usually seen.

SCT Performance

Another popular handheld programmer for your Hemi car is the SCT X4 Power Flash tuner. SCT has preloaded the X4 with a few limited-performance enhancing tunes; it is also capable of holding up to 10 custom-tune files. The custom-tunes can be obtained through any SCT authorized dealer. The X4 has a large, easy-to-read screen that provides on-screen data monitoring. The X4 Power Flash also stores your factory tune during the performance tune installation, should you ever need to return your vehicle to the stock program.

The standard pre-programmed tuning files are based on the use of 87- to 91- and 93-octane fuels, and are designed for use on vehicles with minor performance modifications, including cold-air kits, high-flow exhaust systems, and other basic modifications. Cars that have aftermarket superchargers or turbochargers require custom tuning, which can only be handled through authorized SCT dealers.

The available tunes in the SCT X4 allow your Hemi to benefit from preloaded dyno-proven tune files that increase horsepower. Depending on the tune, your Hemi could see an increase of 15 to 20 hp. The X4 also lets you change features, such as the shift firmness of your automatic

CHAPTER 3

The SCT Performance X4 handheld programmer can easily store up to 10 custom tune files that are able to increase horsepower, torque, and even improve fuel mileage. The 10 custom tune files can be loaded by any of SCT's custom tuning dealers. The pre-programmed tuning files that are included are based on the use of 87- to 91- and 93-octane fuels, and are designed for use on vehicles with minor performance modifications such as cold-air kits, high-flow exhaust systems, and other basic modifications. Cars that have aftermarket superchargers or turbochargers require custom tuning, which can be handled only through authorized SCT dealers. Contact SCT to find an authorized dealer/installer near you. The retail price of the controller is about $400. (Photo Courtesy SCT Performance)

transmission, adjust your speedometer if you change tire size, and even give you a performance setting that is specific to your car if you install something simple like a cold-air kit and/or headers.

Programming your vehicle with one of SCT's preloaded performance or fuel economy tunes is as easy as 1-2-3. Simply plug the OBD-II connector into your LX's OBD-II port, select the preloaded tune file using the simple-to-navigate menu, and within minutes the X4 programs your vehicle.

HP Tuners

Programming your Hemi car with HP Tuners uses the VCM suite. This utility allows you to read the powertrain control module (PCM) memory and save it to a binary file. The flash utility allows a valid calibration to be written to the PCM and incorporates an automatic PCM recovery capability for protection against any reflashing problems that may be encountered.

VCM programming allows adjustments to all parameters, such as spark, fuel, RPM limits, electric fan temperatures, transmission shift points and pressures, speedometer settings, and many more. The editor provides an easy-to-use graphical interface and many powerful table manipulation capabilities, including copying, scaling, and shifting to name a few.

This custom tuning is a very intense and thorough reprogramming, and therefore, HP Tuners only allows authorized installers to implement the VCM suite. But, if you are extensively modifying your engine, this is probably the best alternative for tuning your Hemi car.

Custom Tuning

I briefly mentioned custom tuning above, but here are the details. The first thing you need to do is locate an authorized custom tuning shop that handles your tuner.

Custom tuning requires a process of remapping the parameter of your Hemi car's electronic control module (ECM) to change the way it controls the engine. Although your car's ECU doesn't actually need to visualize the ignition and/or fuel map to picture how the computer comes to its conclusions, imagine a piece of graph paper. Now, draw a simple X-Y axis on it: one horizontal line (the X axis), and one vertical line on the left side of it (the Y axis). Numbers running along the X axis represent the engine's RPM range. The Y axis represents the load on the engine (the energy required to do the task at hand).

Now imagine different points scattered throughout that graph that represent different driving situations. That's a fuel map. At each of the hundreds of possible points, the ECU decides what to tell the fuel injectors to do.

The ECU receives input from all of the car's sensors: vehicle speed, air intake, fuel pressure, and temperature, and plots a specific point on the imaginary graph. The computer is programmed to tell the fuel injectors what to do at that very point on the fuel map, and it sends out the appropriate message without any more input from the driver. Once the ECU has received the information from the sensors and figured out what to do based on the fuel map, it can change three basic things to make the engine run at its best: fuel flow rate, spark timing, and idle speed.

An ignition map is similar to a fuel map; it decides what timing is required for a given engine RPM and load.

BOLT-ON PERFORMANCE

Project: DiabloSport I-1000 Installation

Your Hemi car came from the factory with a pre-programmed computer that controls everything your car needs to do. However, you can connect a small handheld device (computer) to upload a new modified program and alter various engine parameters. Initially, handheld tuners were only made available to factory service centers to compensate for minor tuning changes that may have been required. Luckily, in recent years, the aftermarket has made them available to everyone. Now you can upload custom programs that can adjust spark, fuel, and timing for maximum performance. Increasing power is only a part of the story.

Handheld tuners allow you to alter other parameters, such as the speedometer, gear-ratio changes, cooling-fan operation, fuel cut-off speed, and rev limiters. If your car has an automatic transmission, you can even control the shift firmness.

Before you connect your tuner to your vehicle, make sure that the battery is completely charged. Having the battery die halfway through a programming change is a bad thing because a dealer for the tuner might need to get involved, and that could be costly.

1 Plug the tuner into the OBD-II connector (generally located on the driver's side, underneath the dash). Once connected, turn the key to the run position, but do not start the engine. After the tuner acknowledges the connection, it directs you to change the tuning program or to alter other parameters. That's all there is to it.

This DiabloSport inTune is lightweight, smaller than most smart phones and about the size of an MP3 player. It comes preloaded with several tunes for different performance gains based on the fuel you plan to run in your Challenger, Charger, Magnum, or 300 (87 to 91 octane). The inTune comes with a full-color touch screen; just follow the instructions to easily program your vehicle.

2 Your new DiabloSport inTune comes with everything you need to tune your Hemi car: the cable to connect the tuner to your computer for updates, the cable to connect to your car's OBD-II port, and the tuner itself.

3 Before you connect the inTune tuner to your car, you need to connect it to your home computer to make sure that it has the latest updates. Once you plug the tuner into your computer, it goes to the DiabloSport website and downloads any updates it needs. While updating your inTune, be sure that the computer connection is not interrupted. Updating can sometimes take 20 minutes or more.

DODGE CHALLENGER AND CHARGER: HOW TO BUILD AND MODIFY

CHAPTER 3

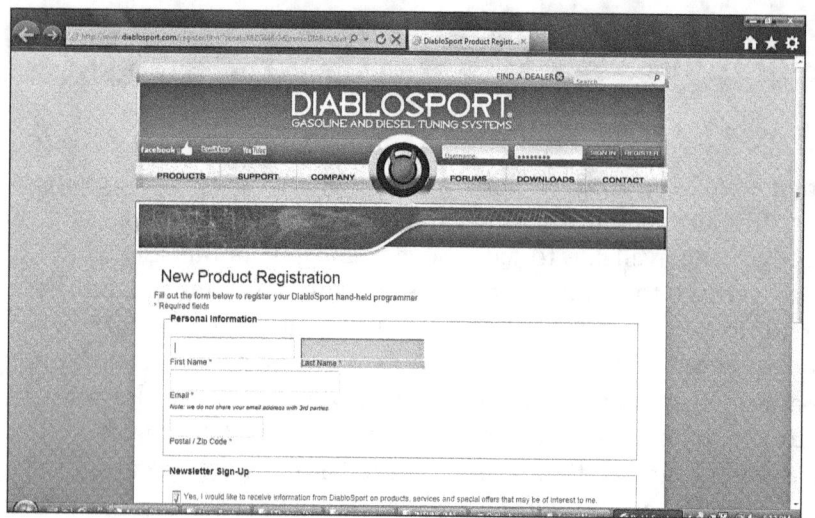

4 Although registration is not required to use the tuner, it is recommended. Registration helps with any warranty issues or technical questions you might have in the future. It only takes a couple of minutes to register.

5 In 1996, the diagnostic port on all automobiles made in North America was standardized. The OBD-II port on your Charger, Challenger, Magnum, or 300C is under the dash, closer to the driver's side of the driver's compartment.

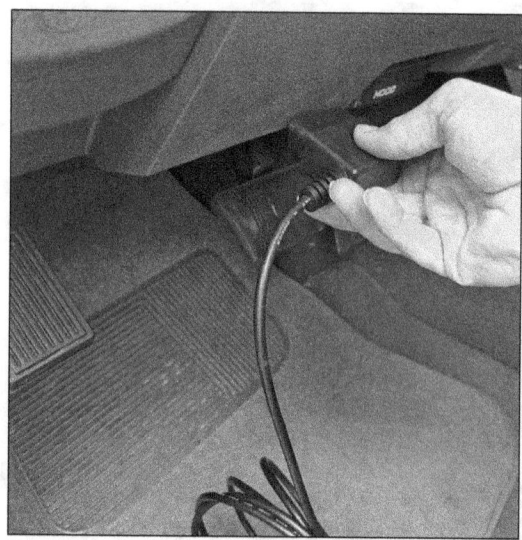

6 Begin by plugging in the supplied OBD-II cable to the inTuner handheld tuner, and then connect the other end of the cable to the OBD-II port. Make sure the ignition is turned off; do not turn the ignition on until inTune gives you the instructions on the screen to do so.

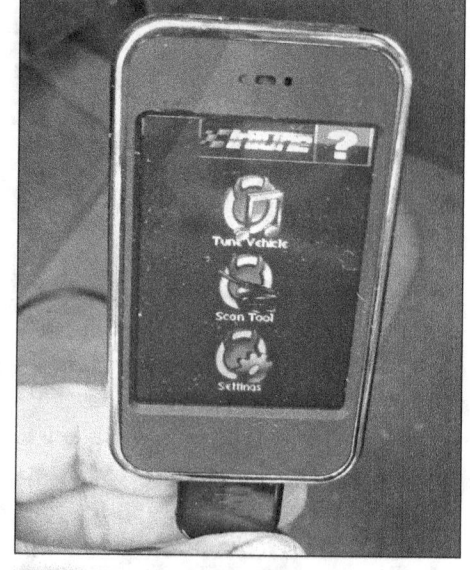

7 Once the tuner is plugged in and connected to the OBD-II port it turns on by itself. When it does it prompts you to turn on the ignition (do not start the car). This allows the inTune to determine what vehicle it is connected to and what tuning parameters are available for the application.

8 Once the inTune tuner configures itself for your vehicle, the tuner screen displays the available options. You can choose from tuning the vehicle, scanning for trouble codes, and going to the settings menu. "Tune Vehicle" does just what it implies. You can select from various pre-programmed tunes. The "Scan Tool" function allows you to scan for trouble codes that may be present in the ECM. "Settings" is just that, the settings of the inTune tuner.

54   DODGE CHALLENGER AND CHARGER: HOW TO BUILD AND MODIFY

BOLT-ON PERFORMANCE

9 When prompted, turn the key to the On position. Do not start the engine. At this time, the inTune tuner attempts to recognize your vehicle by communicating with the ECM. Do not unplug the tuner or turn off the ignition during this process. When it is time, read and accept the disclaimer on the screen. Once your vehicle has been identified, the tuner displays your vehicle's VIN along with any tunes that are available for your car.

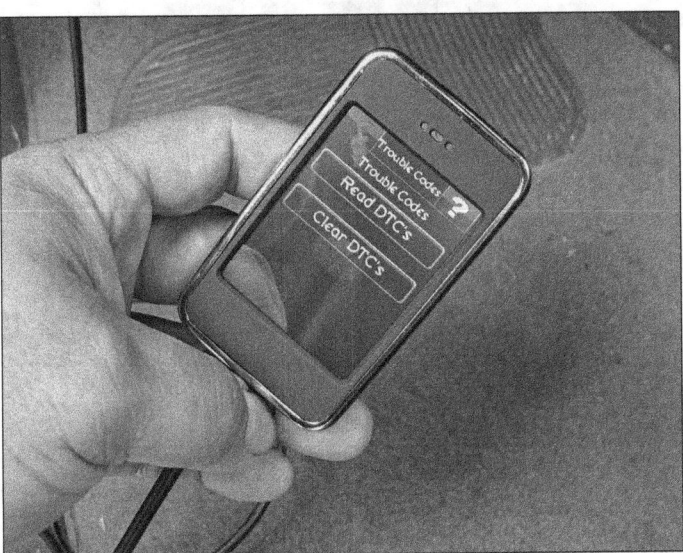

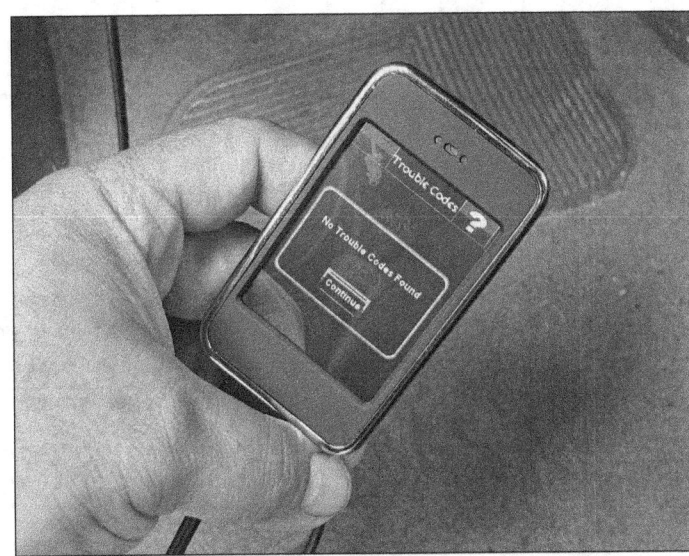

10 Before you actually install a tune, scan the ECU for any trouble codes. If no trouble codes are found, you can proceed.

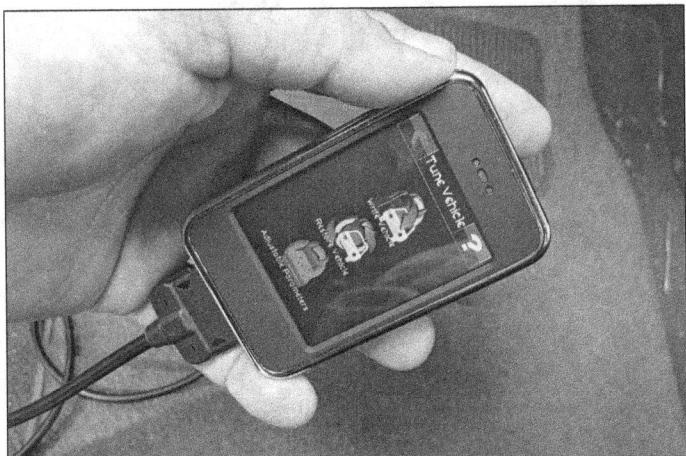

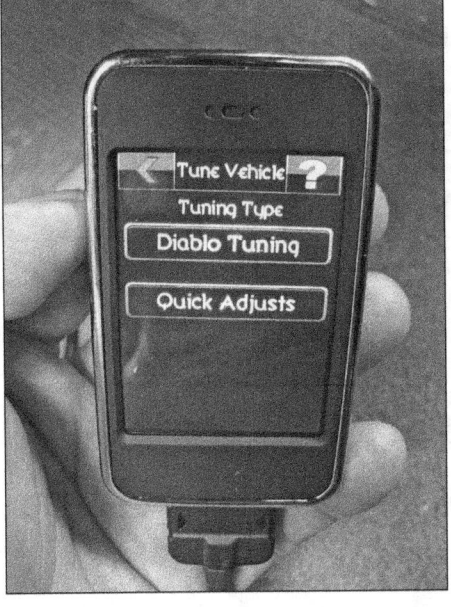

11 With the code scan out of the way, it's time to install one of DiabloSport's tunes. To do this, you first need to follow further screen prompts. At this point, you can either write the vehicle (tune it), or restore the factory settings.

12 If you choose Write Vehicle, you see this screen. From here, you can choose Diablo Tuning to access the available tunes for the car. If you choose Quick Adjusts, you can alter parameters such as tire size, RPM limit, etc.

DODGE CHALLENGER AND CHARGER: HOW TO BUILD AND MODIFY

CHAPTER 3

13 The inTune gives you the option to tune for use with 93-octane fuel, 87-octane fuel, or to get the best mileage. If you want to check the mileage booster first, choose that setting.

14 Before the inTune tuner reprograms your computer, it saves the factory tune parameters. This is done so you can return your car to stock. If you need to take it to the dealer for repair work you can remove the DiabloSport tune and the dealer will never know it was there.

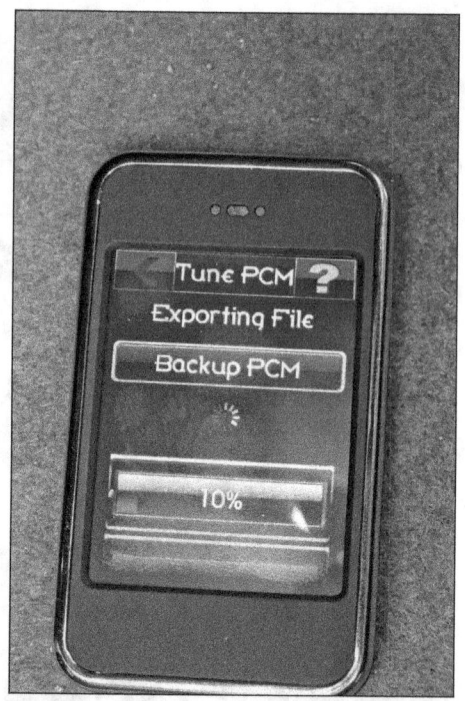

15 It takes a few minutes for the tuner to back up and save the original factory tune. Again, make sure that you do not disturb the inTune connections or turn off the key.

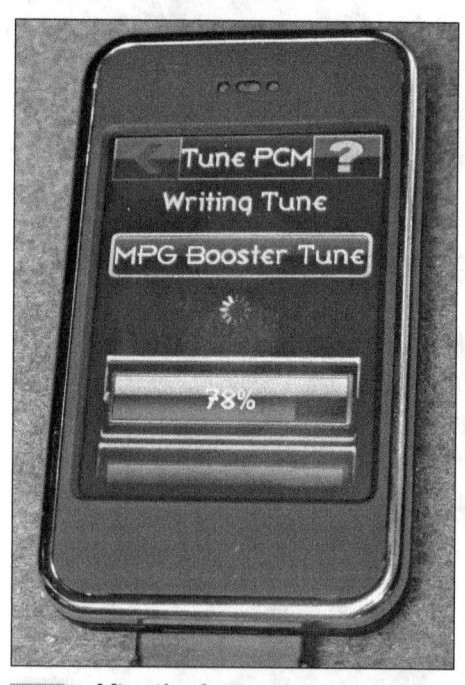

16 After the factory tune is safely stored within the inTune tuner, it starts to upload the tune you have chosen for your vehicle. Uploading should take only a minute or two.

17 Once the tune is uploaded into your vehicle, you are prompted to cycle the ignition. This means that you turn off and then turn on the ignition. Just as before, do not start the engine at this time.

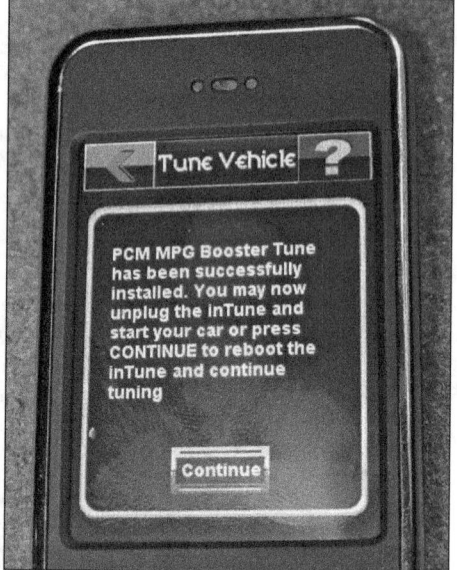

18 Voila, you are finished. Now you can either unplug the inTune tuner or continue to experiment with the parameters of your tuner and vehicle. To end your session simply unplug the tuner. If you wish to continue push "Continue."

DODGE CHALLENGER AND CHARGER: HOW TO BUILD AND MODIFY

BOLT-ON PERFORMANCE

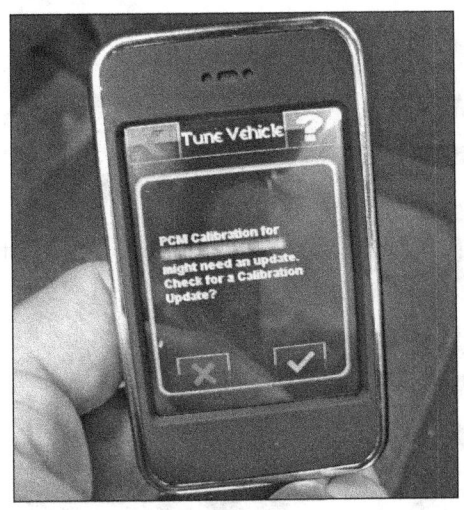
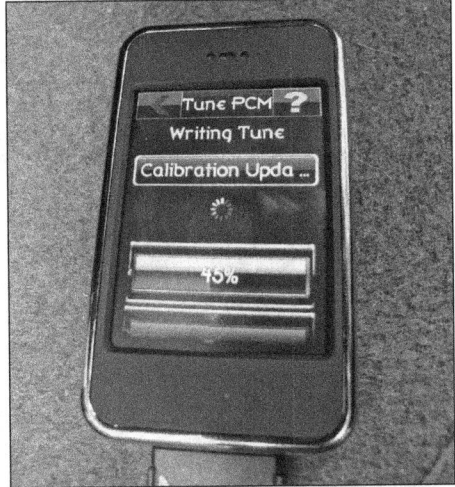

19 After you receive your new inTune immediately connect it to your home computer for updating. As soon as you plug it in to your car's OBD-II port, the screen on your inTune tells you that your powertrain control module (PCM) needs calibration.

This means that your inTune handheld tuner needs to be connected to your home computer again to download an update for your vehicle. Once it is downloaded you hook up the tuner to the car and it updates the vehicle to the newest calibration from Dodge.

Cold-Air Intakes

Cold, dense air produces a more efficient burn in the combustion chamber. A car's air-intake system supplies air to the engine but must also suppress noise, and even look good. Factory-designed air-intake systems feature baffles and chambers that are designed to slow the incoming air and reduce the noise created by fast-moving air. As the air travels through the factory air intake (typically corrugated plastic tubing), it runs into these restrictions and becomes disturbed. This disturbance (turbulence) causes air to lose some of its velocity and density, and this inhibits the engine from reaching peak efficiency. By making the flow of air through the filtration system "quieter," a certain amount of performance is sacrificed.

The factory air intake is an even bigger concern if your Hemi-powered ride has had performance modifications such as a free-flowing exhaust or ported cylinder heads. If the cylinder heads of your Hemi are flowing 15-percent more air than they did from the factory, your performance gains may be reduced when using the restrictive factory air intake. The reason is that the factory intake restriction is still in place, and the extra flow capability of the heads cannot be realized. Even simply changing from exhaust manifolds to headers increases engine airflow enough that a cold-air kit is required.

What I am getting at is that any modifications made to your Hemi-powered ride need to be carefully considered because other parts can and do have an overall effect.

Denser air produces a more complete burn, and less gasoline is wasted and pumped out of the exhaust. With less fuel waste, carbon deposits are minimized, which also adds to the performance improvement of the engine. Throttle response improvement may also be noticed, along with getting more oomph from the engine. Getting cooler, denser air into the engine is possible by only one method: Remove the factory air-filtration system and install a cold-air kit.

Engineers of aftermarket cold-air kits concentrate more on performance gains than on a quiet, neatly packaged system. That doesn't mean that cold-air kits don't improve the underhood appearance of your Challenger,

The LX car's stock air-intake system was designed to fit the underhood area, and it's not a performance-oriented air-delivery system. Performance air-intake kits are an easy-to-install and affordable product for improving horsepower, torque, and fuel economy.

Charger, 300C, or Magnum, however; the end user buys them because of the results that they produce.

Cold-air kits typically use air filters that have a larger surface area than that of a factory filter, metal or smooth plastic tubing, and sometimes, specially-engineered air-intake boxes. These parts are designed for the air to move through the system and into the engine's intake manifold with a minimum amount of turbulence.

Installing an aftermarket cold-air kit on your vehicle is simple, and it might be one of the most beneficial upgrades you can make. A good cold-air kit can provide many benefits, such as increased torque, increased fuel economy, a more aggressive engine sound at higher RPM, and yes, improved appearance under the hood. If you are looking for a large increase in horsepower, just adding a cold-air kit might not give you the results that you are looking for. That being said, the cold-air kit *if* used in conjunction with a handheld tuner/programmer has the potential to produce a solid horsepower increase; I have heard claims made of 20-hp increases.

It is a common misunderstanding that any aftermarket intake has the same results. This couldn't be further from the truth. Some companies spend a great deal more time researching and designing their intakes, and the result is higher horsepower gains throughout the power band.

All of the benefits of improved engine performance directly correlate to the improved efficiency of the engine. A more complete burn means it does not require as much fuel to produce the same amount of horsepower. Less wasted fuel means more of the fuel is burned for the purpose of creating combustion, again saving fuel. Engine computer controls are sensitive and sophisticated enough to recognize the changes provided by a performance air-intake system; the computer reduces injector spray and adjusts consumption demand. When you continue to drive the vehicle in the same manner as before the performance enhancement occurred, you are likely to see an increase in fuel economy.

Many companies offer a cold-air intake for Hemi-powered cars. The following are the most popular among Hemi car owners.

Advanced Flow Engineering

The Advanced Flow Engineering (AFE) Magnumforce Stage II cold-air kit out-flows the factory intake by 57

> ### PCV System
>
> The positive crankcase ventilation (PCV) system on your Hemi car vents the crankcase into the induction system, which helps lower emissions and provides a constant vacuum in the crankcase, aiding piston ring seal. The downside to this method of crankcase ventilation, however, is that small amounts of oil and oil vapor can be sucked into the induction system, and then into the engine's combustion chambers.
>
> This problem is made worse in engines with high crankcase pressures, such as those that are turbocharged or supercharged. A solution to this problem is to install an air/oil separator.

As the PCV system works, the oil that would normally travel back into the engine is captured in the separator.

This Stage II intake system from Advanced Flow Engineering (AFE) features a molded plastic intake tube that replaces the stock intake tract. By replacing the accordion-style intake tube, the AFE tube can increase airflow for maximum performance. The one-piece heat shield that comes with the kit requires minimal assembly, and the filter is constructed with 100-percent polyurethane. AFE has developed this intake to provide a hassle-free installation and is 50-state legal (CARB E.O. D-550-2/14). The retail price is about $330. (Photo Courtesy Advanced Flow Engineering)

BOLT-ON PERFORMANCE

If you want to keep your Charger, Challenger, Magnum, or 300 all Mopar, the Mopar cold-air kit is the answer. With this kit, you get increased airflow, which gives you more power; even better, many people report better fuel mileage after it is installed. This cold-air intake is street legal in all 50 states and has been tested to comply with emissions standards. The intakes are easy to install with a screwdriver, pliers, and a ratchet set in 30 minutes or less. The retail price is about $370. (Photo Courtesy Mopar Performance)

Airaid offers the MXP cold-air intake systems that improve horsepower and torque while delivering better fuel economy. The Airaid MXP system has a one-piece roto-molded cold-air box that is designed to keep engine heat away from the filter while allowing cooler air to get to the intake. It even uses the factory cold-air inlets in the body. The filter is available with either an oiled, red composite material or dry filtration technology in red, blue, or black. Each filter is constructed with a special blend of urethane that does not crack or warp and is washable and reusable. Installation times vary depending on the kit, but 20 to 25 minutes is average. The retail price is about $233. (Photo Courtesy Airaid)

percent. Included in this system is an 18-gauge powder-coated heat shield and washable and reusable oiled conical air filter. This intake system also features a molded plastic tube that replaces the stock intake tract. The one-piece heat shield requires minimal assembly, and the filter is constructed with 100-percent polyurethane for long life and multiple cleaning cycles. Installation times vary, depending on the kit, but 15 to 25 minutes is average.

Mopar

If you want to keep your car all Mopar, check this out: Mopar says that its intake increases airflow to your engine by as much as 20 percent and is one of the best dollars-to-horsepower investments you can make. It is Mopar-tested to boost horsepower and torque. This gain in power doesn't sacrifice anything, and actually improves fuel economy by 1 to 2 mpg depending on driving style. This cold-air intake is street legal in all 50 states and has been tested to comply with emissions standards. The intakes are easy to install with a screwdriver, pliers, and a ratchet set.

Airaid

The Airaid MXP system is designed around a one-piece cold-air box that keeps engine heat away from the filter. The box increases the amount of cooler air available, and even uses the factory cold-air inlets underneath it. The intake includes a large 4-inch-diameter intake tube that eliminates airflow restrictions.

The heart of Airaid's system is the massive air filter, which provides the engine with a steady supply of clean, cold air. The filter is available with either oiled red composite material or dry filtration technology in red, blue, or black. Each filter is constructed with a special blend of urethane that does not crack or warp and is washable and reusable. Installation times vary depending on the kit, but 20 to 25 minutes is average.

Corsa Performance

Corsa takes the cold-air intake one step further by completely encasing the filter, protecting it from engine heat. Starting with a Donaldson PowerCore Air Filter, Corsa was able to increase airflow without compromising air quality. The Corsa intake tube is made from heavy-duty large-diameter piping for silky-smooth transitions, reduced turbulence, and optimal flow dynamics. The air duct is joined with high-grade silicone couplers, which makes fitting the Corsa intake to your manifold a painless procedure. Best of all,

CHAPTER 3

Corsa's cold-air kit is the epitome of high performance. Inside its air filter enclosure is a cleanable and reusable five-layer protection air filter. This kit design allows the highest airflow rate possible and long filter life. Each filter comes pre-oiled and ready for use. Use a two-stage cleaning kit to thoroughly clean and re-oil the filter. You can get one for about $250. (Photo Courtesy Corsa Performance)

Engineers of aftermarket cold-air kits, such as this Corsa unit, concentrate more on performance gains than on a quiet, neatly packaged system. That doesn't mean that cold-air kits don't improve the under-hood appearance; however, the end user buys them because of the results that they produce. Cold-air kits typically use air filters with a larger surface area than that of a factory filter (metal or smooth plastic tubing), and sometimes, specially engineered air-intake boxes.

Corsa cold-air intakes include a one-year warranty.

Designed by the factory, this kit uses factory provisions and hardware, a powder-coated aluminum intake tube, high-quality clamps, and contains a divider and seal between the air box and intake tube. The air filter is a dry construction, which means that it can only be replaced, not cleaned and re-oiled. Installation times vary, depending on the kit, but 20 to 30 minutes is average.

Legmaker Intakes

The Legmaker Hammer design is constructed of carbon fiber. The fabrication process results in a smooth inner surface of the inlet tube which helps increase airflow. The kit is also designed to fit stock and 90-mm throttle bodies, so the kit stays with you through your upgrades. Installation times vary, depending on the kit used, but 15 to 25 minutes is normal.

If you prefer the high-tech look, Legmaker cold-air kits is the answer. The carbon-fiber inlet tube is great looking and effectively increases airflow roughly 20 percent, which improves throttle response and fuel mileage. This kit uses factory provisions and hardware, with a powder-coated aluminum intake tube (carbon-fiber version shown), high-quality clamps, and a divider and seal between the air box and intake tube. The air filter is available in either dry- or oil-type construction. Installation times vary depending on the kit, but 20 to 30 minutes is average. These kits cost about $300.

BOLT-ON PERFORMANCE

Project: Cold-Air Kit Installation

One of the first things that many car enthusiasts install to increase their car's performance is a cold-air kit. Although such a kit doesn't actually deliver cold air, it does deliver air to the engine that is cooler than what is available under the hood. A cold-air kit is an inexpensive and easier-to-install modification than most other engine mods. Although it doesn't add as much power as, let's say, a supercharger, a cold-air kit does deliver an increase in power and helps your engine in other ways.

The following installation of an Airaid cold-air kit (PN 350-210) can be accomplished in about an hour, and the cost is around $230. For such a minimal investment of time and money, you achieve a significant boost in performance.

Most cold-air kits remove the bulky and restrictive factory air boxes and flexible, accordion-style inlet tube that the factory installed. A free-flowing air filter and a large-diameter intake tube replace it. These have a smoother profile with fewer bends and are often wider than the factory units (shown). Some cars do not benefit much from replacing the factory air inlet tube, and simply get a new box and filter; it depends on the car and the factory inlet that it came with.

1 *The Airaid kit (PN 350-210) is designed for use on 2011–2014 Chargers and Challengers with either a 5.7-liter or a 6.4-liter Hemi. Before you begin, it is always a good idea to disconnect the negative battery terminal. You don't need to accidentally short something while you're working. Next, loosen the hose clamp that holds the factory intake tube to the air box. Now, disconnect the crankcase breather hose from the air box top, and you can remove the three air box screws securing the lid. With the lid removed, you can remove the bolt securing the lower half of the air box and remove the box from the vehicle.*

2 *A speed clip is located on the core support that holds the air box in place. This bolt will be in the way in a later step, so remove it now. If you seldom throw things away, you can keep it for a future project; it will not be reused during this upgrade.*

CHAPTER 3

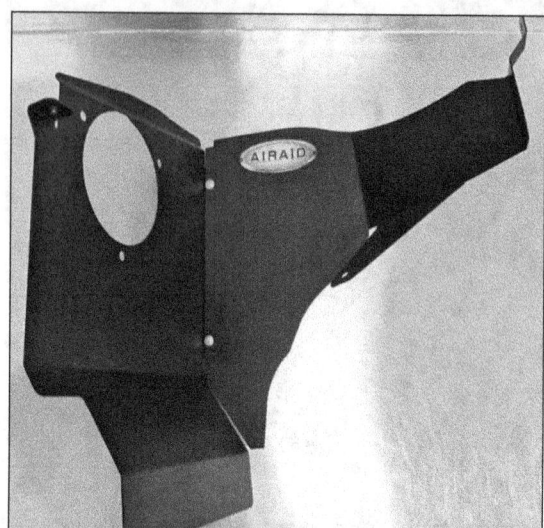

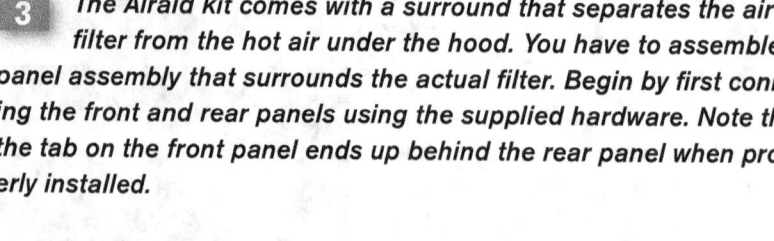

3 The Airaid kit comes with a surround that separates the air filter from the hot air under the hood. You have to assemble this panel assembly that surrounds the actual filter. Begin by first connecting the front and rear panels using the supplied hardware. Note that the tab on the front panel ends up behind the rear panel when properly installed.

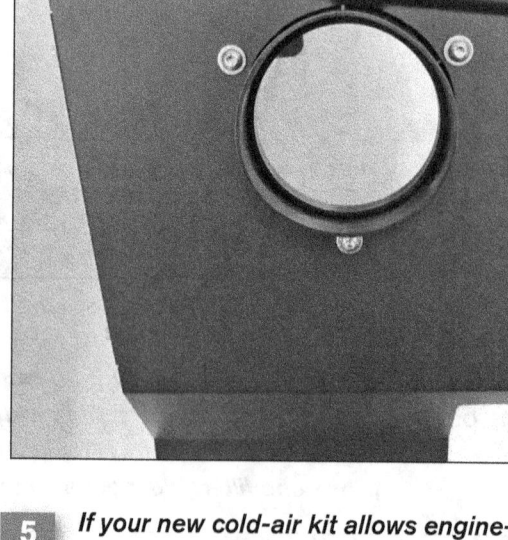

4 The new filter can't be allowed to move inside the enclosure, so to keep the new filter from bouncing around, you need to install the filter adapter onto the front panel (shown). The air filter attaches to this adapter.

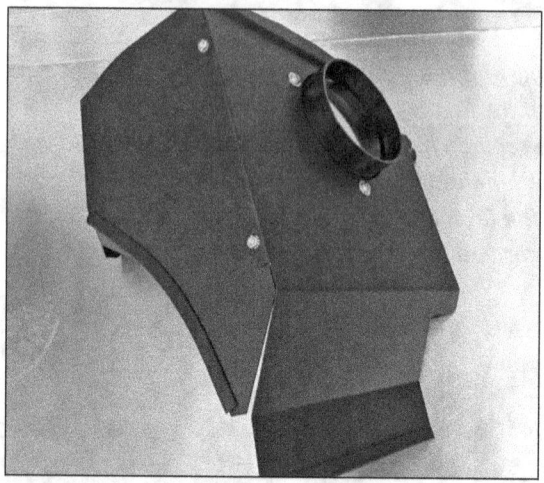

5 If your new cold-air kit allows engine-heated air to enter to your filter, and ultimately your engine, why are you even wasting your time and money doing this? That's why Airaid supplies a weatherstrip-type material to seal the air box surround from engine heat. Install one piece of the seal on the curved edge of the rear panel and the other piece on the bottom of the front panel.

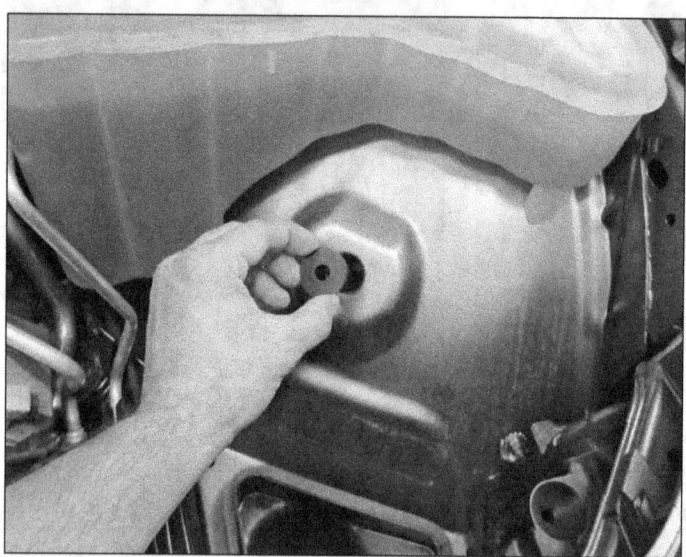

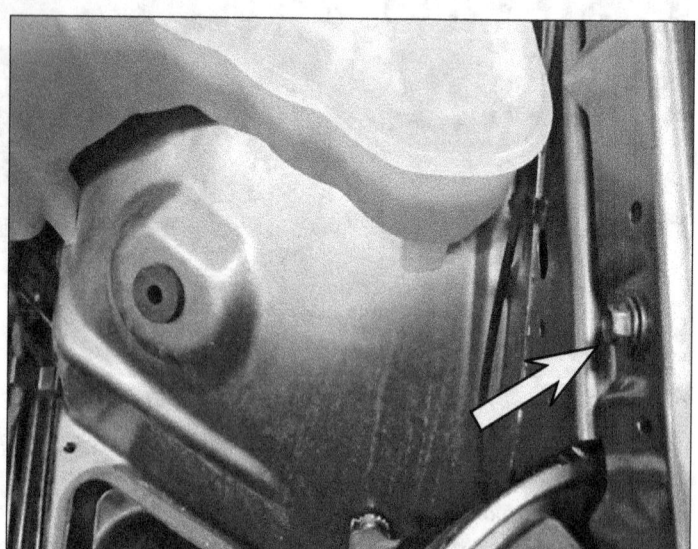

6 Place the supplied 3/8-inch well nut into the factory hole that is located in the inner fender. It will be fully secured in a later step.

7 Remove the factory 6-mm fender bolt and keep it somewhere safe so you don't lose it. You will reinstall it later.

DODGE CHALLENGER AND CHARGER: HOW TO BUILD AND MODIFY

BOLT-ON PERFORMANCE

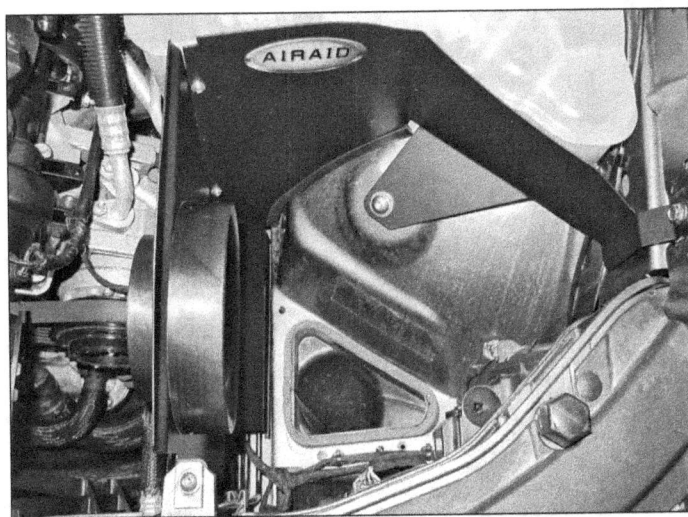

8 Lower the panel-surround assembly that you previously assembled into the inner fender area and align the mounting holes. Be sure to insert the bottom of the front panel between the anti-lock brake system (ABS) brake line and the car's sheet metal. Secure the assembly using the supplied hardware. Install the fender bolt that you saved into the previously placed well nut.

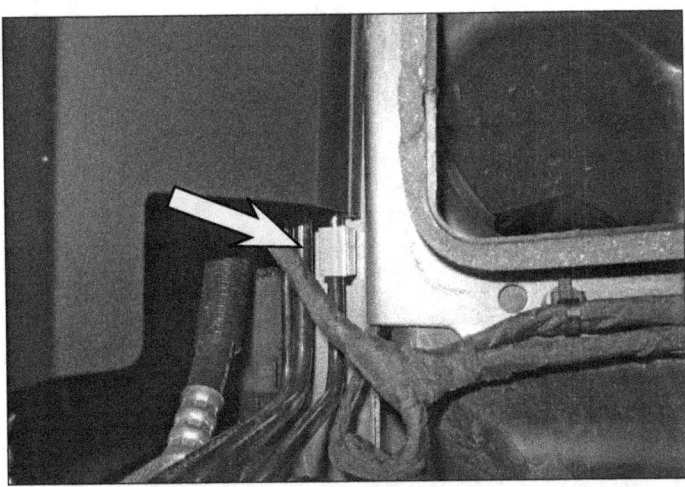

9 A supplied clip serves as a line holder. Snap it onto the ABS line (arrow) closest to the panel assembly and remove the adhesive backing so it sticks to the inner fender of the car. Next, gently push the surround panel away from the brake line, and slide the line holder behind the panel. Once that is done, let go of the panel and allow the adhesive on the clip to bond to the panel. This clip isolates the panels and prevents contact with the ABS line.

10 The Airaid kit is designed to fit multiple Hemi engine configurations including the 5.7- and 6.4-liter Hemi. When installing the cold-air kit, be sure to use the correct intake tube. If a 6.4-liter Hemi engine powers your car, use the inlet tube that is marked KIT-210-8T. If a 6.4-liter Hemi engine powers your Charger, Challenger, or 300, use the intake tube that is marked KIT-210-8T.

Once you have identified the correct tube for your engine, insert the larger, 3/4-inch grommet and one of the larger, 3/4-inch barbed fittings into the side of the tube. Now you can complete the tube assembly by installing the 2½-inch piece of 3/4-inch hose onto the tube fitting. Finally, finish by inserting the second 3/4-inch barbed fitting (shown).

DODGE CHALLENGER AND CHARGER: HOW TO BUILD AND MODIFY

CHAPTER 3

11 The next part of the process is to install the "hump hose" and the clamps. This hose is used as the transition that connects the filter to the inlet tube. The hump hose connects to the filter adapter. When assembling the hump hose, leave the clamps loose for now, as some adjusting may be required during final fitment.

12 Connect the assembled intake tube into the rubber hump hose and factory intake tube. When properly installed, the location lug in the factory tube mates with the notch in the Airaid intake tube. Tighten the clamps and connect the crankcase breather tube to the intake tube.

13 Install the supplied weatherstrip to surround the top edge of the air box panels. Attach the weatherstrip so its contour rolls outward, away from the open air filter area. Complete the installation by attaching Airaid's filter to the filter adapter.

Dyno Results

These graphs show that a horsepower and torque increase throughout the entire RPM range, not just at peak RPM. This means that the Airaid cold-air kit helps peak power and improves power where most people need it most, in the driving/cruising RPM range.

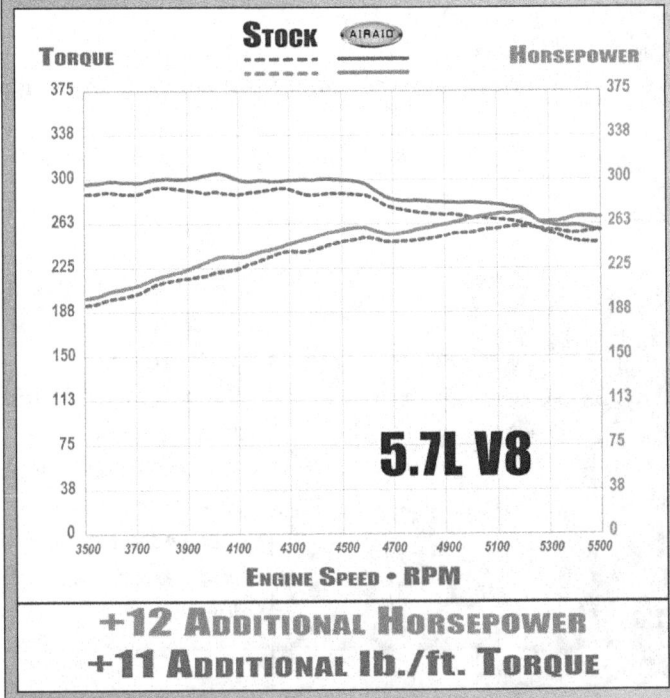

+12 Additional Horsepower
+11 Additional lb./ft. Torque

During dyno testing, a 2011 Charger with a 5.7-liter Hemi showed an improvement of 12 hp and 11 ft-lbs of torque with the Airaid kit installed. (Graph Courtesy Airaid)

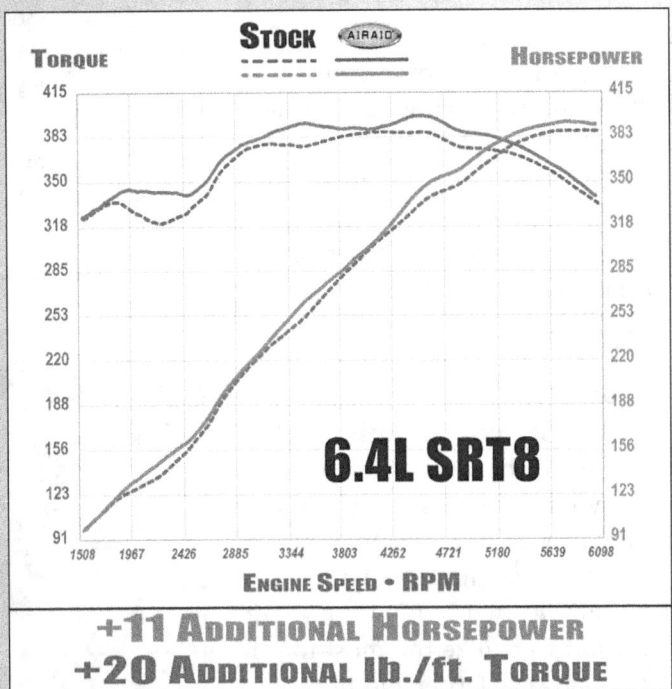

+11 Additional Horsepower
+20 Additional lb./ft. Torque

When tested on a 6.4-liter equipped 2011 Challenger, the Hemi increased to 11 hp and 20 ft-lbs of torque. (Graph Courtesy Airaid)

Headers

A performance-designed exhaust typically works better than a factory system because it is designed to manipulate the pressure waves that assist with engine cylinder-filling and scavenging. From the factory, your Hemi engine came with exhaust manifolds, not headers. That being said, the 6.1-liter Hemi did have a manifold that resembled a shorty-style header. A great way to upgrade your engine and increase performance is to add a set of headers and/or a performance exhaust, unless you live in California, where if it is not approved by the California Air Resources Board (CARB), it's not legal.

Exhaust manifolds are cast iron. Because the material is thick, it does a good job of retaining heat. This heat retention helps eliminate emissions in the exhaust. The rough interior casting surface does not enhance exhaust flow and this reduces the efficiency and ultimately the power of the engine because the exhaust gases must go out to allow fresh fuel and air to come in.

Headers are made from stainless steel or steel, are much lighter, and use individual steel tubes to release combusted air from each cylinder. These tubes are smooth, usually of equal length, and each one connects to a single collector. Because each cylinder fires at a different time, having each tube the same length ensures that the gases from each cylinder reach the collector at different times, avoiding a "collision" of gases, and increased back-pressure.

This benefit, though, can be lost if other exhaust components are not also upgraded. If the exhaust pipe that follows the headers is too restrictive, it can introduce back-pressure and diminish the power advantage of the headers.

Another characteristic of headers is that because of their thinner wall construction, they do not absorb as much sound as cast-iron exhaust manifolds. This can result in making the engine seem louder (although some may see this as an advantage).

Again, it is difficult to give a hard, fast number when it comes to horsepower increases when using headers, but typically, 10 to 15 hp can be gained when a good set of headers is installed. Keep in mind, headers increase airflow out of the engine, so airflow into the engine must be able to increase as well.

This is where compatible parts working together come into play. The true potential of headers might not be realized without also using a cold-air kit.

Header Selection

The first thing to consider when shopping for headers is the intended use of your vehicle. Are you building a daily driver, an occasional bracket racer, or a dedicated quarter-mile race car? At what RPM range do you want to realize the most torque and/or power? Other modifications and installing power adders (camshaft, supercharger, cylinder heads, nitrous, etc.) are equally important factors.

When choosing a header it's easy to think that the bigger the tube the better, but that's not always the case. Primary tubes that are too large for a given engine combination can actually cost you torque and horsepower by slowing the velocity at which the exhaust gas travels through the header. Every time the exhaust leaves the combustion chamber, it is being forced into the primary tube for that cylinder.

Although a small-diameter pipe flows less volume than a larger one, the exhaust in that smaller pipe also flows faster. Until you reach the engine RPM where the volume of exhaust gases requires bigger primary tube diameters, smaller tubes scavenge the cylinders more efficiently.

> **Selecting Headers**
>
> Before you select a set of headers, be sure you know the answers to the following questions.
>
> - What is your engine's expected horsepower output?
> - What is the intended use of your vehicle (street, street/strip, or racing)?
> - What is the average operating RPM range (where the engine spends most of its time)?
> - Do you have (or are you expecting to install) power adders, such as nitrous oxide or a supercharger?

Cast manifolds were never designed as a performance item. Not only is the inside of the manifold "as-cast," but this protrusion causes even more turbulence to the exhaust flow.

If your engine spends most of its time in the 1,500- to 3,500-rpm range, which is typical for a street-driven vehicle, you probably want to use 1 5/8- to 1 7/8-inch primary tubes. Any bigger, and you lose a considerable amount of low-end torque. Small tube headers don't typically lose their edge in horsepower and torque until you exceed 5,500 rpm.

I've talked about tube size and how it affects performance of a Hemi car, but what does it all mean for a street-driven car?. It's a well-known fact that late-model Challengers, Chargers, 300Cs, and Magnums are heavy vehicles. Because it takes torque to move these heavy cars, and most of the time the engine does not exceed 5,500 rpm, you might be wondering if a particular header style produces more torque than another. It is widely agreed that a "shorty" header typically produces more low-end torque than a long-tube design.

Long- and short-tube headers are prevalent in the late-model Hemi performance arena, and both have pros and cons for a given application. For a variety of reasons, long-tube headers do the best job of building horsepower and torque from mid-range to high RPM. These are great for high-revving machines and race cars, but they do sacrifice some low-RPM horsepower.

Shorty headers deliver more horsepower and torque from idle to the mid-RPM range. This makes shorty headers ideal for your Hemi car when used for a daily commute or in-town cruising. Also short-tube headers can be easier to install, as many of them bolt to the engine and

BOLT-ON PERFORMANCE

directly to the factory-installed catalytic converter. Some, however, do not, and require welding.

The cast exhaust manifolds that came on your Hemi are not designed for performance, the inside of the manifolds is rough-cast, which causes turbulence, and for some reason, some of them have a protrusion sticking into the exhaust flow. Upgrading to headers is a wise option.

Many companies offer headers for Hemi-powered cars. The following are the most popular among Hemi car owners.

Tube Technologies Inc.

A good set of headers, such as those from Tube Technologies (TTi), feature a 3/8-inch-thick and laser-cut header-to-head flange to prevent leakage and warpage from engine heat. The primary tubes are made of .065-inch-thick 304 stainless steel tubing and use a ball and socket collector with a 3-inch floating flange. The tubes are mandrel bent on computer-controlled machines for a precise fit and uninterrupted exhaust flow. As with all long-tube headers, unless you use a complete kit from a manufacturer, the exhaust must be modified to fit the headers.

JBA Performance Exhaust

JBA designed their long-tube stainless steel headers with thick 3/8-inch flanges that resist warping and leaks because of heat, and the oversized exhaust ports help direct the exhaust into the mandrel-bent tubing. All four tubes have JBA's patented Firecone collector that maximizes exhaust scavenging for the ultimate in flow.

The JBA Firecone collector eases the transition from individual tubes to the collector, helping to maintain the direction and speed of the exhaust flow. The result is a noticeable increase in power and efficiency. On a 2006 5.7-liter Hemi, dyno testing showed an increase of 18 hp and 28 ft-lbs of torque at peak power, and also showed an increase in both throughout the RPM range.

These headers typically take the do-it-yourselfer an entire day to install. Some modification of the wiring for the oxygen sensor is usually required, as it must be relocated.

Shorty headers, such as those from JBA, are a great performance upgrade available for any application. Although a long-tube header produces more power at high RPM, JBA shorty headers are significantly less restrictive than stock manifolds and dramatically increase the power and efficiency of an engine. Made of stainless steel and with heavy-duty features, these headers have been proven to produce more power than any other shorty header on the market.

You can install this "shorty" design in about half a day, and they fit with your factory exhaust. In dyno testing on a 2003 5.7-liter Hemi it is typical to see an increase of 12 to 15 hp, and 10 to 14 ft-lbs of torque.

SLP Performance

SLP Performance has been increasing engine performance for decades. Their headers are made of

Tube Technologies Inc. (TTi) has been building headers for Mopar cars for years; Mopar is all they do. These are one of the best-fitting headers on the market. The late-model Hemi versions are available in either a raw finish or ceramic coated (polished and unpolished). I've seen power increase by 25 hp (when used with a tune), and around 10 to 12 when no tuning is added. The primary tubes are made of .065-inch-thick 304 stainless steel tubing and use a ball and socket collector with a 3-inch floating flange. These headers retail for about $800. (Photo Courtesy Tube Technologies Inc.)

CHAPTER 3

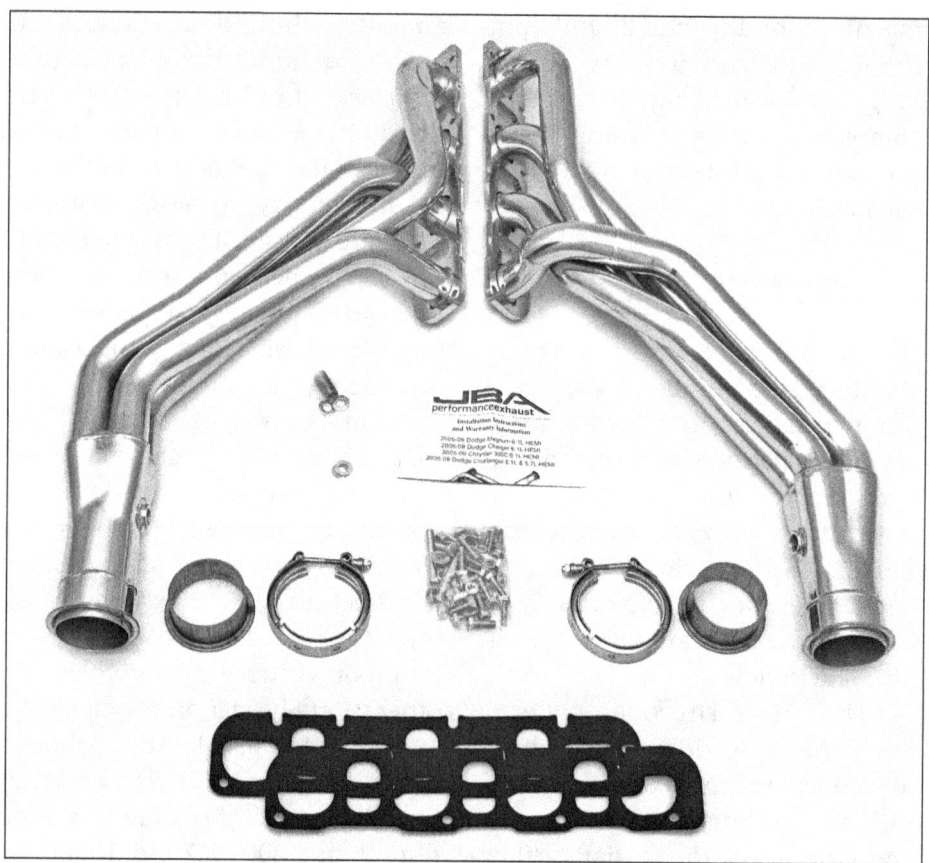

JBA's long-tube headers are made from stainless steel and the construction is top notch. They have applications to fit Challengers, Chargers, 300Cs, and Magnum wagons. The headers have been known to deliver a noticeable increase in power and efficiency, and on a 2006 5.7-liter Hemi, dyno testing showed an increase of 18 hp and 28 ft-lbs of torque at peak RPM, and an increase of both throughout the entire RPM range. You must have patience while installing all long-tube headers because accessing the header-to-head bolts is challenging at best. JBA long-tube headers retail for about $600. (Photo Courtesy JBA Performance Exhaust)

JBA shorty headers are significantly less restrictive than the stock manifolds and dramatically increase the power and efficiency of an engine. They are made from stainless steel that can survive the abuse of racing and daily driving. Each set includes high-quality hardware and thorough instructions for a professional no-leak installation. The retail price is about $400 for raw, and $510 for ceramic coated versions. (Photo Courtesy JBA Performance Exhaust)

mandrel-bent stainless steel, and are then ceramic coated to keep heat in, exhaust velocity up, and underhood temperatures down. The header's flanges are laser cut from 3/8-inch-thick metal, and the headers come with a limited lifetime warranty.

These headers also come with a pair of 3-inch high-flow catalytic converters that connect to 3-inch down pipes that are then sized to bolt to your factory cat-back exhaust system. As with all long-tube headers for LX cars, installation is easier from underneath the car. Once in the car, access to the bolt attaching it to the engine can be accessed from underneath and from the top.

Horsepower gains vary depending on the modification to the engine, but typically, an increase of 10 to 12 hp is realized.

Stock Exhaust System

The stock exhaust system (not including the manifolds or SRT headers) is also not optimized for

BOLT-ON PERFORMANCE

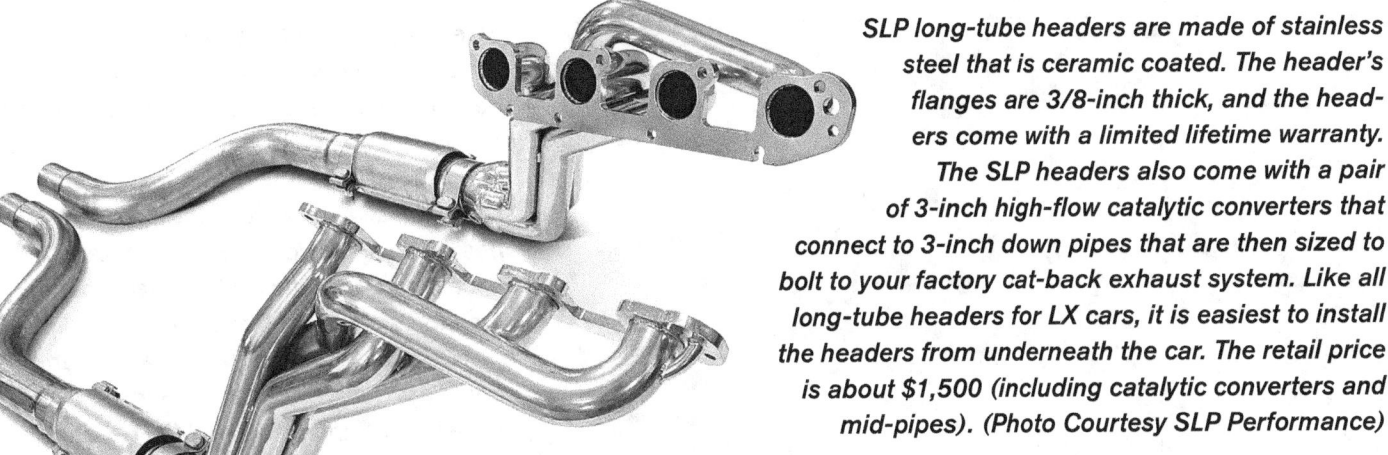

SLP long-tube headers are made of stainless steel that is ceramic coated. The header's flanges are 3/8-inch thick, and the headers come with a limited lifetime warranty. The SLP headers also come with a pair of 3-inch high-flow catalytic converters that connect to 3-inch down pipes that are then sized to bolt to your factory cat-back exhaust system. Like all long-tube headers for LX cars, it is easiest to install the headers from underneath the car. The retail price is about $1,500 (including catalytic converters and mid-pipes). (Photo Courtesy SLP Performance)

the best flow possible. It seems as if the designers spent more time thinking about the shape and placement of the radio and air conditioning controls than they did planning the exhaust system. That lack of performance thinking means that your engine has to work harder after combustion has occurred to get the exhaust gases out of the system. This robs it of horsepower, torque, and fuel economy. A performance exhaust system harnesses the potential power that your engine is wasting because of its inefficient stock exhaust. One of the reasons that the factory exhaust is not very efficient is because of the restrictions in the system. This inefficiency is the result of multiple factors.

First, the factory's run-of-the-mill muffler is the main source of exhaust silencing. It is a combination of tuning chambers, formed by partitions and ventilated and solid tubes. It is designed to effectively contain, absorb, and dissipate noise while moving the exhaust gases out of the tailpipe. The design that a stock muffler uses to dissipate noise is not suited to performance applications.

Another restriction is the exhaust pipe itself. Auto manufacturers use "press-bent" or "crush-bent" pipes for LX cars. This type of bending causes restrictions in the exhaust pipe that hinder flow by reducing the pipe's diameter at each bend.

Although technically a dual exhaust, the restrictive factory exhaust system on a Challenger, Charger, 300C, or Magnum is far from performance oriented. It is not designed to deliver performance, but rather, a quiet ride, and simply a way to exit the exhaust fumes.

The muffler itself is located in the middle of the car, and both banks of the engine expel gases through it. It is not only a huge restriction, but just before the exhaust gases exit the rear of the car, a pair of resonators is also installed. This design works very well as a sound-muffling device, but performance is definitely hampered. By swapping the exhaust, your vehicle can experience a substantial gain in power.

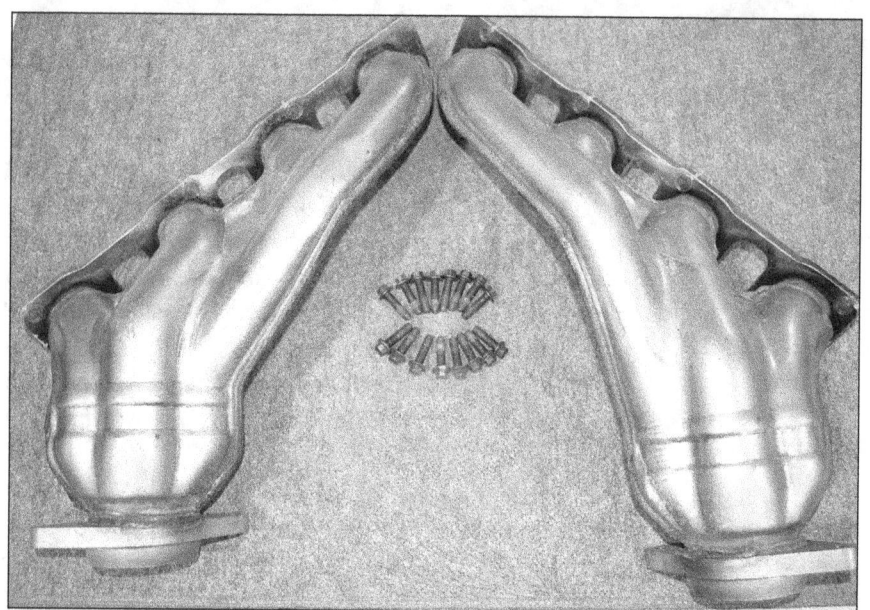

When the 6.1-liter Hemi was introduced in 2008, the SRT group designed and engineered a set of exhaust manifolds that were capable of out-flowing any Mopar manifold used at the time. The manifolds are an SRT exclusive, and are really a shorty-style header with individual tubes that are encased in a stainless steel shell. These manifolds are unique to the 6.1-liter Hemi.

Because the stock 5.7 exhaust manifolds are definitely a huge restriction in the engine's ability to expel the exhaust flow, many enthusiasts have added 6.1-liter manifolds to their 5.7 Hemi. Keep in mind, the collector size on the SRT manifolds is different from that of the R/T models.

To accomplish the swap, you need the manifolds, new mid-pipes, and other miscellaneous items. By the time you add up the cost of the 6.1-specific pieces, you might as well just buy a set of shorty headers that are designed to fit your car.

Catalytic Converter

Although not covered in this book, catalytic converters are part of the exhaust system, and are an emissions control device that converts toxic pollutants into an inert exhaust gas, creating less toxic pollutants.

As exhaust gas flows through the catalytic converters it flows over a catalyst (usually platinum and/or palladium). This catalyst is bonded onto a ceramic honeycomb or ceramic beads that are housed in a muffler-like package. In a Hemi car, these are attached to the exhaust manifolds. The catalyst helps to convert carbon monoxide and hydrocarbons into carbon dioxide.

A catalytic converter is typically more of an exhaust blockage, than either the muffler or the manifolds. One way to cure the problem is by using high-flow catalytic converters. High-flow cats, such as these from Dynomax, do the same thing as the stock units but accomplish the task more efficiently. With high-flow cats, increasing the overall cross section of the honeycomb or widening the passages allows you to elevate the flow rate of the exhaust. This affords the converter more passages where the chemical reaction can take place or allows exhaust gases to flow more freely.

Designs with larger cross sections have to be engineered to fit within the allotted space on the car, and designs with larger passages have to contain more catalyst metal so they can quicken the catalytic reaction. Either way, it's important that the unit does not sacrifice effectiveness for greater efficiency or increases carbon dioxide exhaust emissions.

Always make sure that any catalytic converter you buy is from a reputable source, and that it complies with the emissions laws in your state. Consult with an emissions repair shop to make sure that you select a setup that is both legal and effective. ■

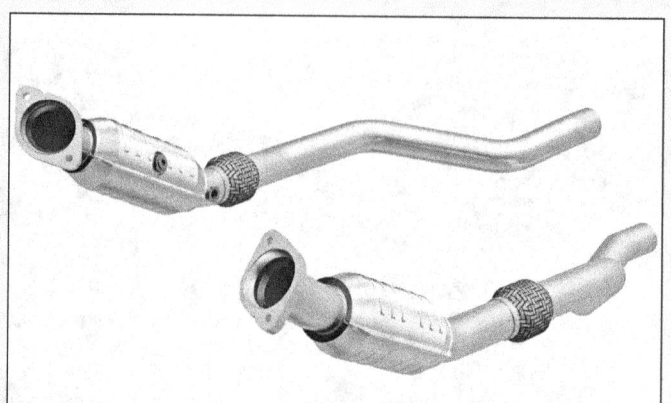

The OEM catalytic converters on your car are a bottleneck for exhaust flow. If you want to add performance, many times adding a set of high-flowing cats significantly increases the engine's horsepower output.

Performance Exhaust Systems

However, a better way does exist to form an exhaust system for your vehicle, and most aftermarket exhaust systems are bent with this preferred method. Performance exhaust systems generally use a mandrel bending process. When the pipe is bent using a mandrel method, the pipe does not change diameter (crushing). This makes mandrel bending much better.

Pipe Size

The way your pipes are bent is a serious consideration, but their actual size (diameter) affects how much horsepower your engine can deliver to your tires. Most performance exhaust systems use pipes with a larger diameter than the factory pipes. The larger diameter allows the maximum amount of exhaust to flow.

The diameter of the pipe is based on your engine size and power output. Again, bigger is not always better. A good performance exhaust is properly sized for your particular vehicle. A guide to determine the correct size or diameter of pipe to use is to consider the fact that your exhaust system needs to flow 2¼ cfm for every 1 hp the engine produces.

Material and Cost

After you decide to install a performance exhaust you must consider that the materials used to make it can dramatically affect the price. Two types of materials are primarily used to make exhaust parts: aluminized steel and stainless steel.

Aluminized steel is used for most factory-installed exhausts. It's inexpensive and it works. However, it corrodes and rusts over time. Dealers' and parts store replacement parts for exhaust systems also use aluminized steel.

If you decide that you want a better-quality material for your exhaust, you can step up to stainless steel. Then you need to decide whether you want T409 stainless or T304 stainless steel. T409 stainless steel contains added chromium and nickel that gives it a little more resistance to rust and corrosion and is the most commonly used material in aftermarket exhaust systems.

T304 stainless steel contains more chromium and significantly more nickel than T409. The material is lightweight, and can maintain its appearance over the course of many years of rugged use. It is the highest grade of stainless steel used in automotive parts.

Exhaust Pipe Sizing

To get a rough idea of the pipe you need, you can use this formula:

$$CFM = RPM \times displacement \div 2$$

This gives you the proper volume of air (CFM) for the exhaust system. If you really want to go further with the math, you can correct for thermal expansion, but you need to know the exhaust temperature to calculate it.

To make pipe selection easy, the following table shows the amount of air flowed in some common pipe sizes, as well as the estimated maximum horsepower for each pipe size.

Pipe Diameter (inches)	Pipe Area (in²)	Total CFM (est.)	Max HP Per Pipe	Max HP For A Dual Pipe System
1½	1.48	171	78	155
1⅝	1.77	203	92	185
1¾	2.07	239	108	217
2	2.76	318	144	289
2¼	3.55	408	185	371
2½	4.43	509	232	463
2¾	5.41	622	283	566
3	6.49	747	339	679
3¼	7.67	882	401	802
3½	8.95	1,029	468	935

Fuel Rails

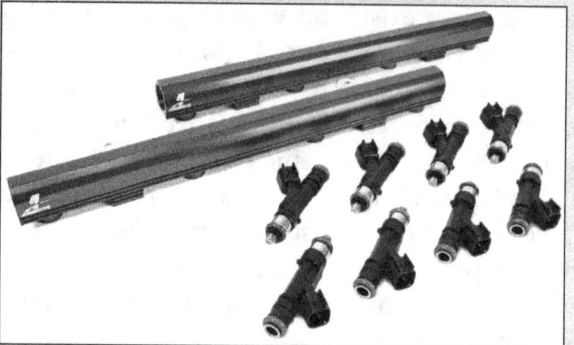

You can purchase quality fuel rails from Aeromotive (shown), Modern Muscle, shopHemi.com, among others. Swapping fuel rails usually takes a couple of hours, but can be done at home. The retail price starts at about $250. (Photo Courtesy Aeromotive)

Although fuel rails do not actually add horsepower, they do typically feature a larger internal diameter that dampens the reverbing injector pulses, and the larger diameter also provides a small increase in fuel volume.

Two things may lead you to replace your stock fuel rails: the power level of your engine and their lack of visual appeal. A good power level for upgrading is around 500 rear-wheel horsepower. Most aftermarket rails are of decent quality and allow you to run large cross-over lines and a fuel return if you have a high-horsepower fuel system.

Performance System Types

Challenger, Charger, 300C, and Magnum exhaust systems come in three types: full, cat-back system, and axle-back.

Full systems (headers and exhaust) are available from companies such as TTi and SLP. These systems come with everything that you need (header, hardware, pipes, and mufflers). They cost more than a cat-back system because they have more parts. They are also more involved to install because they include headers.

Cat-back systems (from the manifolds/headers back) are a replacement exhaust that begins at the catalytic converter/mid-pipe and run to the rear bumper. A cat-back exhaust provides more horsepower.

Axle-back systems (from rear axle to rear bumper) are primarily designed to improve the sound and look of a vehicle.

Full Exhaust Systems

As you know, a set of headers or a cat-back exhaust system can increase the performance of a Hemi car. But if you swap out the stock manifolds *and* the exhaust system, you have developed a path of less resistance for the wasted exhaust gases to escape the engine. When the stock exhaust components are replaced to improve the flow of exhaust gases out of the engine, you reduce "pumping losses."

Pumping losses refers to the amount of horsepower that is used to push the exhaust gases out of the engine's cylinders during the engine's exhaust stroke. Because a free-flowing exhaust reduces the amount of exhaust gas from being pushed out of the engine, more horsepower is now available at the flywheel. An added benefit of reducing pumping losses is that fuel mileage also increases.

Many companies offer full exhaust systems for Hemi-powered cars. The following are the most popular among Hemi car owners.

SLP Performance

SLP's Hemi-powered Challenger, Charger, Magnum, and Chrysler 300C headers are mandrel bent from stainless steel. Then they are ceramic coated to keep heat in, exhaust velocity

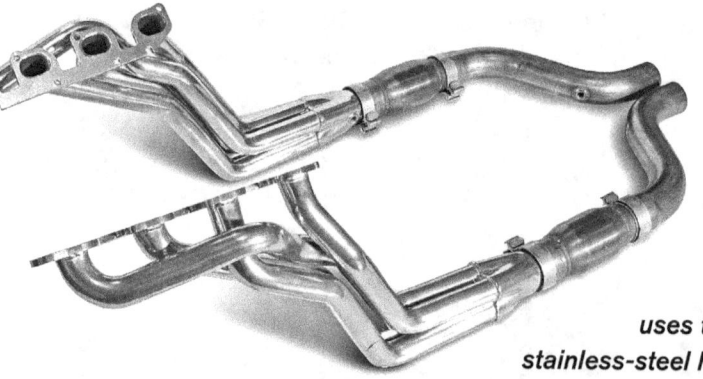

SLP has a complete exhaust system for the Hemi-powered Challenger, Charger, Magnum, and Chrysler 300C. The kit uses their mandrel-bent stainless-steel headers, which are ceramic coated. The headers are also compatible with the factory exhaust gas recirculation (EGR) system. (Photo Courtesy SLP Performance)

BOLT-ON PERFORMANCE

Included in SLP's exhaust is a pair of 3-inch high-flow bullet catalytic converters, which flow into a full 3-inch down pipe that bolts to SLP's D31004 or D31005 exhaust. All necessary hardware and installation instructions are included, and the headers are backed by their limited lifetime warranty. Installation takes the better part of a day, but typical hand tools should get the job done. The retail price is about $2,200. (Photo Courtesy SLP Performance)

up, and underhood temperatures down.

The primary tubes are 1¾ inches, and they are compatible with the factory exhaust gas recirculation (EGR) system. Also included is a pair of 3-inch high-flow bullet catalytic converters, which flow into a full 3-inch down pipe that is sized to bolt to SLP's D31004 or D31005 exhaust.

All necessary hardware and installation instructions are included, and the headers are backed by a lifetime warranty. When tested on a 2006 Daytona, SLP's headers and exhaust yielded an additional 20 hp and 32 ft-lbs of torque over the factory system.

Tube Technologies Inc.

TTi offers a complete exhaust (or individual parts) for 5.7- or 6.1-liter Hemis. The headers feature 1⅞-inch primary tubes and are available ceramic coated. The entire exhaust system (cats included) is made of 3-inch mandrel-bent pipe and comes with everything needed for a complete install including polished tips.

Plan on most of the day for installing this complete kit.

Cat-Back Systems

The second most common upgrade, after the addition of a cold-air intake system, is to install an aftermarket cat-back system. This type of exhaust system attaches to the factory catalytic converter and mid-pipe, and then runs to the rear of the car.

Installing this style of exhaust is fairly simple. For most applica-

TTi offers a complete exhaust system with ceramic-coated headers, and an exhaust system with 3-inch-diameter pipes. To make this a complete kit, TTi even includes new catalytic converters. The retail price is about $1,629 with uncoated headers, and $2,500 with coated headers. (Photo Courtesy Tube Technologies Inc.)

tions a cat-back exhaust includes mandrel-bent piping, clamps, and muffler(s). The Challenger, Charger, Magnum, and 300 all came with resonators at the rear of the exhaust, and a cat-back system eliminates the resonator, allowing better flow, performance, and sound.

Many companies offer cat-back exhaust systems for Hemi-powered cars. The following are the most popular among Hemi car owners.

DynoMax Performance Exhaust

DynoMax has been building their Super Turbo mufflers for years, and now they offer them with a cat-back kit for Challenger, Charger, 300C, and Magnum. Unlike a chamber-style muffler, the Super Turbo uses a channel to direct exhaust gases and eliminate turbulence. The large internal flow tubes improve exhaust flow and reduce back-pressure; each muffler uses fiberglass matting to absorb unwanted interior resonance while maintaining a performance tone.

DynoMax Super Turbo mufflers are backed by a limited lifetime warranty and exclusive 90-day performance and sound guarantee. If you are not happy with the performance or sound within 90 days, you can return it (restrictions apply).

This cat-back system can be installed in a few hours in your driveway, so your vehicle's exhaust can be quickly and easily customized with an emissions-legal premium performance system. I've seen this system post a gain of 13 hp and 24 ft-lbs of torque in recent dyno testing.

Flowmaster

Flowmaster's cat-back DOR (dual out rear) exhaust, Force II, offers excellent performance. The system delivers a moderate exterior tone and a moderate-to-mild interior tone. It is suited to customers looking for efficiency improvements without a lot of noise. Like all Flowmaster systems, the benefits include improved throttle response and power and mileage increases.

Flowmaster offers a DOR (dual out rear) kit that delivers a moderate exterior sound, with a moderate-to-mild interior tone. The Flowmaster cat-back exhaust connects to the factory mid-pipe, just behind the factory catalytic converters. The retail price is about $750. (Photo Courtesy Flowmaster)

Designed for an easy fit, this system includes all necessary parts and hardware for easy installation. The mandrel-bent 16-gauge aluminized tubing connects after the factory catalytic converter. Again, installation can be done a couple of hours. And you can expect approximately a 15 hp and torque increase.

Corsa Performance

Corsa cat-back systems come in 2½- and 2¾-inch diameters and feature either a mellow (Sport), or "extreme" tone, depending on which you choose.

This system is designed to fit, and can be installed in a couple of hours or so. Corsa says that you can expect to gain approximately 10 hp and 13 ft-lbs of torque.

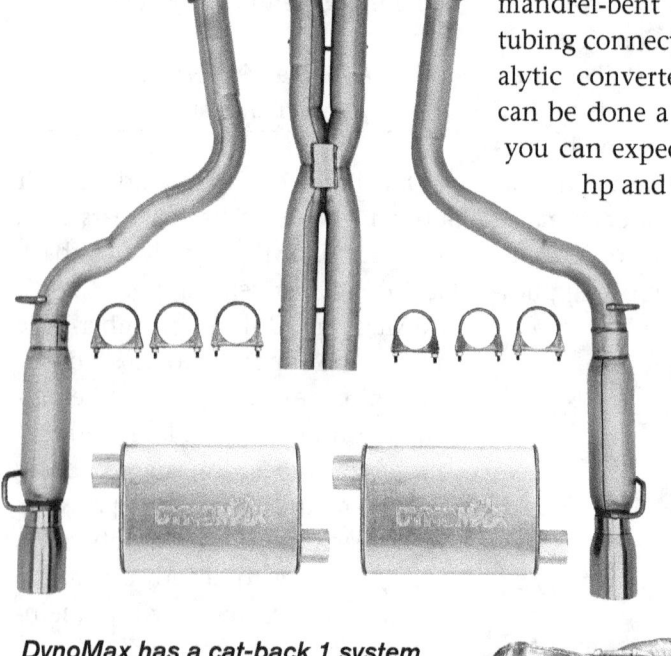

DynoMax has a cat-back 1 system that features either their Super Turbo or Ultra Flo mufflers. The internal flow tubes of the mufflers reduce back-pressure, and the sound is impressive. The muffler "muffles" unwanted resonance, but delivers a deep, performance tone. The retail price is about $700. (Photo Courtesy Dynomax Performance Exhaust)

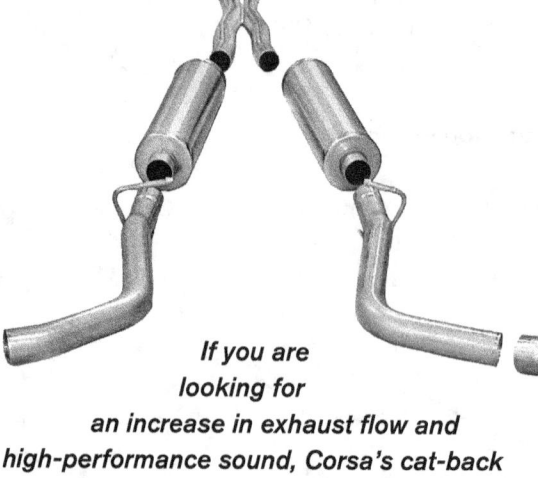

If you are looking for an increase in exhaust flow and high-performance sound, Corsa's cat-back systems deliver either a moderate or a more aggressive exhaust note (depending on muffler choice). The kit is a bolt-on installation and includes all the necessary parts. The retail price is about $1,800. (Photo Courtesy Corsa Performance)

JBA Performance

JBA has a complete 3-inch cat-back exhaust system that fits a Hemi-powered Challenger, Charger, 300C, or Magnum. This kit is a mandrel-bent stainless steel system with JBA's proprietary mufflers for an exclusive JBA sound. The kit offers an increase in flow and performance, and is designed to accommodate the popular factory exhaust tips.

Once again, installation can be completed in a few hours. When tested on a 2006 Magnum SRT, the 6.1 Hemi saw an increase of 17 hp and 22 ft-lbs of torque.

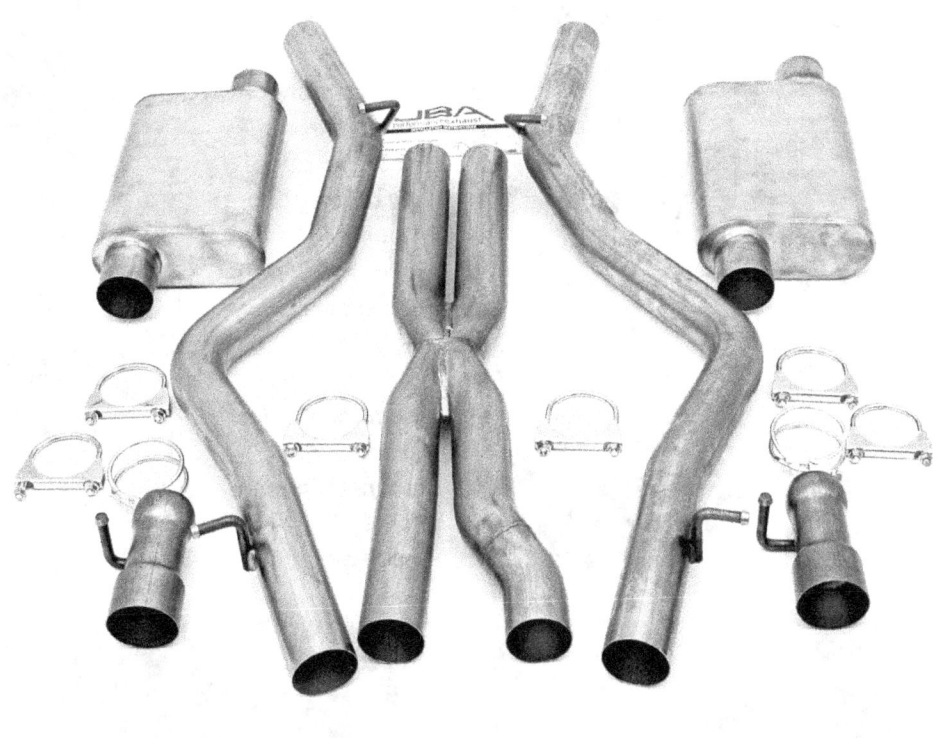

JBA's 3-inch cat-back system for Hemi-powered cars uses all mandrel-bent stainless and patented JBA mufflers. Their mufflers give you an exclusive sound that only JBA can deliver. The retail price is about $600. (Photo Courtesy JBA Performance Exhaust)

Project: TTi Full Exhaust Installation

Most automobile manufacturers leave a lot to be desired when it comes to improving the performance of the modern muscle car, including the Charger, Challenger, Magnum, and 300 Hemi car. I'm not saying that the buyer was cheated when it comes to performance, but manufacturers chose the least expensive alternative for items such as the exhaust system. An aftermarket performance exhaust, such as one from Tube Technologies, frees some of the power from the engine and makes the car sound great at the same time.

The TTi system allows for a smoother, more efficient path for exhaust gases to escape, so your engine breathes better. This means that more fuel and air can be burned to create more power. One of the most noticeable improvements (and the main reason a lot of folks change their exhaust) is the subtle, but distinctly more-aggressive, exhaust note.

Another factor to consider is the material used to make the system. Most factory exhaust systems are made of mild steel, so they have a tendency to deteriorate over time.

When researching exhaust systems, the diameter of the header primary tubes and the exhaust pipes is another thing to keep in mind. This is especially important if you plan to add more aftermarket parts (such as a supercharger). Although most Hemi cars benefit from slightly larger piping, if you use a pipe that is too big you can actually hurt your vehicle's performance. On the other hand, if you are eventually adding a supercharger, you want to go with larger pipes so that you can use the same exhaust after the boost is added.

Because most factory-made systems were formed using a "crush-bend" technique, exhaust gas-flow is restricted. The TTi exhaust uses a mandrel bending process, which is smooth and allows the pipe to remains at a constant diameter throughout the bend. That means there's less resistance, so you get more efficient airflow and better performance.

When I installed the complete TTi exhaust it took me a full day; plan accordingly. Finally, before purchasing any aftermarket exhaust system, find out what is and is not legal in your state. Some states allow a modified exhaust (headers) and some do not.

CHAPTER 3

1 Start removing the exhaust by unhooking the exhaust hangers. To do this, use a small pry bar to pry off the rubber mounts from the factory exhaust. Leave the rubber hangers on the car, as you need them for the new exhaust. A two-person team makes the job much easier.

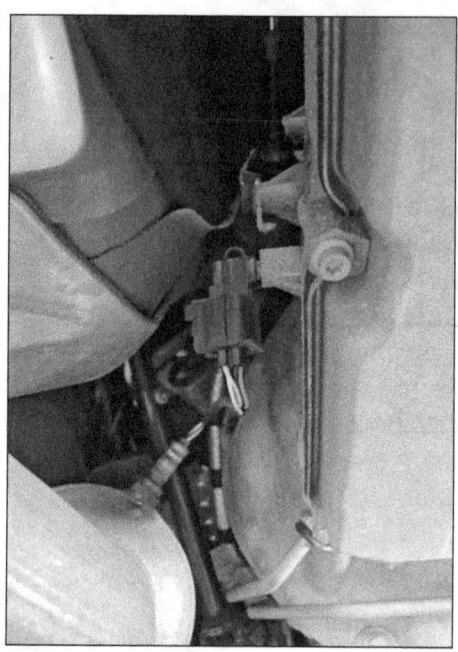

2 Oxygen sensors are before and after the catalytic converters. Before you can remove the exhaust, you need to unplug them from the car's wire harness. Be very careful not to damage the oxygen sensors; your car needs them, and they are fairly expensive to replace.

3 Unhooking the exhaust from the factory exhaust manifolds can be tough. If the nuts are rusted to the studs, they could either round-off the nut when you try to remove it, or break the stud in the manifold. If you're replacing the manifolds with headers, a broken stud is no problem. A rounded nut, on the other hand, can be a problem. It might help to spray the stud and the nut with a good penetrating oil and let it soak.

4 Protruding into the manifold is the oxygen sensor. The sensor is part of the emission control system. Your Hemi engine burns the gasoline present with the oxygen. The air and gasoline ratio of around 14.5:1 for standard pump gas is perfectly balanced. If there is less air than this ideal ratio, there will be extra fuel left over after combustion that didn't burn. A rich mixture like this is bad because the unburned fuel creates pollution.

If there is more air than fuel required for this ideal ratio, then there is excess oxygen. This is called a lean mixture. A lean mixture tends to produce more nitrogen-oxide pollutants, and in some cases, it can cause poor performance and even engine damage. The goal of the sensor is to help the engine run as efficiently as possible and to produce as few emission contaminants as possible.

The oxygen sensor is positioned in the exhaust pipe to detect rich and lean mixtures. These oxygen sensors generate a voltage, and the engine's computer looks at the voltage to determine if the mixture is rich or lean. The computer then adjusts the amount of fuel entering the engine accordingly. The reason the engine needs the oxygen sensor is because the amount of oxygen that the engine can pull in depends on all sorts of things, including altitude, air temperature, engine temperature, barometric pressure, engine load, etc. When the oxygen sensor fails, the computer can no longer sense the air/fuel ratio, so it ends up guessing. Your car performs poorly and uses more fuel than it needs to.

BOLT-ON PERFORMANCE

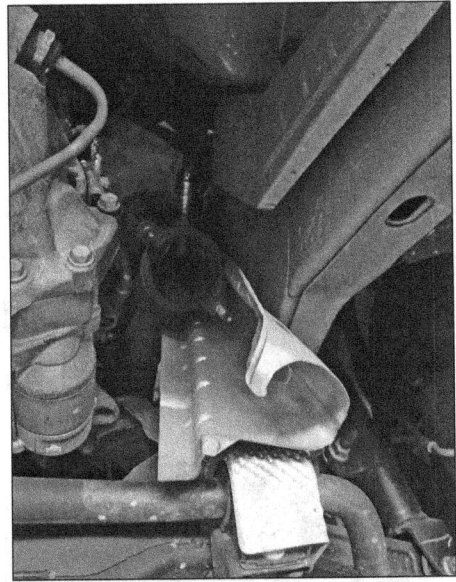

5 The factory heat shield needs to be removed to get to all of the exhaust manifold bolts. You don't have much room to get your hands up in where they need to be. Once the bolts are removed, the shields can be moved out of the way. You will not be reusing the shields, so if they are "tweaked" while being removed, it's no great loss.

6 As I mentioned earlier, some of the manifold/header bolts can be tough to access. Before you start to remove the bolts from the factory manifolds, give them a good shot of penetrating fluid. It is not very likely that these bolts are rusted fast, but the penetrating fluid helps keep them from galling as you remove them. If for some reason you feel the need to use a torch, these bolts are in very tight quarters, with wiring very close by. A torch is not recommended.

7 One of the bolts holding the factory manifold in place on the passenger's side helps support the oil dipstick tube. The dipstick tube needs to be removed from the engine to make room for manifold removal.

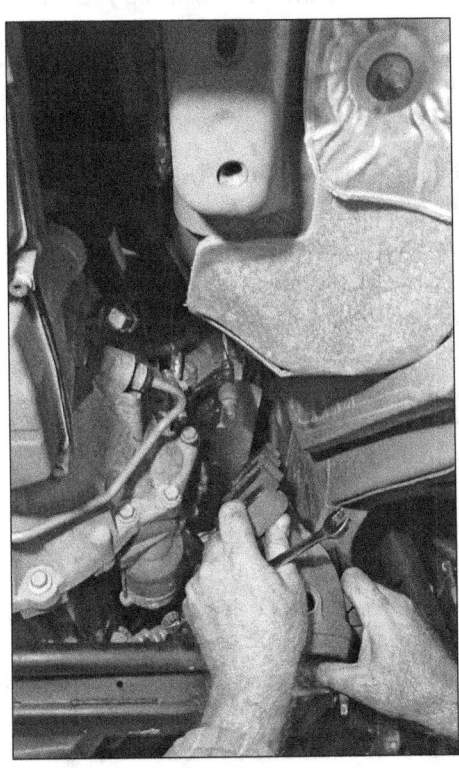

8 Once the bolts are removed from the manifold, it comes out easily.

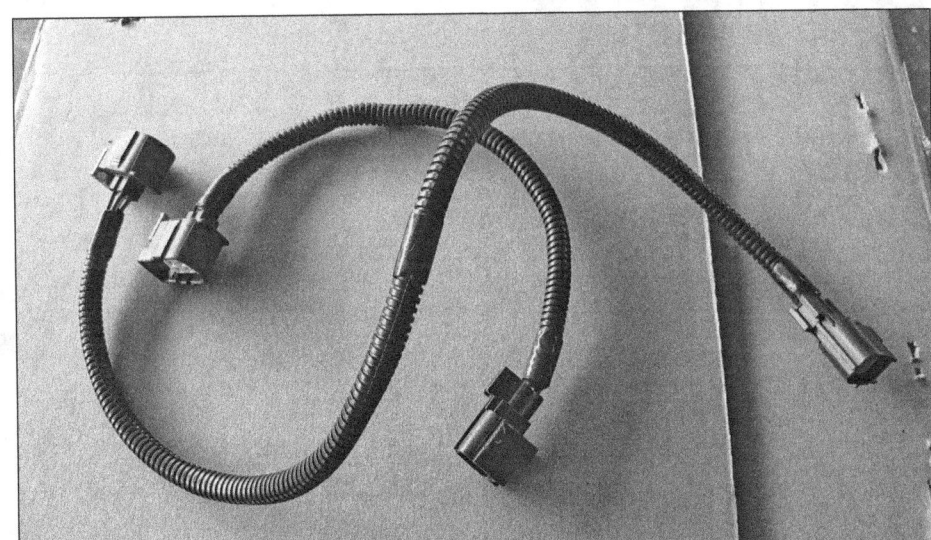

9 When installing headers, the oxygen sensor needs to be relocated. The TTi headers come with oxygen lead-extensions that are required in order to reconnect the sensors.

DODGE CHALLENGER AND CHARGER: HOW TO BUILD AND MODIFY

CHAPTER 3

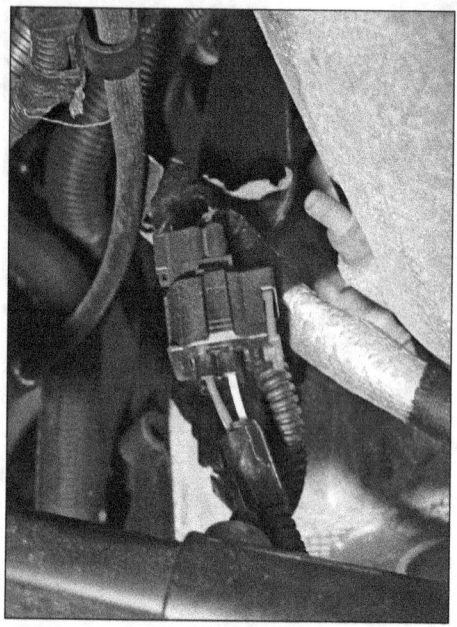

10 Plug the lead-in extensions into the main wiring harness.

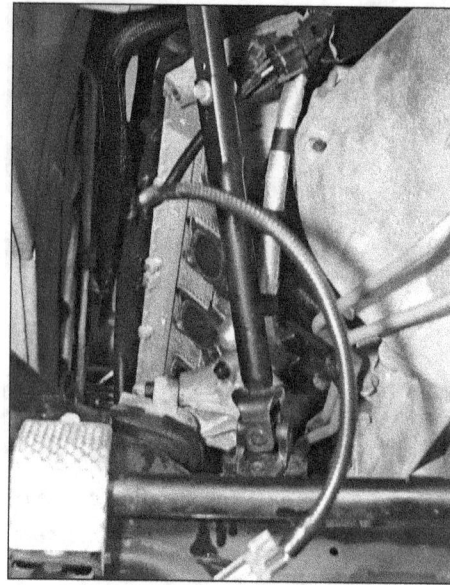

11 Then plug the other end of the wiring harness extension into the O2 sensor.

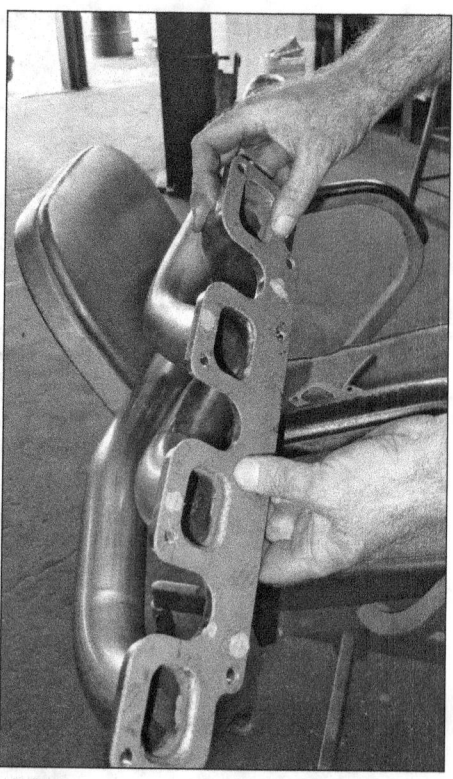

13 This 3-inch exhaust kit (PN CH30HWCM) comes with a pair of Magnaflow "high-performance" catalytic converters. Each converter has a ribbed design with funneled inlets and outlets.

12 Installing the header gaskets after the header is in place is a tough proposition. To make it easy, you can either place a couple of small dabs of silicone on the gasket so it "sticks" to the header while you install it, or you can take some sewing thread and tie the header gasket to the header by using the bolt holes.

14 The Magnaflow converters have a stainless-steel body and heat shield that contain a flow-efficient, monolithic honeycomb catalyst that's designed for maximum flow and surface area. Although a stock engine might not see any gain in performance by adding just a "high-flow" catalytic converter, a modified engine needs more flow, so it could see greater gains if used. Add to it a performance exhaust, and exhaust flow becomes a non-issue. This is because it's all about back-pressure and exhaust scavenging. The TTi exhaust size and length is tuned with the Magnaflow cats to pull burned gases most efficiently from the engine.

BOLT-ON PERFORMANCE

15 *While my helper, Richard, was working on tightening the header bolts, I started to install the exhaust system. This is why I said that using a drive-on lift would make things easier. First of all, the header bolts cannot be accessed from the top of the engine. And second, I was able to use supports (dead man) to hold the exhaust in place while I installed the bolts.*

16 *The TTi exhaust connects to the headers with this ball and socket flange. The ball and socket is not as prone to leaking as a flat gasket–fitted coupling system. Loosely install the bolts just to hold the cats in place. Do not tighten any exhaust bolts or clamps until the exhaust system is completely installed.*

17 *Once I finished the exhaust, I was more than happy with the exhaust note, which had a deep growl at idle and made its presence know when I hit the loud pedal. In addition, there is no drone inside the car when driving.*

DODGE CHALLENGER AND CHARGER: HOW TO BUILD AND MODIFY

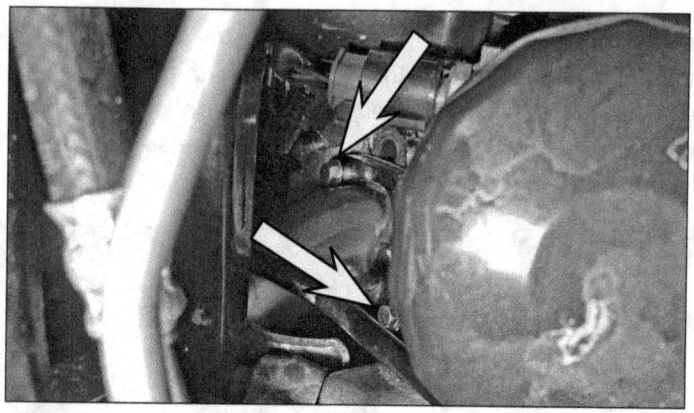

18 Remember I said that some of the header bolts (arrows) are difficult to get to for tightening? This is one of the easy ones!

19 When you finish loosely hanging the exhaust, you hang the tailpipes by the factory rubber isolators. With a light coating of penetrating oil, the hanger slides over the pin.

20 Once you have the exhaust completely in place, you can tighten the bolts and clamps. Notice that Richard is still tightening header bolts. In no way is the header bolt situation any fault of TTi! The design of the engine and the routing constraints of the primary tubes in the engine bay dictate what space is available. It does not matter what long-tube headers are installed, getting to the bolts is still a pain.

In a comparison between a completely stock exhaust and the TTi 1⅞-inch headers with the 3-inch exhaust, power was up nearly 20 hp at a peak of 5,700 rpm. The mid-range saw an equally impressive improvement. In the torque department, there was a 35–ft-lb increase at peak, and just slightly less than 50 ft-lbs of torque at 4,200 rpm.

Nitrous Oxide

If you're looking for instant power on demand, then bolting a nitrous oxide kit to your Hemi might be something for you to consider. Nitrous oxide (sometimes known as laughing gas, nitrous, or NOS) is a chemical compound. Outside of the automotive world it is used as an anesthesia in surgery and dentistry. For car guys, it is used to increase the power output of an engine.

Dry or Wet

The two main types of nitrous oxide systems for a Hemi car are dry and wet. A dry nitrous system only controls the delivery of the nitrous oxide; the fuel is delivered via the existing OEM fuel injection system. The extra fuel required by the addition of the nitrous is increased by either increasing the fuel-delivery pressure or by extending the time during which the fuel injector is held open.

Single-injector dry systems are sometimes referred to as dry manifold systems because the additional fuel that is required with nitrous does not pass through the intake manifold as it does with a wet system. A dry system is good for about a 100-hp shot of nitrous. The mounting location for the nozzle is typically in the air inlet tube about 2 to 6 inches before the throttle body.

The introduction of fuel and nitrous to the intake causes the intake

BOLT-ON PERFORMANCE

When activating a nitrous oxide system, you are adding both nitrous oxide and more fuel to the engine. Contrary to popular belief, nitrous oxide does not burn, rather, it's simply an oxidizer. As such it provides the engine with more oxygen, which allows additional fuel to be added and burned. Together, the increased air and fuel produce more power. Simply bolt your bottle in place, plumb the system, connect the wires, and hang on.

Two types of nitrous kits are available for Hemi-powered cars: wet and dry. The black nozzle indicates this is a wet nozzle, which sprays both nitrous oxide and fuel into the engine (note the two threaded inlet openings). Wet nozzles add both fuel and nitrous, and are used for both big and small shots of nitrous. Most common nitrous users prefer wet shots on bigger and direct-port nitrous systems. (Photo Courtesy Holley Performance Products)

The gold nozzle indicates this is a dry nozzle and is capable of shooting only nitrous oxide into the engine. Dry nozzles are often used for smaller shots of nitrous. Some people prefer to use dry nozzles because they feel that they can control the fuel better through the injectors with advanced engine management systems, and can tune the vehicle better through this method. (Photo Courtesy Holley Performance Products)

Whether you use a wet or dry nitrous oxide system, the nitrous and fuel need to be regulated. You need metering jets for the nitrous oxide (and fuel with a wet kit). These metering jets can be interchanged with other jets that have a larger or smaller orifice to regulate the amount of nitrous oxide (and fuel) introduced into the engine. These jet changes are responsible for the horsepower rating of the nitrous oxide kit.

If you're running a 100-hp nitrous kit, by changing the metering jets to the appropriate size(s) you can effectively add another 100 hp for a total of 200.

Often you hear the horsepower rating referred to as a "shot." This is merely a slang term for the amount of horsepower a system is producing. A 100 shot produces roughly 100 hp. (Photo Courtesy Holley Performance Products)

manifold to become "wet" with fuel. A wet single-point nitrous system has a nozzle that introduces the fuel and the nitrous into the engine simultaneously. This nozzle is also mounted just before the throttle body, and this introduction of fuel and nitrous to the intake causes the intake manifold to become "wet" with fuel.

Because the intake on Hemi engines is designed to operate in a dry condition, adding fuel can sometimes result in fuel distribution problems. This is because dry intakes are designed to move only air, which travels through smaller openings and tighter turns with less pressure. Wet nitrous systems are capable of producing more power than dry systems, but in many cases, can be more expensive and difficult to install because the process involves tapping into the fuel delivery system of a car, many of which are high pressure (45 to 50 psi).

Application Variations

Deciding which kit is best for your Hemi-powered LX car depends on the application, just like everything else. It really doesn't matter if you're running a 5.7-, 6.1-, or 6.4-liter Hemi, a nitrous kit doesn't distinguish among them.

A wet kit is ideal for both naturally aspirated engines and engines with forced induction. A dry kit is excellent for naturally aspirated combinations that have a return-style fuel system. They are both very easy to install and are a great first-time nitrous system. It is not recommended that dry systems be used on forced-induction engines.

A direct-port nitrous system introduces nitrous and fuel directly into each intake port on the engine. Usually, these systems combine nitrous and fuel through several nozzles that are similar in design to a wet single-point nozzle. These nozzles individually mix and meter the nitrous and fuel that is delivered to each cylinder. Different types of nozzles are available for a direct-port injection kit, and placement requires drilling and tapping the manifold.

A multi-point nitrous system produces the most power, because of the placement of the nozzle in each runner, as well as the ability to use more and higher-capacity solenoids. Wet multi-point kits can be used in two, three, or even four stages. These systems are also the most complex and expensive of nitrous systems, requiring significant modification to the engine, including adding distribution blocks and plumbing for each cylinder. These systems are typically used in racing applications.

A recent improvement on the staged concept is the progressive delivery system, which allows a system to deliver a smooth, progressive increase in power that is adjustable to suit user requirements.

Timing Guidelines

When nitrous is injected into an engine, be sure that the timing has been properly set. Running nitrous oxide requires that the timing be backed off (retarded), and a good rule is to retard the timing 1½ to 2 degrees for every 50 hp of added nitrous.

The reason you retard timing with nitrous is that the air charge becomes more oxygen-dense, resulting in the air/fuel mixture burning at a much higher rate. This causes peak cylinder pressure to happen much earlier. Retarding the timing ensures that peak cylinder pressure occurs at the point that is most beneficial to making power. Retarding the

A multi-port fogger unit delivers unrivaled performance. A multi-port (wet) nitrous system introduces nitrous oxide and fuel directly into each intake port. These systems are able to combine the nitrous oxide and fuel through several nozzles, which are able to mix and meter the nitrous and fuel that is delivered to each cylinder. This is accomplished individually, allowing each cylinder's nitrous/fuel ratio to be adjusted without affecting the other cylinders. A multi-point system is the most capable of producing large power increases because of the placement of the nozzle in each intake runner. They also use more powerful and higher-capacity solenoid valves. These systems are also the most complex and expensive systems you can use, requiring significant modification to the engine, including adding distribution blocks and solenoid assemblies, as well as drilling, tapping, and constructing the plumbing for each cylinder runner. The retail price starts at about $900. (Photo Courtesy Nitrous Outlet)

timing too much causes peak cylinder pressure to occur much later in the combustion cycle, and that energy is wasted.

Although you can't easily change the timing on a late-model Hemi without a custom tune, you should realize that if you are using an aftermarket chip or programmer that is not programmed for use with nitrous, you cause damage to your engine. Typical performance reprogramming adds more ignition timing to increase performance, and when combined with nitrous, could lead to engine damage.

Spark Plug Considerations

Adding a nitrous system to your engine also forces you to pay attention to the spark-plug heat range, reach, and gap. The widely accepted standard is to lower the heat range of your spark plugs one heat range for every 100 hp of nitrous added. It is also best to use a non–projected-tip spark plug. Projected plugs allow a greater portion of the electrode to be exposed to combustion gases, and that can cause detonation.

The spark plug gap also plays an important part in nitrous-fed engine performance. The increased cylinder pressure created by the additional nitrous and fuel makes it harder for the spark to jump the gap between the ground strap and the electrode, causing misfires and a loss of power.

Stress Factors

As with any modification to increase power, the use of nitrous oxide carries with it concerns about the engine's reliability and lifespan. Because of the increased cylinder pressures, the engine as a whole is placed under greater stress, and an engine with components not able to

You need to know a few basic facts about spark plugs so that you can intelligently choose the correct one for your nitrous-equipped engine. Using a projected-tip spark plug is a no-no, as it can produce a misfire condition after just a few seconds of using the nitrous. Using an improper heat range plug does not cause a misfire, but rather, the misfire occurs because the ground strap of the spark plug starts glowing. This happens when the projected tip is too long and is unable to dissipate the extra heat that is being produced by the nitrous-accelerated ignition burn.

The proper way to fix this condition is to replace the spark plugs with ones that do not have a nose that projects as far into the cylinder. If you simply introduce a spark plug with a colder heat range (but still has a projected tip), you will surely still have a misfire problem.

Stock coils are easily removed for upgrades. If your coil has one spark plug wire attached to it (early design), just unplug the wire from the coil, remove the bolts holding the coil to the valve cover, and lift the coil out. This is a later design coil that does not have the spark plug wire attached. For this design, simply unplug the electrical connection, remove the bolts holding it to the valve cover, and pull it off.

Companies such as Performance Distributors have developed aftermarket coils to provide performance junkies with better economy and a more complete combustion burn. These Sultans of Spark coils improve upon the factory design with better conductivity and use of better quality materials. These coils are direct replacements for the stock coils, but offer up to 50-percent more spark, up to 40,000 volts. The higher voltage and spark duration allow you to open up the gap on your spark plugs to .065 inch, which gives you a bigger and hotter spark inside the cylinder.

cope with the increased stress from the nitrous system can experience minor or even major engine damage, such as cracked or destroyed pistons, bent connecting rods, or even damage to the crankshaft. Even if the engine is up to the task, severe damage can occur if a problem presents itself in the fuel system.

For example, if the engine's fuel supply were diminished (even for a brief moment), it would cause the engine to run lean by whatever degree the fuel delivery was reduced, and this could lead to engine knock or detonation. Depending on the engine, major damage can occur in a matter of seconds. It is recommended that some sort of sensor or controller be incorporated into the ignition system to disable the nitrous system when a knock sensor detects spark knock. High-octane premium fuel is also recommended to avoid detonation.

Legal Issues

Although possessing nitrous oxide might not necessarily be illegal where you live, Johnny Law could contend that when carrying a compressed gas the container needs to be carried outside of the occupant area of the vehicle in an upright position. That tends to be the sticking point on it because that is the most dangerous thing about it. Some states might also consider it illegal because it is injected into the intake manifold, which often makes it fail the visual part of some emissions tests.

Many companies offer nitrous oxide systems for Hemi-powered cars. The following are the most popular among Hemi car owners.

Zex

The Zex Blackout Nitrous System is designed to provide anywhere from 75 to 125 additional hp to your engine. The kit can be installed on an engine that is stock, or even one that is turbocharged or supercharged, in around two hours. All necessary components come with the kit, including tuning jets, required fuel fittings, and a nitrous management unit that contains solenoids, filters, and electronics.

This nitrous system's active fuel control feature automatically adjusts fuel delivery to compensate for changes in nitrous-bottle pressure so that your engine never runs too rich or too lean while spraying the nitrous. In addition, the system offers an electronic throttle position sensor (TPS) switch for reliable system activation at wide-open throttle (WOT).

Nitrous Oxide Systems

Although this company was not popular until the *Fast and Furious* movie franchise featured it, Nitrous Oxide Systems (NOS) has been delivering power-enhancing systems for years. Their wet nitrous kit (PN 05135NOS) is designed specifically for cars with drive-by-wire systems, which feature adjustable high- and low-RPM switches and an adjustable TPS activation point. This allows you to custom-tailor the shot of nitrous for any situation.

This kit is capable of delivering an increase of horsepower in the 75 to 150 range. More power can be achieved if upgraded solenoids are installed.

Nitrous Outlet

This company has both a dual-nozzle dry nitrous system and a wet-plate system. The dry kit offers horsepower gains up to 150, and the wet kit is capable of up to 400. Nitrous Outlet systems come complete with a high-flow bottle valve with dual accessory ports, large solenoids with purge port design, and a limited

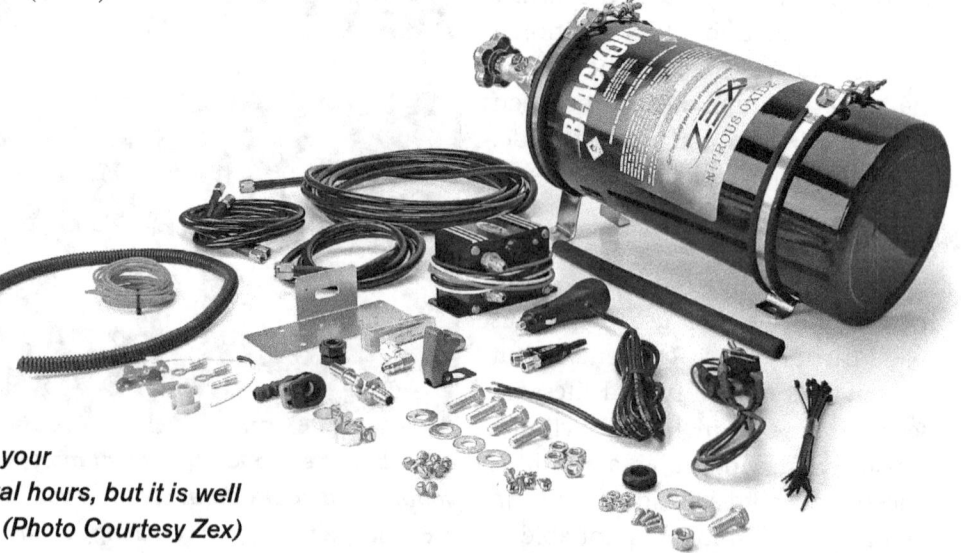

Zex's Blackout Nitrous System (wet shown) is versatile enough to be installed on anything from a stock engine to one that is highly modified. It offers the ability to adjust fuel pressure, which is a useful option if future engine upgrades are in your plans. Installing the Zex kit takes several hours, but it is well worth it. The retail price is about $650. (Photo Courtesy Zex)

BOLT-ON PERFORMANCE

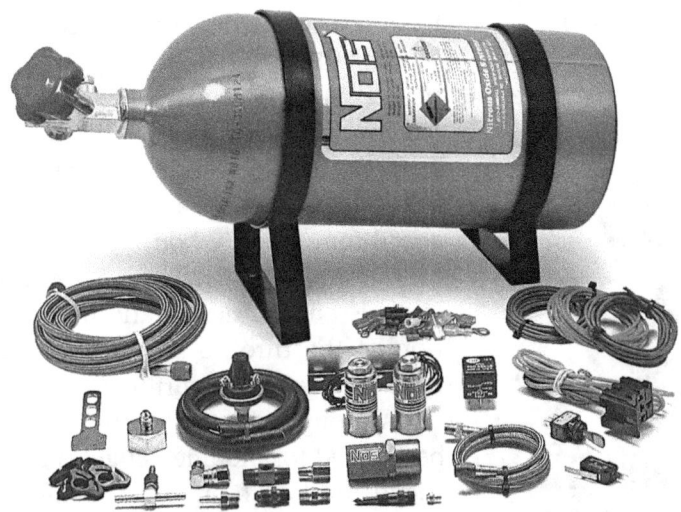

Nitrous Oxide System's kit (PN 05135NOS) is designed specifically for cars with drive-by-wire systems. It features adjustability so you can custom-tailor the nitrous. Although the base kit delivers 75 to 150 hp, more power can be added if larger solenoids are installed. The retail price is about $750. (Photo Courtesy Nitrous Oxide System)

Nitrous Outlet nitrous oxide kits (both wet and dry) come as either nozzle or plate systems. The simple-to-install dry kit can be installed in a couple of hours; the wet kit takes at least four to six hours. Although nitrous greatly increases power, keep in mind that the more you use it the more often you have to refill the bottle. The retail price of the kit is about $360 to $550. (Photo Courtesy Nitrous Outlet)

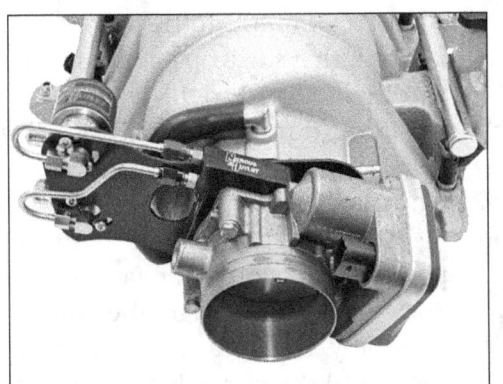

This plate conversion kit from Nitrous Outlet installs directly behind the throttle body. It includes all of the needed hardware and jetting to convert a single-nozzle wet system to a plate system. This plate also works with any brand of wet system and has 3AN inlet fittings for fuel and nitrous. (Photo Courtesy Nitrous Outlet)

This nitrous injection plate from Nitrous Outlet has six specially designed nitrous and fuel discharge ports that saturate the air-intake charge with the best-atomized mixture possible. For higher horsepower levels proper distribution into the air steam is critical for cylinder-to-cylinder distribution. In fact, large droplets of fuel do not disperse very well. The plates are machined from billet aluminum, have a black anodized finish, and are flow tested to ensure proper function and flow characteristics. (Photo Courtesy Nitrous Outlet)

lifetime warranty. Like any nitrous oxide kit, it requires aftermarket tuning software that tells the computer to add the extra needed fuel.

Like all other dry nitrous kits, the version from Nitrous Outlet uses a nozzle that is mounted into the intake tract to introduce the nitrous. If you use the wet-plate system, the plate with the nozzles mounts between the throttle body and the intake.

Throttle Body

In a fuel-injected engine, such as your Hemi, the throttle body is the part of the air-intake system that regulates the amount of air that flows into the engine. This is done in response to the driver pushing the accelerator pedal. The throttle body is located between the air-filter box and the intake manifold.

The throttle body is a cast-and-machined piece of aluminum that (in OEM applications) mounts directly to the intake manifold. Inside the throttle body is the throttle plate (also called a butterfly), which regulates the incoming airflow. When you press the accelerator pedal, the throttle plate opens a percentage of its opening capability relative to the throttle pedal's movement.

CHAPTER 3

The throttle body controls the air needed to run a 5.7-, 6.1-, or 6.4-liter Hemi. This serves as a control valve, regulating the amount of air flowing into the engine. The opening on the throttle body becomes larger or smaller in relation to the amount of pressure applied to the throttle pedal by the driver.

From 2005 through 2012, Hemi engines used a VDO-style throttle body (right). In 2013, Chrysler made the switch to a Magneti-Marelli throttle body (left).

In cars such as the Charger, Challenger, 300, and Magnum that have electronic throttle control (also known as drive-by-wire), an electric motor controls the movement of the throttle plate. The accelerator pedal connects not to the throttle body, but to a sensor that sends an electronic signal to the engine control unit (ECU) that relates to the throttle pedal's actual position (in percent of travel).

Aftermarket Upgrade Benefits

But what about installing an aftermarket throttle body? Is this a good modification? For some vehicles it is, but some vehicles benefit very little from an aftermarket throttle body.

From 2005 through 2012, Hemi engines used a Continental Corporation VDO-style throttle body. In 2013, a Magneti-Marelli throttle body was employed.

How much of an increase in power is a throttle body upgrade worth? Although the question seems simple, the answer definitely lies in a gray area. I've seen power gains range from as little as 2 hp to as much as 25 to 30 hp. That might seem like a big disparity for a simple bolt-on, but as I said, this is a gray area. So, the question isn't about whether or not swapping a throttle body can net an increase in power, but rather, why the disparity?

As you know, a throttle body is nothing more than an air valve. There is no magic to how it works. But there is some magic to maximizing the airflow rate that goes through it. A given opening flows a certain amount of air, and it's no surprise that a 90-mm throttle body should outflow an 80-mm throttle body. That being said, would you be surprised to know that it is possible for an 80-mm throttle body to outflow a 90-mm piece? That might sound strange, but the design and preparation of the throttle body's opening has a huge effect on airflow.

Although a larger throttle body is best suited for modified engines that spend most of their time at higher RPM, a larger throttle body does not necessarily hurt low-RPM power. That being said, it can have a dramatic effect on throttle response. When a large throttle body is compared to a smaller one, any comparable throttle position offers an increase in airflow.

For example, if you open the venturi of a 90-mm throttle body 3 to 5 percent, that's like opening a smaller throttle body 10 to 12 percent. But the larger throttle body has less flow velocity, and the effect could make part-throttle driving difficult.

The first obstacle in terms of power production is the fact that air does not pass through the throttle body only. That means the flow rate of the throttle body is only as efficient as the rest of the air-intake components. Installing a performance-designed, larger throttle body does not yield the performance results when used with a stock air cleaner, camshaft, and exhaust, as it would in conjunction with using the aforementioned performance-enhancing items.

In other words, a stock engine does not have the air volume requirement of a modified engine, and only ingests the amount of air that it needs. If it only needs 900 cfm of air, and the aftermarket throttle body flows 1,200, no discernible results

BOLT-ON PERFORMANCE

Selecting a Throttle Body

Choose a throttle body based on CFM and not on a metric measurement. The following chart is based on engine displacement and RPM.

Engine	CFM at 6,000 rpm	CFM at 6,500 rpm	CFM at 7,000 rpm
5.7-liter	608	658	709
6.1-liter	642	696	749
6.4-liter	677	734	790
6.7-liter (426)	747	809	871

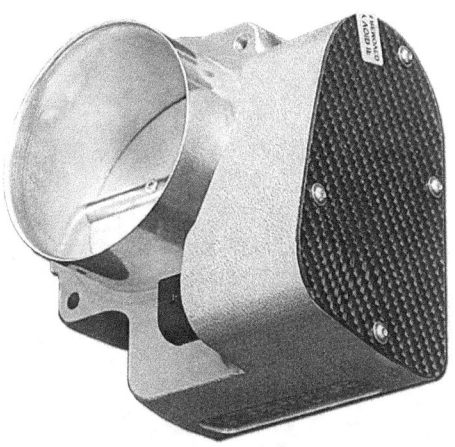

Arrington's 90-mm VDO-style throttle body is a quick bolt-on application that increases performance when used on a modified engine. A stock engine will not see a benefit. Install is easy; just unhook the intake tube and drive-by-wire plug, take out the four mounting bolts, then reverse those steps to install the new throttle body. A throttle body swap can be completed in about an hour. The retail price is about $479. (Photo Courtesy Arrington Performance/ShopHemi.com)

are realized because airflow velocity is diminished because of the larger opening.

When a Hemi engine is supercharged, throttle body sizing and maximum flow is less critical than it is with a naturally aspirated engine. This is because the pressurizing of the air at the throttle body can artificially increase the actual flow rate of the throttle body. The reason for this is the pressurization created by the supercharger. Basically, a stock throttle body has less of a restriction on a supercharged engine than it does on a naturally aspirated engine.

Instead of asking, "What size throttle body do I need?" you might instead ask "How much CFM of air does my engine need?" The problem with choosing a throttle body according to CFM usage is that throttle bodies are not rated by CFM. Throttle body manufacturers list their throttle bodies by the measurement of the inside diameter of the throttle body's opening near the throttle blade (in millimeters).

As a general rule, an 80-mm throttle body (which is stock on 5.7-, 6.1-, and 6.4-liter Hemi engines) flows nearly 1,000 cfm.

Keep in mind that a throttle body is only a small part of the entire air-intake system. Don't expect huge gains if the factory air filtration system is still in use, as that can hamper the airflow more than the stock throttle body. Also, when upgrading the entire air inlet system and throttle body, a tune should be considered.

Many companies offer throttle bodies for Hemi-powered cars. The following are the most popular among Hemi car owners.

Arrington Performance/ShopHemi.com

The 2013 and newer Hemi cars used a newly designed Magneti-Marelli throttle body. Arrington's billet throttle bodies are a completely new unit and come in venturi sizes from 84 to 88 mm. (Before 2013, Hemi engines used a VDO-designed throttle body.) Arrington's 90-mm cast VDO throttle body is a quick bolt-on application for better performance with a modified engine. Just unhook the intake tube and drive-by-wire plug, take out the four mounting bolts, then reverse those steps to install the new throttle body. The cast throttle body is engineered and tested for the best results.

Arrington Performance/ShopHemi.com originated big-bore throttle bodies for the late-model Hemi. Their "full-bore" throttle bodies for 2013 and newer Dodge and Chrysler Hemi V-8 engines feature billet housings that are manufactured in-house. These are not re-worked factory housings. Because of this, they can design and build throttle bodies that deliver the advertised diameter throughout the bore and at the blade. The retail price is about $560.

CHAPTER 3

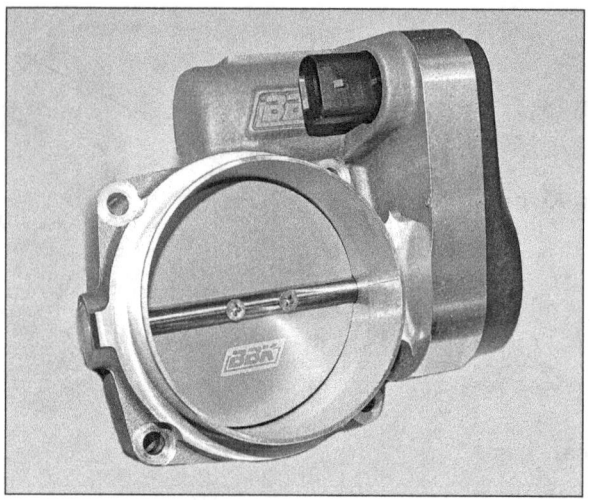

BBK's VDO-style throttle body can add horsepower without sacrificing fuel mileage or drivability. The Power+Plus Series is made from brand-new CNC-machined aluminum housings with OEM throttle controls. Installation is a simple bolt-on procedure with no modifications and can be completed with simple hand tools. The retail price starts about $360.

BBK Performance

The engineers at BBK have tweaked the VDO-style throttle body, and according to them, it adds between 12 and 24 hp without sacrificing mileage or drivability. It's available in 85- and 90-mm versions. The Power+Plus Series are brand-new CNC-machined aluminum housings that are fitted with new factory OEM electronic throttle controls, making installation a true bolt-on with no modifications.

Modern Muscle

Modern Muscle can upgrade the existing stock throttle body and give you a performance throttle body that fits your application. Modern Muscle is able to improve airflow through the stock throttle body, which allows for more power. Some basic tuning is recommended to increase fuel when at wide-open throttle (WOT). The retail price is between $330 and $670.

Modern Muscle has pioneered throttle body upgrading. With their five-axis CNC porting capability, they can deliver a throttle body from 83 to 90 mm. In some modified applications, the 80-mm throttle body has shown to be a restriction on Hemi engines, but with Modern Muscle's new venturi-like design, airflow through the stock throttle body has been increased, allowing even more power from a bolt-on part. It is fully plug-and-play, and only basic tuning is recommended at WOT

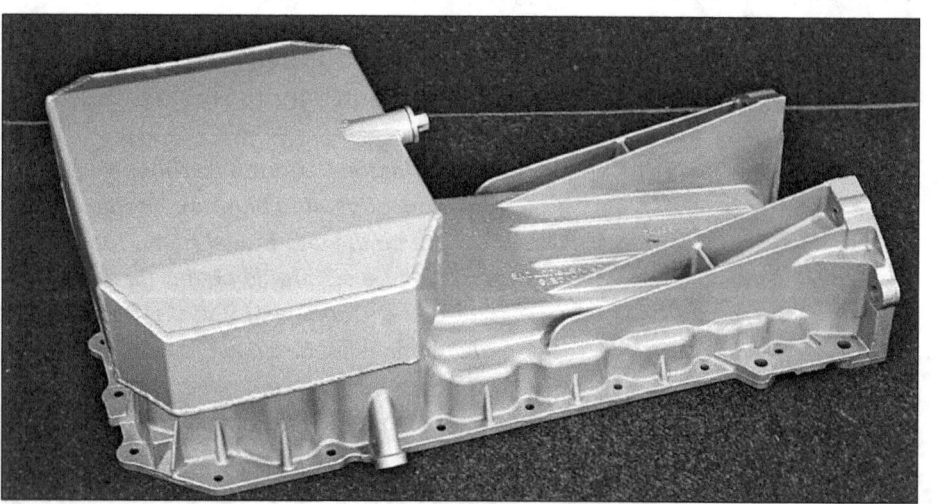

Keeping your Hemi engine well lubricated is a necessity to ensure a long life. Modern Muscle's custom-built high-capacity oil pan adds to the oil capacity of your engine for high-horsepower fast-revving applications. This extra capacity is the cure for an engine that may starve for oil because of inefficient oil return. You also get better oil cooling from the added volume and sump surface area. This is a modified "stock" pan, and by retaining the stock pan you do not sacrifice the structural integrity between the engine and transmission. Internal baffles keep oil at the pick-up, and this pan adds 3½ quarts to the stock capacity. Use of a stock oil-pick-up tube is not recommended. (Photo Courtesy Modern Muscle Performance Group)

BOLT-ON PERFORMANCE

In basic function, the purpose of the clutch is to provide smooth drivability not only when leaving from a stop, but also at high power levels that were previously not available from OEM parts. This means that the clutch in your Challenger must be able to smoothly apply pressure to the flywheel, and keep that pressure applied even when the engine is spinning at the upper end of the RPM limit. Sometimes the factory clutch wears out prematurely and is unable to do either. That's when a replacement clutch assembly comes into play.

to compensate for the additional airflow to optimize power. Their throttle bodies are developed using brand-new CNC-ported OEM units. Both Magneti-Marelli and VDO throttle bodies are available.

Clutch Assembly

Imagine that you are sitting in your Challenger at a red light, your foot firmly holding the clutch pedal to the floor. You are planning to annihilate the rear tires when the light turns green. You know your car can do it; the supercharger will make it happen. When the light goes green, you slide your left foot off the clutch pedal to begin your smoke show.

But for some reason, something isn't right. You can see the smoke billowing out from under your car, but the smell is different. It doesn't smell like tire smoke. You see the guy filming video of you trying to do a burnout and smoking the stock clutch instead. You, my friend, are about to go viral on YouTube as an epic fail.

Although the OEM clutch in your Challenger performed well when your car was all OEM, upgrades tend to put more stress on parts. Your Challenger came equipped from the factory with a single-disc clutch that comprises a flywheel, clutch disc, and pressure plate. When you push the clutch pedal, the pressure plate releases the pressure on the clutch disc, and you can shift gears. When you release the pedal, pressure is applied, and your car moves.

Anyway, now that the only thing left of your factory clutch is the smell, you need to figure out how to fix this problem. Replacing the clutch with another OEM unit yields the same results, so it's time to step up. But stepping up requires a little knowledge. How do you know what you need, if you don't know what's available?

Hurst Shifters

Hurst's Billet/Plus2 manual shifter is the industry standard in upgraded shifters and delivers firm, confident shifts for floor-shifted models.

Their automatic shifter comes with a CNC-machined knob, classic-looking Hurst stainless steel stick sleeve, and a CNC-machined console plate.

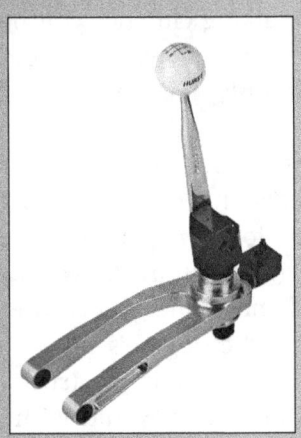

The Hurst Billet/Plus2 performance short-throw shifter kit is precision engineered and CNC machined from billet alloys. This kit comes with a chromed Hurst stick and white knob but does accept the factory knob or a classic Hurst pistol grip handle. A moderate reduction in shift throw allows you to rip through the gears with quicker and more precise shifts. The retail price is about $380. (Photo Courtesy B&M Corporation)

Hurst's automatic shifter is compatible with all automatic-equipped LX cars, even those with the Autostick feature. The retail price is about $225. (Photo Courtesy B&M Corporation)

Clutch Materials

As the performance of your Challenger increases, so should the characteristics and durability of the clutch material. The following is a brief synopsis of the clutch materials available and when each should be employed.

Organic material is used to make stock-style clutch discs; it is fine for normal driving conditions and usage, but as operating temperatures rise or you place the clutch under high loads (which is usually accompanied by slippage), its clamping ability fades. This is because its coefficient of friction drops off. In addition, at high RPM and/or when hot, organic clutch discs tend to fail structurally.

Kevlar material offers a much higher coefficient of friction than organic material, but with some loss in drivability (i.e., it gets grabby when releasing the pedal). As the coefficient of friction goes up in the material used to make the disc, so does the aggressiveness of the material when the clutch is engaged. This usually results in clutch "chatter."

Because Kevlar is compatible with stock flywheels and pressure plates, it makes a good upgrade choice, but using it takes some getting used to in regard to pedal releasing.

Bronze metallic materials are the most aggressive for producing clutch friction. Because it is aggressive, it offers an extended life over Kevlar and organic materials. Bronze metallic materials provide a quick, clean clutch engagement by reducing static pressures.

Because bronze metallic is the most aggressive material, it also causes the quickest wear on the flywheel and pressure plate surfaces. Therefore, it should only be used with steel or nodular-iron friction surfaces (pressure plate and flywheel). If used on the street, this material causes chatter when the clutch is engaged.

Sintered iron is suited for street use, as it has an exceptional ability to withstand some slippage and not lose its friction coefficient. Sintered iron clutch material withstands high-horsepower applications and is ideal for drag racing.

Single- or Twin-Disc Design

In addition to choosing the material for your clutch disc you also must decide if you need one or two discs. Clutches are generally rated by their torque-holding capacity. A single-disc clutch inherently has less holding capacity than a twin-disc, based solely on surface area.

Twin-disc clutches are designed to have a lower inertia but have higher torque-holding capabilities; they spread the load across more surface area. Twin-disc clutches tend to be noisier than their single-disc counterparts, simply because there are more plates and separators in the package.

A good rule to remember is that a single-disc clutch is a good all-around performance clutch on a stock or mildly modified engine. Depending on the clutch material used, it has OEM-like engagement and shifting qualities. Twin discs are designed to handle a lot more torque than a stock or even aftermarket single disc; therefore, they are a better fit in high-horsepower applications.

To make the correct choice, you need to know the torque capability of your engine and consult the clutch manufacturer.

Flywheel Type

When talking clutches you have to factor in the flywheel. The flywheel not only has the teeth for starter engagement, it is also an energy-storing device. A heavy flywheel causes the engine's RPM to climb at a slower rate than that of a lighter (aluminum) flywheel. It also stores more energy because of its mass, so the engine's RPM does not drop as dramatically (such as between shifts) as it would with an aluminum flywheel.

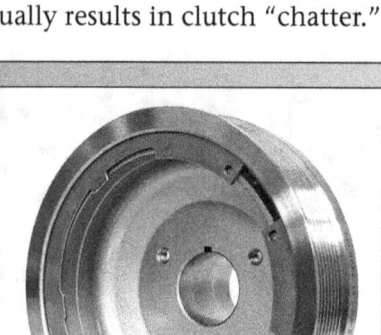

An underdrive pulley slows accessories, and this has an effect on their performance. (Photo Courtesy Pro Race Performance Products)

Underdrive Pulley

If you are thinking about installing an underdrive pulley on your Hemi, you need to consider a few things. First, it is definitely an inexpensive mod that gives you some benefit. But, if you drive in a lot of stop-and-go traffic where the temperatures become hot, you can expect your car to run warmer than usual. Depending on the heat and traffic, it could reach a dangerous level. Also, at night when you come to a stop sign or red light and idle, you might notice that your lights become dim, and then brighten when you leave idle. Finally, if you have any kind of upgraded stereo system, expect charging issues.

On the other hand, a lighter flywheel allows the engine to spin faster, but a more dramatic drop in RPM is noticed (such as between shifts). The lighter weight could also be a problem for daily driving because the lower inertial mass of the lighter (aluminum) flywheel means that the car is more difficult to get moving from a stop sign or traffic light. Aluminum is generally used in road race/drag race applications where the engine is kept at higher RPM.

Pressure Plate Selection

Without a pressure plate, the clutch does not work, period. The pressure plate applies the clamping force that squeezes the clutch disc between the pressure plate and the flywheel. The three main types of pressure plates are long, Borg & Beck, and diaphragm.

The long-style pressure plate is identified by the three thin fingers that contact the release (throw out) bearing. This plate is typically used in drag race applications and has a hard pedal feel.

The Borg & Beck style is similar to the long style, but while it too functions via three fingers, they can be identified by the somewhat-wider three fingers that release plate pressure. The Borg & Beck also uses rollers under the pressure plate cover that are forced outward under centrifugal force. This increases the plate load (pressure) with increasing RPM.

A diaphragm pressure plate uses a series of "fingers" (also called a Belleville spring) that completely encompass the center opening of the pressure plate. The main advantage to this style of flywheel is that holding the clutch pedal down at a stoplight is much easier than it is with either a long or Borg & Beck pressure plate.

Project: Ram Clutches Performance Clutch Installation

So, which flywheel, pressure plate, and clutch material do you think you need now that you've smoked your clutch and become a YouTube favorite? That imagined car is a popular combination so a replacement/upgrade should be readily available, correct?

The following steps take you through the installation of a Ram Clutches street dual-disc system. It is specifically engineered for today's late-model performance cars.

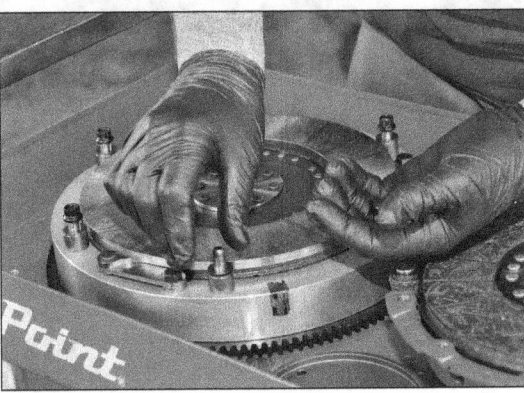

1 After you remove the new clutch-flywheel assembly from the package it needs to be dismantled prior to installation. Black marks align the cover assembly with the flywheel, ensuring that the pressure plate straps and floater-plate straps are properly located. If improperly located, you experience disengagement troubles.

2 The installed height of the pressure plate is a critical measurement. It is the distance between the pressure plate and the flywheel. The height is determined by using spacers and shims. To ensure that the hydraulic clutch system functions properly, it is imperative that the spacers and shims remain in place during assembly.

3 The floater plate is located between the inner and outer clutch discs. It is connected to the aluminum flywheel by three straps. During initial disassembly once out of the box, mark the floater plate to make sure that it is reinstalled correctly. Note that a properly finished floater plate is characterized by Blanchard grinding marks on both sides. This irregular finish ensures effective seating between the floater plate and the clutch discs.

4 The inner disc that comes with the Ram clutch (left) has no springs in the center core. To deliver a cushioned, smooth drive, Ram added eight springs to the outer clutch disc (right). Ram's dark-colored clutch linings are their 300-series organic discs that support up to 900 ft-lbs of rear-wheel torque.

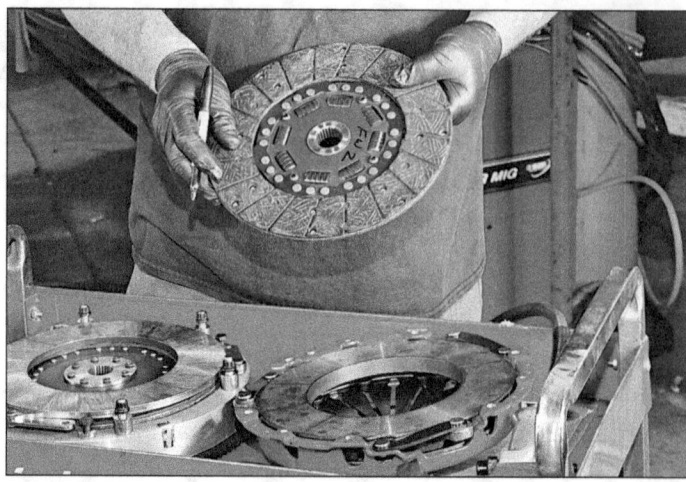

5 While removing the clutch kit from the box, be sure to mark both of the clutch friction plates to ensure they are installed in the proper sequence.

6 Made from 6061 aluminum, Ram's flywheel sheds approximately 14 pounds of surplus rotating weight. By lowering the moment of inertia, this flywheel allows the engine to accelerate faster.

7 The two major advantages of installing an upgraded clutch over the original assembly are increased holding capacity (think launching and not slipping the clutch) and serviceability in the future. The new, upgraded unit handles twice the power as the OEM unit. Because the original clutch is riveted together, it can only be replaced as a complete unit.

8 Compared to the original cast-iron flywheel (left), the aluminum replacement (right) is almost 30-percent lighter, and dissipates heat much faster. This is done by virtue of the 1/4-inch-thick steel insert that is embedded in the alloy flywheel. This steel insert (ring) contacts the inner clutch disc.

9 After installing a new pilot bearing, hoist the new aluminum flywheel into place and attach it to the crankshaft flange with the original 12-mm bolts. Be sure to use red Loctite on the bolts.

BOLT-ON PERFORMANCE

10 When tightening the flywheel bolts to the proper torque, do so in a crisscross pattern (tighten the bolts to 85 ft-lbs). Ram's fasteners, spacers, and shims are secured around the perimeter of the flywheel. They attach the floater plate and cover assembly to the flywheel.

11 With the flywheel torqued, insert a clutch alignment tool into the pilot bearing in the crankshaft. Once that is in place, slip the inner clutch disc over it, install the floater plate, and tighten the fasteners to 35 ft-lbs. Once that is done, install the outer clutch disc on the clutch alignment tool.

12 Using the correct spacers and shims that were provided in the kit, attach the pressure plate cover assembly to the flywheel. Now tighten the assembly using a crisscross pattern. Avoid potential misalignment by ensuring the clutch alignment tool slides back and forth during the tightening process.

13 To make sure that the clutch release bearing has sufficient travel to properly operate the clutch fingers of the cover/pressure plate assembly, install this round anodized spacer behind the internal slave assembly, which includes a green bellows and a clutch release bearing. Position the floating spacer on the transmission side of the bearing with an alignment pin.

14 A quick-disconnect hydraulic coupler is located between the clutch master cylinder and the internal clutch release bearing. Before sliding the transmission completely into place, you need to reconnect it. Slide the coupler collar away from the end of the coupler, and then insert the hose that is connected to the bearing into the collar/coupler and release the collar. This allows fluid that is trapped in the slave cylinder assembly to return to the master cylinder, easing the installation process of the transmission.

CHAPTER 3

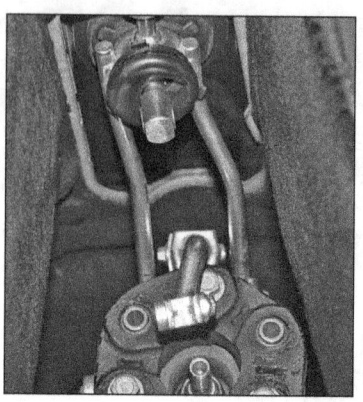

15 Remount the starter motor and connect the shift lever mountings and shift lever mechanism. When reconnecting the shifter to the transmission, start by sliding the front of the shifter bracket into the transmission, and then reinstall the two lock pins and clip retainers. Now you can reinstall the shift-change rod bolt and torque it to 15 ft-lbs. Don't forget to plug in the electronics. The plug is on the driver's side of the transmission.

16 An arrow on the cast crossmember indicates which way the crossmember goes back in. With either a wrench or a ratchet and socket, reinstall it to the chassis with the original four bolts. Then connect the transmission's two rear mounting points to the crossmember.

17 This step is easier with two people. First, reattach the front driveshaft yoke to the transmission using the factory bolts. Bolt the center carrier bearing back in place in the transmission tunnel. Connect the rear yoke to the rear end. Finally, reinstall the exhaust in the reverse order in which you removed it.

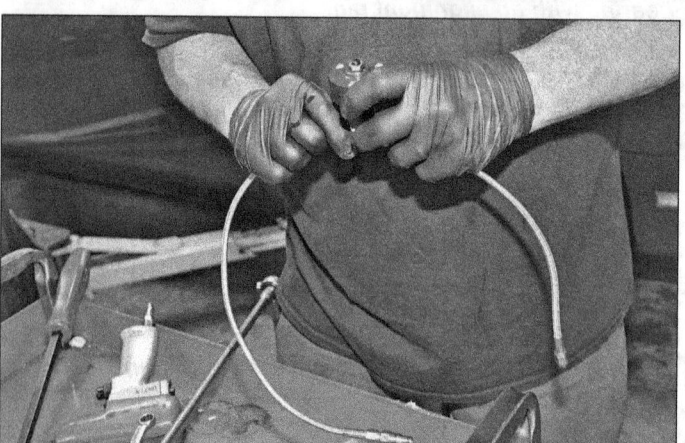

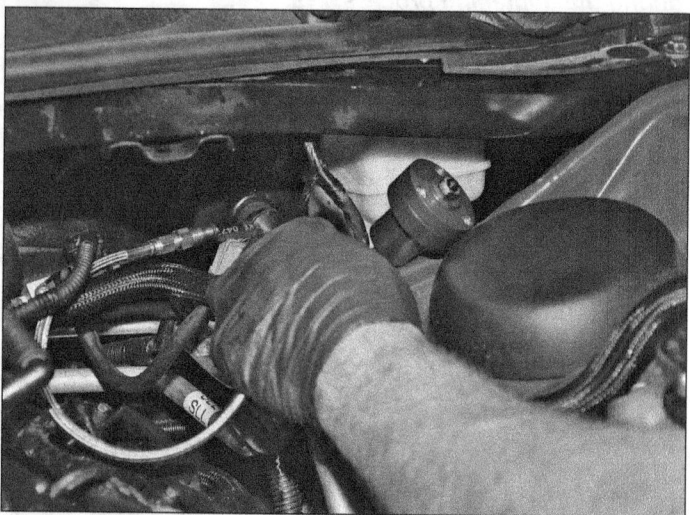

18 The height of the clutch pedal on some Challengers can be uncomfortably high for some drivers. Ram has resolved the issue by producing a clutch pedal adjuster that is situated within the hydraulic line between the slave cylinder and the master cylinder.

19 To adjust the pedal height, simply reset the adjuster nut that is located on top of the hydraulic cylinder to lower the height of the clutch pedal.

CHAPTER 4

MODIFYING YOUR ENGINE

Okay, so you're now back home with your "new" car, and although the drive was fun, you have decided that just adding a few bolt-on items isn't going to be enough to satisfy that lead foot of yours. That's not a problem; you can have your cold-air kit and even more power to boot. You need a comprehensive plan about what goals you have for your Challenger, Charger, 300C, or Magnum before you buy parts. You need to make sure that all the parts complement and support one another, so you can realize the car's maximum performance.

The biggest issue when building a car is that you typically need to make a compromise. Most of the time you want to be able to drive your vehicle every day *and* race it on the weekends. Because racing and street driving require different characteristics in a car, compromises must be made. Every step in part selection is different, according to what you *really* want to accomplish with your car. So having a pre-build plan helps you save money and ensures that the parts you purchase work well together and complement each other.

If you take a look at the late-model Hemi in reference to horsepower per cubic inches (hp/ci), the 5.7-liter Hemi is 345 ci, and in 2005 made 340 hp. That is just shy of 1 hp/ci. That's not bad for a production engine. The 6.1-liter Hemi that was available in SRT models carried a few more ponies than its little brother, making 425 hp. That's a tire-shredding 1.14 hp/ci. The early 5.7 Hemi not only made 390 ft-lbs of peak torque, it also made more than 300 ft-lbs of that torque starting at 1,200 rpm.

Those are not bad numbers for a factory-built car that can be driven every day and still get the blood pumping on the weekend. When the 6.4-liter Hemi was introduced in production cars in 2011, the 470-hp rating gave you 1.19 hp/ci. To say that the late-model Hemi has definitely solidified itself as a true performance engine is an understatement.

But, what are the limitations of the late-model Hemi if you want to add some horsepower-increasing modifications? Are there any concerns that you need to take care of

If you want to squeeze the most performance possible out of your Hemi engine, you really need to plan on getting your hands dirty and getting inside to make some real modifications. The Hemi engine in your Challenger, Charger, 300C, or Magnum wagon responds really well to engine-upgrade modifications. I've seen as much as a 27-hp increase just by swapping the camshaft in a 5.7.

in the name of longevity before you make any modifications? You have already determined that simple bolt-on items can reliably enhance the performance of your Hemi-powered ride, but what if you want more power than those simple bolt-on items can produce? Have you thought about adding a supercharger, ported cylinder heads, or a lumpy camshaft? If so, you need to consider a few things.

Case in point: Did you know that adding parts such as a supercharger or headers and exhaust typically requires a tuning program of some kind? Often, getting deeper into your engine for a performance build requires the use of many bolt-on items as well.

Each part within an engine must be compatible with all of the other parts of the same engine. Buying a bunch of aftermarket parts because your buddy recommended them can result in an engine that doesn't perform as it should; it will also empty your wallet.

Supercharger and Turbocharger Design

Two supercharger design choices are available for your late-model Hemi: twin-screw and centrifugal. Twin-screw superchargers operate by pulling air through a pair of meshing rotors that resemble a set of worm gears. The air inside a twin-screw supercharger is trapped in "pockets" that are created by spinning the rotor lobes. A twin-screw supercharger compresses the air inside the rotor housing because the spinning rotors have a conical taper that pushes the air through the housing, forcing it out of the supercharger and into the engine.

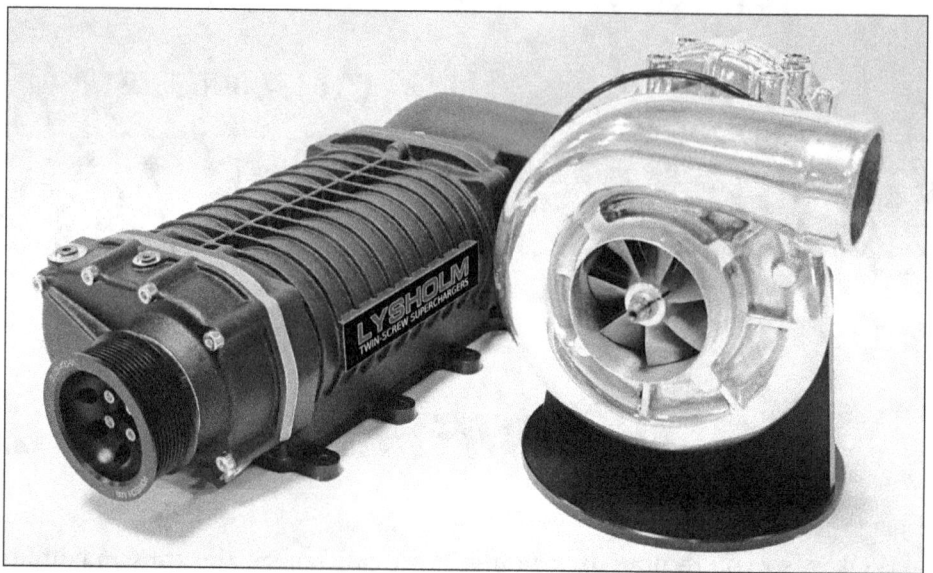

When supercharging a Hemi, you can use either a twin-screw style (left) or a centrifugal style (right). Although a twin-screw supercharger makes boost right off idle, a disadvantage to this type of blower is decreased fuel mileage. Every time you touch the throttle, the computer has to add fuel and remove timing to prevent detonation. Even at light throttle the computer has to go into this mode.

The centrifugal supercharger basically freewheels until you put enough load on the engine to drop the vacuum to near zero. At that point, the blow-off valve closes, and the supercharger starts making boost. Until boost pressure is finally created, the computer is still in cruise mode with full timing and a lean fuel mixture. (Photo Courtesy Lysholm Technologies)

The turning of these screws causes the air pockets to decrease in size as the air moves from the inlet to the discharge side of the supercharger. As the air pockets shrink, the air is squeezed (compressed) into a smaller space. A twin-screw supercharger sits above the engine, and makes what many consider more noise than a centrifugal supercharger when the engine is running.

A centrifugal supercharger has an impeller inside the housing that spins at very high speeds to draw air into the small compressor housing. Although the engine usually spins up to 6,000 rpm, impeller speeds can reach as high as 50,000 to 60,000 rpm. As the air is drawn into the impeller, the centrifugal forces of that impeller force it outward into a diffuser. When the air leaves the impeller, it is traveling at a high rate of speed, but it is at low pressure.

The diffuser is a set of stationary vanes that surround the impeller and convert this high-speed, low-pressure air into low-speed, high-pressure air. The air is slowed when it hits the vanes, which reduces the velocity of the airflow but increases its pressure.

Centrifugal units are small, lightweight, and attach to the front of the engine instead of mounting on top of it. Like a twin-screw supercharger, they also make a distinctive whine as the engine revs up, but depending on the manufacturer, the whine can be minimized. Some centrifugal supercharger kits require that you tap into the engine's oil system to supply

MODIFYING YOUR ENGINE

If you want to change the amount of boost that is delivered to your Hemi, change the supercharger's drive pulley. A smaller pulley causes the supercharger to spin faster, resulting in higher boost pressures. For example, if your stock supercharger creates 8 psi of boost, using a smaller pulley may net you 12 psi of boost.

Keep in mind that increasing boost requires a retune or reflash to support the change in boost pressure. You also want to consider the fuel system, as upgrades may be required.

the supercharger with lubricant, and some kits are self-contained.

The biggest disadvantage of a supercharger is also its defining characteristic. Because they are driven by the crankshaft, they use some of the engine's horsepower just to operate. A supercharger can consume as much as 20 percent of an engine's total power output, but can also generate as much as 46 percent of additional horsepower.

The key difference between a supercharger and a turbocharger is that a supercharger is mechanically driven by the engine, and a turbocharger is powered by a turbine that is driven by the engine's exhaust gases. Compared to a mechanically driven supercharger, turbochargers tend to be more efficient but less responsive because of the requirement of having to build exhaust-gas pressure to operate.

One often-asked question is, "Are superchargers and turbochargers legal?" It varies from state to state and also by the kit. Some kits are CARB compliant and can be used in all 50 states. The best advice I can give is that when you decide what kit you want for your car, talk to the manufacturer or dealer. You probably find more smog-legal supercharger kits than smog-legal turbo kits, because a supercharger doesn't integrate into the exhaust as a turbocharger does.

Supercharger Installation Tips

Installing a supercharger on a stock or modified Hemi engine is a cost-effective way to increase the power under the hood of a Challenger, Charger, Magnum, or 300C. When planning to install a supercharger in a vehicle that you are going to drive every day, you want to make sure to keep the car street legal. This is a concern especially in California because of the strict emissions standards. Keep in mind that some superchargers are designed for racing use only and do not pass standard street-legal considerations. Most Pro-Charger systems are 50-state legal.

An efficient supercharger system can produce yesterday's muscle car performance while using today's lesser quality gasoline. Not only do you get a substantial increase of power, but today's supercharged muscle cars deliver exceptional reliability and minimal impact on fuel economy. Superchargers are easy to install (relatively speaking), especially when compared to pulling, rebuilding, and fine-tuning an engine. And they are simple to maintain.

Once a supercharger is installed, you have virtually no more expense or hassle associated with performance. This is unlike a nitrous oxide kit that needs to have the bottle refilled frequently. In short, supercharging delivers exceptional performance with little of the hassles traditionally associated with high performance.

Although some manufacturers claim a specific horsepower increase at will, superchargers actually add horsepower only as a percentage gain (percentage of actual atmospheric pressure). For example, let's say that you install a supercharger on an engine with a compression ratio of around 9.0:1 and running pump gas.

If a supercharger supplies your engine with 7½ pounds of boost (approximately 1/2 of atmospheric pressure), you see around a 35- to 40-percent gain in horsepower and torque compared with a non-supercharged Hemi's maximum horsepower RPM. If detonation forces you to use an ignition/timing retard system, you of course see less of a gain because when backing off several degrees of timing you greatly reduce an engine's power output.

Twin-Screw Superchargers

Many companies offer twin-screw superchargers for Hemi-powered cars. The following are the most popular among Hemi car owners.

Edelbrock

Edelbrock has been building performance parts for cars since cars were first built, and your Hemi ride can be another happy recipient. Edelbrock's complete supercharger

Turbocharger versus Supercharger

If you're still not exactly sure whether a turbocharger or supercharger is right for you, here are some considerations in deciding which one is the correct choice:

- Turbochargers must be fitted as close as possible to the cylinder head, within the exhaust.
- Turbochargers run very hot because they rely on the exhaust gas velocity. Therefore, the area surrounding a turbocharger must be well insulated from the radiating heat. It is advisable to let the engine idle for a short period of time after heavy use before turning off the engine. This allows the turbocharger to cool down.
- Turbochargers have turbo lag (i.e., the time it takes to wind up the impeller). This is less noticeable in a car at speed with an automatic transmission but is very noticeable with a manually shifted car or during a standing start. Another way to explain turbo lag is that a turbocharger works on the chain-reaction principle.

When the engine idles, so does the turbocharger. At idle, the boost pressure is zero. Now, if you open the throttle to a particular point and keep it there, the engine RPM increases and makes the turbocharger spin. Lag is the brief moment it takes the turbocharger impeller to "catch up" to the speed of the engine.

- Turbochargers require connecting an oil supply line to the engine to keep the turbocharger oiled.
- Two turbochargers can be used on a single application if they are chosen carefully. You also need to consider that you have twice the radiation heat problem and twice the cost.
- Turbochargers require special exhaust connections.
- Because a supercharger is connected directly to the crankshaft of the engine, it supplies immediate boost with no lag. It can also build more boost at a lower RPM.
- Superchargers generally do not heat the incoming air as much as a turbocharger, and do not require an intercooler in some cases (although they are recommended). Some supercharger kits do not require lubrication from the engine oil.
- Superchargers are easier to install.
- Depending on the type of supercharger, the fitment varies from complicated to as easy as fitting an air-conditioner pump.

The selection of the correct size of either a turbocharger or supercharger should be left to the experts. That's why many manufacturers have kits that are ready to go, and free advice is available from the manufacturers if you simply give them a call.

Superchargers can be used with automatic or manual transmissions and do not increase transmission wear (again, under normal driving conditions). When racing, the additional torque provided by a turbocharger or a supercharger places additional load on the transmission, especially when increased traction is present, such as when using slicks. This impact is minimized when the boost increases with engine RPM, as is the case with centrifugal supercharging and turbocharging.

A centrifugal supercharger yields approximately the same fuel economy as normally aspirated engines under normal driving conditions. When racing, however, fuel economy decreases given the supercharged engine's ability to consume additional fuel and produce more horsepower. ∎

---

systems come in two versions, Street and Professional Tuner.

Street systems are 50-state emissions legal and provide the best combination for a daily driver. Professional Tuner systems include all of the essential components that a racer or tuner needs to build a custom supercharged racing setup. They offer the flexibility of choosing the right pulley, cold-air intake, etc. for any custom supercharged installation. Keep in mind that the tuner kit is for competition racing use only.

Edelbrock's E-Force supercharger system fits under the factory hood, as the supercharger assembly is integrated into the intake manifold. Edelbrock's inverted supercharger assembly is uniquely oriented, allowing for an incredible amount of intake runner length for maximizing low-end torque.

Installing a twin-screw supercharger is a little more involved than installing a centrifugal unit; the factory intake has to be removed and replaced with the supercharger and its accompanying intake. This adds to the complexity of the install, so a working knowledge of engines and their assembly and disassembly is a must.

On a 2007 5.7-liter Hemi, dyno testing has shown 466 hp and 456 ft-lbs of torque. The same supercharger on a 2012 5.7-liter

MODIFYING YOUR ENGINE

The newest late-model Hemi supercharger kit is the Edelbrock E-Force twin-screw supercharger system. As large as it looks, this kit fits under the hood of a Challenger, Charger, 300C, or Magnum because the supercharger assembly is integrated into the intake manifold. Installing a twin-screw supercharger is a little more involved than installing a centrifugal unit because the factory intake has to be removed and replaced with the supercharger and its accompanying intake. It takes a full day for the do-it-yourselfer to install the Edelbrock kit. The retail price is about $6,500. (Photo Courtesy Edelbrock)

Hemi saw 471 hp and 475 ft-lbs of torque. All numbers are at the rear wheels.

Kenne Bell

Kenne Bell's Mammoth kits push Dodge performance to a new level and come in multiple sizes (2.8, 3.6, and 4.2 liters). Kenne Bell decided that because cooler air makes more power, their kit ensures that your Hemi engine sucks in only cool, dense air from the unique inlet filter that mounts behind the front bumper.

When choosing a supercharger, your first reaction may be to get the biggest one available. Unfortunately, bigger is not always better, or correct. Kenne Bell has several sizes and models; contacting them to get their input could be beneficial.

The Kenne Bell Mammoth is much like the Edelbrock twin-screw supercharger. The factory intake must be removed to install the supercharger and the adjoining intake. The Kenne Bell kit also has a water-to-air intercooler that must also be plumbed into the system, so if you plan to install the kit yourself, it could take a weekend to install.

Although they look completely different, the Kenne Bell supercharger is like the Edelbrock unit in that it, too, is a twin-screw supercharger. That is all that they have in common; the Kenne Bell kit has a water-to-air intercooler that must be plumbed into the system. If you plan to install the kit yourself, it could take from a whole day to the better part of a weekend to complete. The retail price starts at about $7,000.

When dyno-testing an automatic-equipped 2009 Challenger, it netted 340 hp and 337 ft-lbs of torque in stock trim. After adding the Kenne Bell supercharger kit, the numbers jumped to 512 hp and 472 ft-lbs of torque.

Centrifugal Superchargers

Many companies offer centrifugal superchargers for Hemi-powered cars. The following are the most popular among Hemi car owners.

Vortech Engineering

The Vortech supercharging system was designed to operate as a seamless addition to your car. The boost curve that is generated by Vortech's superchargers is matched with today's highly evolved engines, and gives you power when you need it. The superchargers and their tuning fully integrate into the vehicle's existing platform, giving your car a smooth continuity of power and performance.

Most Vortech supercharger systems are capable of passing the most stringent emissions regulations. Most of their "complete systems" can be purchased as tuner kits. These kits delete the fuel system and ECM programming. This allows you several supercharger and performance options so that you can custom build and tune your vehicle for more aggressive use.

CHAPTER 4

If you choose a Vortech supercharger system, keep in mind that the kit requires that you plumb oil lines from the engine to the supercharger. This adds to the complexity of the install, and many people do not want the extra plumbing hassle. A benefit to this type of supercharger lubrication is that when you change the engine oil, the supercharger also receives fresh oil. The retail price is about $6,700. (Photo Courtesy Vortech Superchargers)

ProCharger's superchargers feature a patented design that eliminates the need to plumb oil lines. They feature an internal oil pump. Although this eliminates the extra plumbing, it requires that the supercharger oil be changed approximately every 6,000 miles. The retail price is about $5,500. (Photo Courtesy ProCharger Superchargers)

Their standard supercharger systems include all components required for a bolt-on installation. Most complete systems are even 50-state emissions legal. The high-output systems are similar to the standard systems, but they deliver an even higher level of performance. This supercharger is set at a higher boost level, and an intercooler is usually included with higher rated subsystems to accommodate the higher boost. Appropriate fuel pump and injectors, bypass valves, and other upgrades, along with ECM re-programming, are part of these highly popular systems on most models.

As with all centrifugal kits, depending on your mechanical capabilities, you can plan on it taking at least a day to perform the install.

ProCharger

ProCharger superchargers feature self-lubrication, which means no plumbing of oil lines to feed the supercharger. ProChargers also feature the highest step-up ratio available, exclusive billet impellers, and the industry's only billet gear case for superior rigidity, sealing, and appearance. Certain ProCharger models are durable enough to be backed with a three-year warranty. ProChargers also feature an internal step-up ratio of 4.10:1 for improved belt tracking and traction, and maximum low-RPM boost and power.

The SC series of superchargers (specifically, P-1SC-1) is available for Hemi cars. The P-1SC is the basis for the Hemi kits. Each ProCharger kit also comes with the required tuning (handheld programmer) to ensure that you get the most out of the kit, and that your engine has the proper tuning to work with the supercharger.

MODIFYING YOUR ENGINE

Installing an Arrington Performance/ShopHemi.com twin-turbocharger kit is a very in-depth install of bolt-on parts. They don't sell the kit as a do-it-yourself install, but rather, as a complete package that must be installed at an authorized shopHemi.com dealer. The retail price is about $10,000 installed. (Photo Courtesy Arrington Performance/ShopHemi.com)

When installing a centrifugal supercharger, you can expect to spend at least a full day installing the kit.

Turbochargers

As you well know, turbochargers use exhaust gases to drive a centrifugal compressor to pressurize the airbox and stream more air into the engine. More air forced into the engine equates to more horsepower. You can design or have a shop design a turbo for your car, but several performance shops offer turbo kits for LX cars. If you're an experienced mechanic, it's often feasible to install your own turbo, but these systems have many component parts; or, in other words, a lot of plumbing. Employing a shop to install the system is often a much better option than installing it yourself.

Arrington Performance/ShopHemi.com

The Arrington twin turbocharger kit is available in many configurations and power levels to suit the driving style of any Hemi-powered ride. Their most popular configurations feature 58- or 62-mm turbochargers. Installing a set of twin turbochargers is probably the most in-depth install of bolt-on parts that you can choose. Therefore, it is best left to the professionals; it is a major undertaking. That is why shopHemi.com doesn't sell the kit as a do-it-yourself install, but rather as a complete package that must be installed at an authorized shopHemi.com shop. Horsepower numbers vary depending on the kit.

Project: ProCharger Supercharger Installation

Most ProCharger systems are covered by a one-year warranty, although a three-year extended policy is available for many automotive applications.

When installing a ProCharger kit, keep in mind that most ProCharger systems can be installed in roughly 8 to 10 hours with simple hand tools.

When it comes to supercharging, ProCharger was one of the first companies to deliver complete supercharging kits for the Chrysler 5.7-, 6.1-, and 6.4-liter Hemis. Their superchargers fit great and mount under the hood for a clean look. ProCharger offers Challenger, Charger, Magnum, and 300 owners two levels of performance: the HO and the Stage II.

Unless you are building a dedicated race engine, your Hemi should have the stock engine compression ratio if it is receiving a ProCharger upgrade. If your engine has been modified in any way, please consult a member of the ProCharger staff before proceeding with the installation. For best performance and reliability, always use premium-grade fuel (91 octane or higher).

CHAPTER 4

1 To remove the front fascia from the car, use a Torx-bit screw driver to remove the panel fasteners from the top side of the fascia (I have seen Phillips-head screws used here as well). The lower panel fasteners connecting the front fender wells to the front fascia use the same fasteners.

Unhook the lighting connectors and disconnect the wiring harness running to the front fascia. This eliminates having to unplug the fog lamps and turn signals separately.

Remove the front fascia from the vehicle by pulling outward on each side at the wheel opening, and unsnapping and pulling the fascia straight off the front of the vehicle.

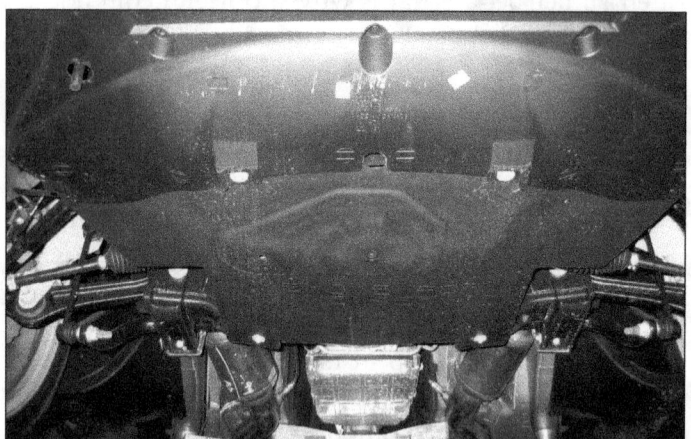 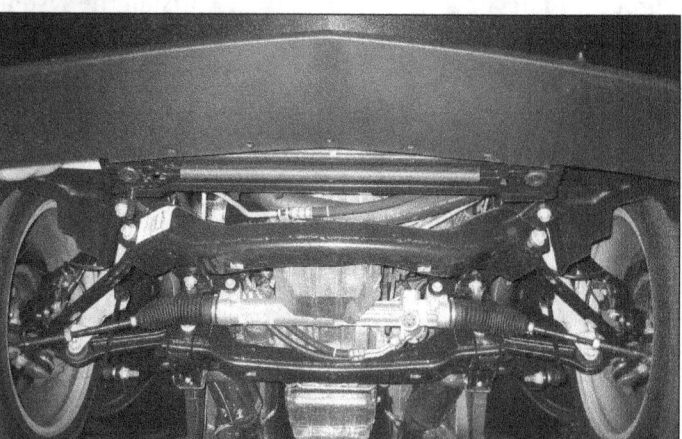

2 You need to gain access underneath the vehicle to remove the underbody splash shield. You can do this with a floor jack and jack stand, but a lift makes the entire job a lot easier. The splash shield is held in place by Torx-head screws across the front of the shield and a couple of bolts near the middle and trailing edge of the shield. Remove the screws and bolts and the shield easily comes off.

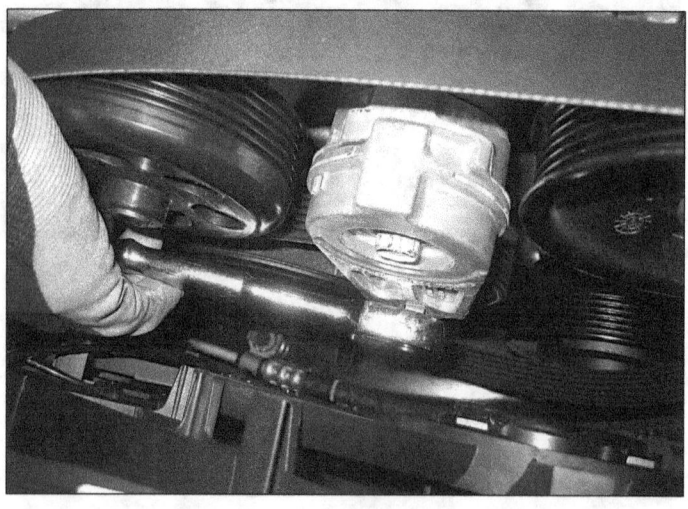

3 With the front fascia and the factory air cleaner assembly out of the way, you can remove the serpentine belt. Use a ratchet with a 15-mm socket and release the spring tension from the serpentine belt tensioner. Using the ratchet and socket, rotate the tensioner away from the belt so the belt can be removed. Do not lose your grip on the ratchet (or tensioner), as the pressure allows the tensioner to spring back violently. Save the tensioner; it will be reused later in the installation.

MODIFYING YOUR ENGINE

4 Using a 13-mm wrench, remove the three bolts that secure the power steering pump assembly to the engine. Once the bolts are removed, pull the assembly upward far enough to access the back of the pump. Once accessible, remove the three 10-mm bolts that secure the power steering reservoir to the pump and separate the reservoir from the pump. This connection is sealed with an O-ring, so do not damage or lose this O-ring.

Drain the excess fluid into a container. The reservoir will no longer be used, so after you remove it and the line that was attached to the cooler on the passenger's side you can discard the reservoir.

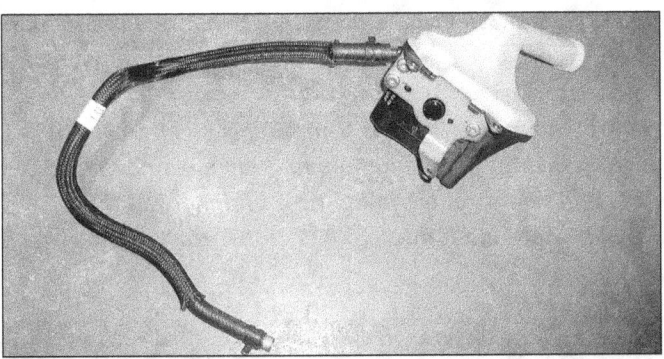

5 Remove the power steering reservoir and the line.

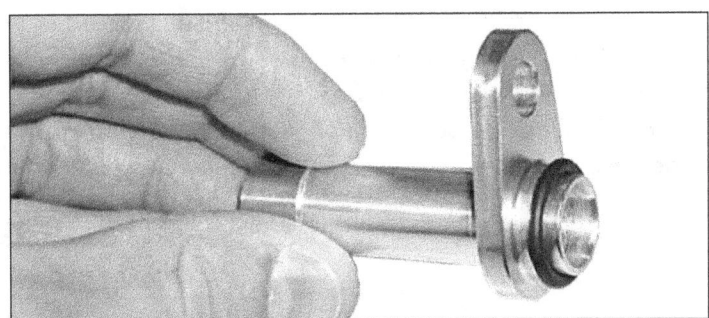

6 You see a factory O-ring on the connection between the factory power steering reservoir and the pump. Slide it onto the ProCharger-supplied adapter. Bolt the adapter to the pump using the provided bolt and washer. Be careful not to damage the O-ring when installing the adapter into the pump. Adding a small amount of oil to the O-ring helps during the install.

7 With the reservoir removed, and the ProCharger hose adapter in place, you can now install the supplied 5-inch section of 5/8-inch hose over the adapter. Secure the hose to the adapter with a hose clamp and then reinstall the pump to the front of the engine.

8 Using the supplied bolts and brackets, mount the new reservoir pump near the throttle body (shown). Attach the supplied 3/8-inch hose to the small port/outlet on the reservoir using a hose clamp. When attached, route the hose from the reservoir to the front of the vehicle on the driver-side and under the driver-side headlamp. This hose will eventually be connected to the power steering cooler that is located behind the fascia.

Position the large port/outlet from the reservoir in line with the 5/8-inch hose that comes from the power steering pump (trim if needed). Attach it with a hose clamp.

Temporarily reinstall the engine covers when positioning the reservoir. Be certain the 5/8-inch line is not pinched. Any restriction in the line causes power steering pump noise and even failure.

DODGE CHALLENGER AND CHARGER: HOW TO BUILD AND MODIFY

CHAPTER 4

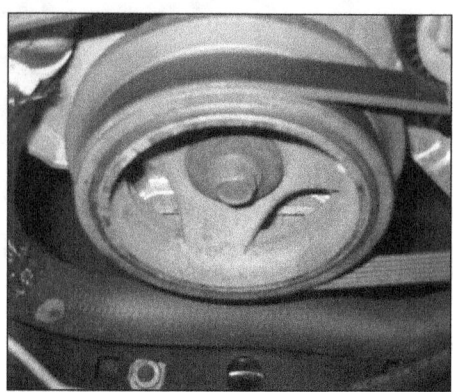

9 Because the crankshaft pulley bolt must be removed for this step, you need to remove the factory cooling fan assembly to gain access. The crankshaft bolt needs to be removed so that the pulley can be modified.

10 To modify the crankshaft pulley, drill the dampener and the crankshaft snout to install the locking pin that secures the blower drive pulley to the crankshaft. Once the bolt is removed, place the supplied drill jig onto the crankshaft pulley and tighten it in place using the supplied bolt and washer.

Wrap a piece of tape around the supplied 1/4-inch drill bit, approximately 1⅝ inches from its tip. Using this taped drill bit, drill a hole in the crankshaft and harmonic balancer, but only deep enough so that you stop at the tape's edge. By doing this, the needed hole is centered on the outside diameter of the crankshaft and the inner diameter of the pulley/dampener. Do not drill deeper than .800 inch into the face of the crankshaft.

After drilling, remove the jig and set it aside. Thoroughly clean the metal chips and drilling debris from inside the drilled hole and the surrounding area. Install the supplied stainless steel dowel pin in the hole that you just drilled. Reinstall the crankshaft pulley bolt and tighten to 129 ft-lbs. You can now replace the cooling fan assembly.

11 Install the main supercharger mounting bracket assembly by inserting the bolt through the main bracket, the sub-bracket, and the bracket brace. Position the bracket assembly in place on the driver's side of the engine, and then thread the bolt into the cylinder head. Install the remaining three fasteners. Once installed, you can tighten the sub-bracket bolts and complete the bracket installation by tightening the main bracket bolts.

12 The supercharger can now be placed into the bracket. Most ProCharger kits have an available drain hose for the supercharger that is used to drain the oil for changing. Although not a required hose, it makes supercharger oil changes a lot easier. Fill the supercharger unit with one of the supplied bottles of oil. Remove the fill plug/dipstick using a flat-head screwdriver. After filling the head unit with oil, replace the fill plug/dipstick.

MODIFYING YOUR ENGINE

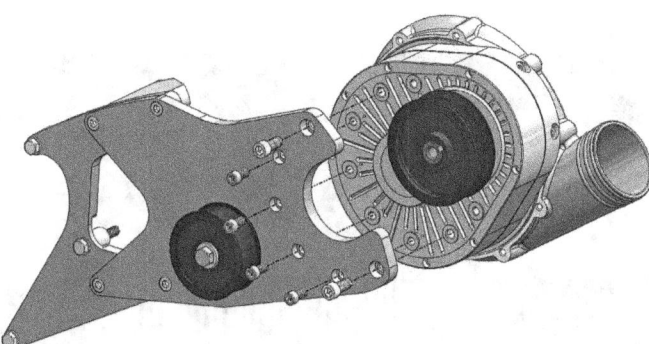

13 This diagram shows how the mounting brackets and supercharger head unit are positioned. (Photo Courtesy Procharger Superchargers)

14 With the supercharger head unit in place, reinstall the factory belt tensioner with the pulley aimed straight downward; tighten the bolt. Install the serpentine belt and tension the belt by adjusting the idler pulley adjustment screw.

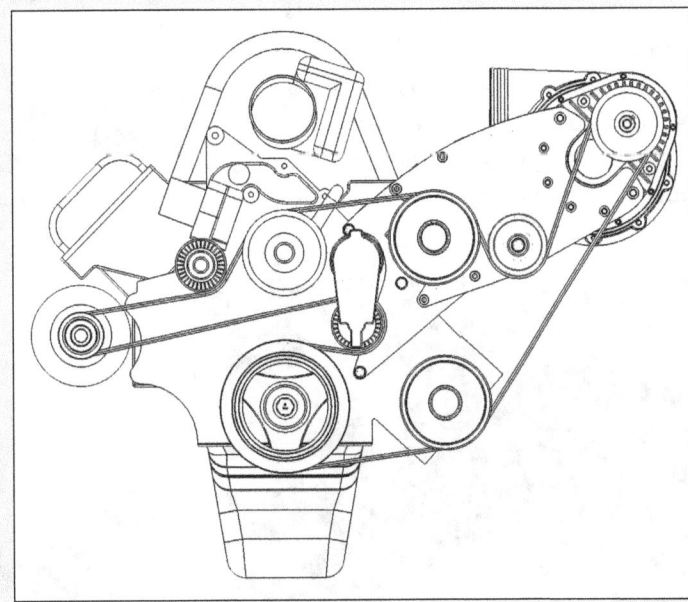

This is the correct routing for the serpentine belt. (Photo Courtesy Procharger Superchargers)

15 To mount the intercooler, first assemble the intercooler brackets using the four M6 x 25–mm bolts. The offset portion of the bracket faces the car. This orientates the intercooler forward to gain room for the condenser. Now you can attach the brackets to the car using the two M8 x 60–mm bolts and washers for the lower connections, and the two M6 x 20–mm bolts and washers for the upper connections. If the body holes do not align perfectly, drill out the top hole to a larger size.

Mount the intercooler horns with the factory 13-mm bolts and washers to the supplied horn relocation bracket. Mount the intercooler to the brackets using the four 3/8-16 x 1–inch bolts and washers. Before installing the passenger-side upper bolt and washer, slide the horn relocation bracket between the bolt and intercooler bracket, and then tighten the assembly.

CHAPTER 4

16 When assembling the intercooler brackets, position the offset portion of the bracket toward the radiator core support. This orientation is required to push the intercooler away from the vehicle to leave space around the air conditioning condenser.

Use the two M8 x 60–mm bolts and washers for the lower end of the bracket, and the two M6 x 20-mm bolts and washers for the upper connections. If the body holes do not allow for proper bracket mounting, drill out the top hole to a larger size.

17 Mount the intercooler to the brackets using the four 3/8-16 x 1–inch bolts and washers.

18 Slide the 3½-to–3-inch silicone reducer onto the throttle body. Use a 3¾-inch T-bolt clamp for the throttle body connection and a 3¼-inch T-bolt clamp for the hose connection. Complete the connection by sliding the throttle body tube (#315) into the open ends of each hose. You might need to rotate the hard tube when installing it into the silicone tubes to gain clearance from the cooling fan and supercharger bracket assembly.

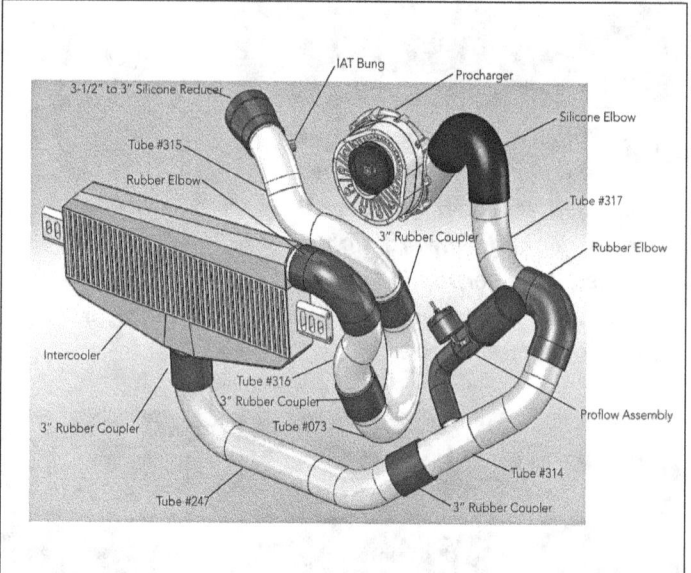

19 You can use this hose routing diagram as reference. (Photo Courtesy Procharger Superchargers)

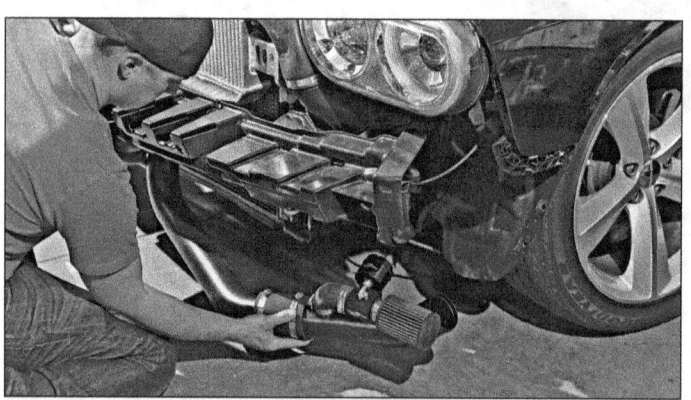

20 Slide the surge valve (commonly called the blow-off valve, or BOV) onto the open end of the rubber elbow in the orientation shown here. Place the filter onto the end of the valve. Using the provided 3/16-inch vacuum line, connect one end to the barb located on the surge valve and route it under the blower. It will later connect to the open barb located on the soon-to-be installed vacuum manifold. Be sure to zip tie the line for clearance and to keep it away from moving components and from the exhaust manifold.

MODIFYING YOUR ENGINE

21 Locate the supplied power steering cooler brackets and hardware. Mount the brackets to the cooler's factory mounting tabs using 3/8-inch bolts. Remount the cooler flat and horizontally between the frame and the radiator, underneath the cooling fan assembly. The brackets mount to the factory nuts in the frame using the factory hardware.

Once the cooler is mounted, reroute the cooler lines to the cooler. It may be necessary to trim the lines for proper fit. Fill the power steering reservoir to the indicated full level.

22 Remove the stud/bolt on the front cover of the engine with a 15-mm wrench, and then loosen but do not remove the top alternator bolt with a 16-mm wrench. Mount the new coolant reservoir by sliding the slotted bracket between the head of the upper alternator bolt and alternator itself. Align the upper bracket with the hole in the front cover where the stud/bolt was removed. Using the factory hardware, secure the reservoir to the vehicle.

The hoses that were running to the factory coolant reservoir must be removed to install the new coolant reservoir. The easiest and cleanest way to do this swap is to empty the factory coolant reservoir and crimp the two hoses running to the reservoir. The factory coolant reservoir will no longer be used.

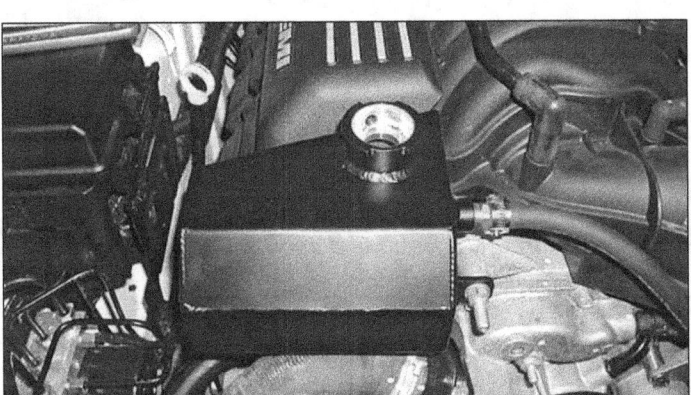

23 The lines from the factory coolant reservoir must be lengthened to reach the outlet on the new reservoir. Install the 3/4 x 3/4–inch barbed fitting into the 3/4-inch factory coolant line. Slide the supplied section of 3/4-inch hose onto the open end of the barb and secure the connections with #12 hose clamps.

Run the new 3/4-inch coolant line under the supercharger, along the bottom of the cooling fan, and then up the passenger's side of the car. Slide it onto the 3/4-inch barbed fitting on the bottom of the new reservoir and secure the connection with a #12 hose clamp.

Install the 3/8 x 3/8–inch barbed fitting onto the 3/8-inch factory coolant line. Slide the longer section of supplied 3/8-inch hose onto the open end of the barb, and secure with #6 hose clamps. Run the 3/8-inch line under the front of the intake manifold and to the side of the reservoir and slide the hose onto the barbed fitting. Secure the connection with a #6 hose clamp.

24 If you have or are installing a boost gauge, do not install the plug, and use an additional barb fitting to connect the gauge. Thread each fitting into the manifold. Locate the brake booster hose on the driver's side near the firewall. Remove a 3½-inch section of this hose so you can place the manifold in-line, in its place. Be sure the brake booster hose connections are tight and that the connection to the booster did not come loose. Connect the 3/16-inch vacuum hose coming from the surge valve.

Remember that improper clamping of the splice into the brake booster hose could cause a vacuum leak and could cause the power brakes to become inoperable. Use extreme caution when installing the vacuum manifold to prevent any possible leaks.

CHAPTER 4

25 The MAP sensor is located on the passenger's side on the rear of the intake manifold. Remove the electrical harness by sliding the red retaining tab back and disconnecting it from the sensor. Use a 7-mm socket to remove the MAP sensor from the intake manifold. Remove the O-ring from the factory MAP sensor and install it onto the supplied MAP adapter fitting. Insert the adapter into the intake manifold and tighten using the factory screw. Install the new supplied sensor into the adapter fitting. Connect the electrical harness to the new sensor.

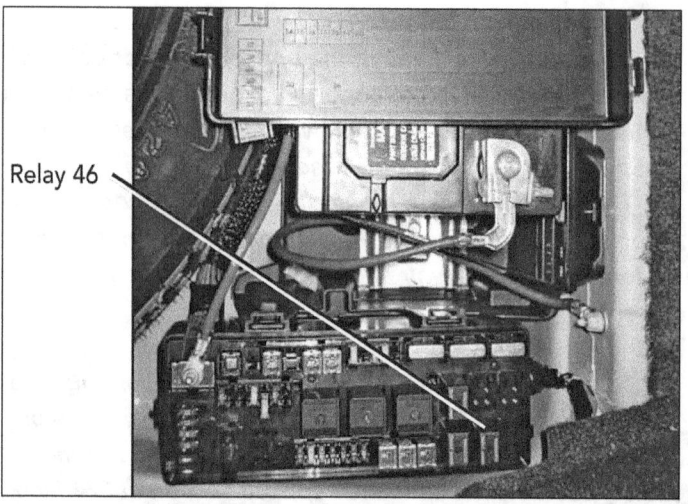

Relay 46

26 Reconnect the battery, and then remove relay #46 from the fuse panel in the trunk. Some models require the removal of the #6 20-amp fuse that is located in the trunk so that power to the fuel pump is turned off. Crank the engine for 15 seconds and then disconnect the battery.

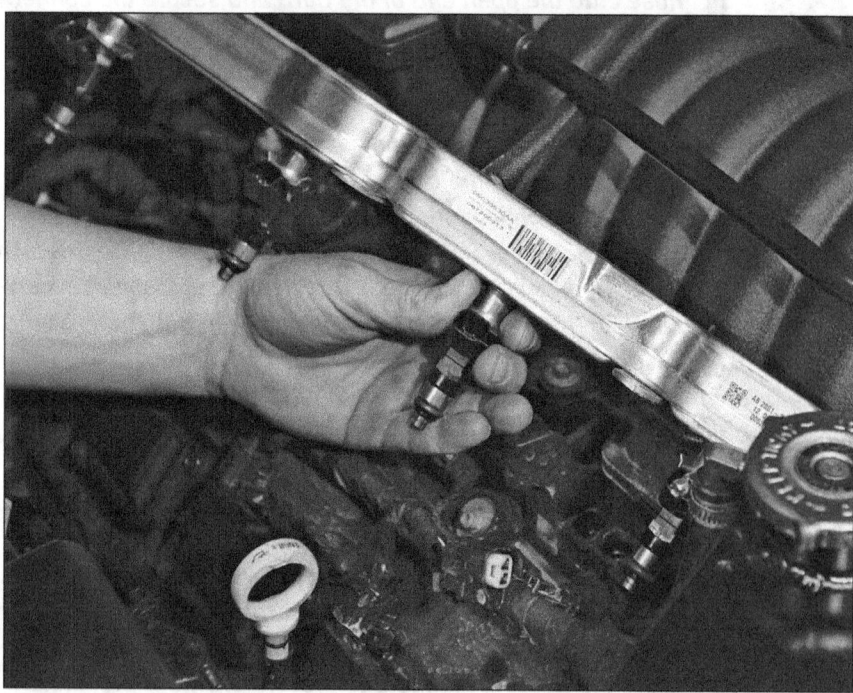

27 Unclip the wiring harnesses from each fuel injector. Remove the four bolts securing the fuel rails to the manifold, and pull the fuel rails upward and off the manifold to gain access to the fuel injectors. Remove the fuel injector retaining clips from each injector and rail. Remove the injectors by pulling them straight out of the rails.

Install the new injectors, followed by the factory retaining clips. Push the injector and rail assembly back into place, and tighten the rails. Reinstall each wiring harness to each injector.

Note that the fuel system mod only applies to complete systems, which include upgraded fuel system components and tuning. If you do not have a full system, an upgraded fuel system and tuning is required before starting the vehicle.

MODIFYING YOUR ENGINE

28 Slide the air filter onto the supercharger, and rotate the assembly so it lays flat over the top of the driver-side engine cover; proper adjustment allows for ample clearance from the hood liner. Tighten all hose clamps.

On the back side of the front fascia, the two plastic deflectors must be removed to gain clearance for the intercooler and tubing. Cut the heads off the five plastic rivets on each deflector. Unclip the harnesses attached to the deflectors and remove them from the fascia.

Reinstall the front fascia in the reverse order it was removed. Connect the wiring harness on the passenger's side of the vehicle that is attached to the fascia. Tighten all hardware. Replace the factory underside cladding using the factory hardware.

I installed and tested the eight-rib ProCharger on a 392 Challenger, and with no other modifications, I saw 616 hp and 566 ft-lbs of torque at the wheels. That's an increase of 161.17 hp and 119.55 ft-lbs of torque. Not only did peak numbers climb, the averages went from 329.67 to 396.44 hp and 403.46 ft-lbs of torque to 496.61. (Photo Courtesy ATI Performance Products)

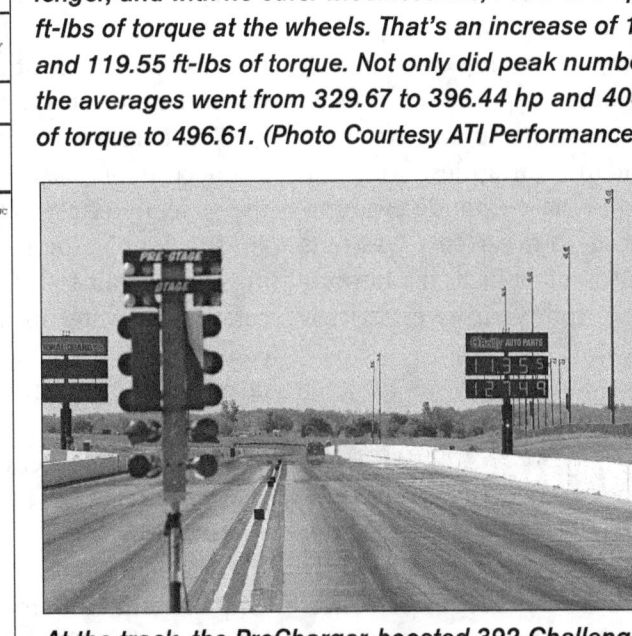

At the track, the ProCharger-boosted 392 Challenger ran a best of 11.35 at 127.49 mph in the quarter-mile. This was with a bone-stock engine with no modifications other than the ProCharger kit.

Fuel Selection

If your Hemi engine is stock, always follow the manufacturer's recommendations as to what fuel to use. When an engine is modified, depending on the modification, a high-octane fuel is recommended. In general terms, the primary factors that determine fuel type for a modified engine are the compression ratio of the engine, the tune that is installed in the engine, and whether or not an added turbocharger or supercharger system is intercooled.

For intercooled Hemi applications with compression ratios less than 9.5:1, boost can safely be added with proper tuning if running premium pump gas. For a Hemi engine with a 9.5:1 or higher compression ratio, running without an intercooler, boost levels above 5 psi require the use of specialized tuning with an ignition/timing retard. Premium pump gas (racing gas) is highly recommended.

Adding more than 12 psi of boost should generally be avoided, even when using race fuel in an engine with a 9.5:1 or higher compression ratio. Of course, lower ratios are able to run more boost, and higher ratios produce less boost (everything else being equal). So when it comes to choosing the fuel for your modified Hemi engine, although it might cost more at the pump each time, the added security of a high-octane fuel is worth the peace of mind.

Although most people use price as a deciding factor for purchasing a kit, warranty availability should also play an important role. A cheap turbocharger or supercharger kit isn't worth the savings if it doesn't include some type of warranty. Reputable manufacturers generally offer standard warranties, with the option to purchase extended warranties. Because your car cost you tens of thousands of dollars, it's important to make sure your investment is protected.

Intercooler

Whether you add a supercharger or turbocharger to your vehicle, the process of compressing air also heats that air, so an intercooler is something to consider. Although the added pressure creates more horsepower, the highly heated air is not as dense as it was before it was compressed and heated. The less dense the air before it mixes with the fuel that enters the combustion chamber, the less power is ultimately generated, and the more likely it is for the engine to detonate.

Adding an intercooler significantly lowers the heated air's temperature, allowing for a more dense (and cooler) air/fuel mixture to enter

When adding boost, an intercooler is definitely something to consider. Compressed air is heated, and adding an intercooler decreases the heated air's temperature. Remember, cool air makes power; hot air hampers power.

the Hemi's combustion chamber, creating more horsepower and eliminating detonation. Similar to an engine's radiator, an intercooler is a simple heat exchanger, built in two primary parts: the core and the end tanks.

The core is made up of tubes and a collection of fins. Each tube radiates the generated heat to the fins, which are then cooled by the outside moving air in an air-to-air unit, or the circulation of water in an air-to-liquid (water) unit. The end tanks simply take the air from the pipe, distribute it to the tubes of the core, and then collect it at the other end.

Intercooler Types

Air-to-air intercoolers are the simplest and least inexpensive style of intercooler. They use the air that is flowing through the intercooler to cool the charged air inside the intercooler. Air-to-liquid intercoolers are much more complex, and therefore more expensive. They use a separate liquid cooling system that encompasses the intercooler to cool the air inside the intercooler. This requires the additional work of installing a water-circulation component to the supercharger.

In a Hemi car, air-to-air intercoolers are placed in the front of the vehicle, behind the bumper and grille. This area of the vehicle allows for larger intercoolers to be used. Front-mounted intercoolers require a large amount of tubing to plumb the intercooler. The charged air must go from the turbocharger or supercharger to the front of the car and then back to the engine intake.

An air-to-liquid intercooler uses a separate water pump, radiator, and heat exchanger. On Hemi applications, the air-to-liquid intercooler is typically located near the engine intake, and although it requires less tubing for the charged air, the coolant connection adds to the complexity of the install.

Intercooler Ratings

Intercoolers are rated by their effectiveness and flow restriction. An intercooler's effectiveness is defined as the ratio of how many degrees of temperature were removed from the charged air by the intercooler as compared to the original temperature of the compressed air. You can easily calculate your intercooler's effectiveness.

For example, if the supercharger compresses and heats the air to a temperature of 140 degrees F, but after passing through the intercooler the air is 115 degrees F, the effectiveness is 82-percent efficiency (115 ÷ 140 = .82).

Typically, superchargers create boost for only a short amount of time, roughly 5 to 20 seconds. Therefore, intercoolers are only needed during those 5 to 20 seconds. Intercoolers are made from aluminum and possess a thermal inertia property. This means that if the metal is cool, it takes time to heat it up.

Let's say that your intercooler is at 70 degrees and you hit the throttle, creating boost. The intercooler started at 70 degrees and does a great job of cooling the heated, compressed air, but as the seconds go by, the intercooler warms up. After 5 seconds, the metal could now be 110 degrees, and its effectiveness has been reduced by 37 percent. From 5 seconds on, the effectiveness may be constant if the intercooler does not become any hotter.

Intercoolers are also a flow restriction, and what good is an intercooler if it chokes 10 psi of your boost pressure as it tries to force the compressed air through it? What you need to look for is an intercooler that is large enough and designed to be free flowing.

Intercoolers can be rated by how much airflow they can pass (cubic feet of air per minute, measured as CFM) at a given pressure drop. This is much like coming up with a carburetor's CFM rating on a flow bench.

Although large intercoolers offer more airflow and have more thermal inertia, a large intercooler is more difficult to package within the constraints of the car, and if using a turbocharger, have a dramatic effect on turbo lag.

Whether you add a turbocharger or supercharger to your Hemi, it needs to be tuned to make sure that it doesn't destroy itself. Proper supercharging and turbocharging kits come complete with the appropriate tuning required. If you choose to not change the ignition timing, please continue to read as I discuss engine internals.

Built-In Durability

Forged crankshafts, connecting rods, and pistons are essential for ensuring durability in your Hemi engine when it is under the higher loads that high-performance engines typically experience. The factory third-generation Hemi engines use powder-metal rods and hypereutectic (cast) pistons that are strong enough when used within the engines' factory-stock operating range, but frankly, are not designed for the demands of displacement combinations that could add 25 percent or more horsepower and torque.

Okay, now that I've said that, I'm sure that you have seen supercharger kits that were installed on cars with stock engines. You're also wondering how they survive after I just said they shouldn't. The answer comes down to tuning. Aside from tuning, the manner in which a car is driven directly affects engine life. Assuming a properly tuned system with proper oil change and engine maintenance, supercharging does not generally shorten the life of an engine. That is also the case with OEM turbocharging (with a proper cool-down period).

Pistons

The piston design of the late-model Hemi engine is not only "cast," but the top ring is close to the top of the piston. This creates a small area (ring land) between the top ring

As you know, spark knock (detonation) can cause severe damage or complete destruction of engine components (especially the pistons). As the combustion process is subjected to irregular ignition, the multiple flame fronts collide and create shock waves that produce a sharp metallic pinging or knocking noise. That is the sound of your pistons being hit with a force equal to or greater than that of a hammer.

A strong foundation is paramount to your Hemi engine's longevity, and a forged crankshaft provides more strength than a cast crankshaft. Although many crankshaft manufacturers produce crankshafts with different strokes, another way to increase the stroke of your engine's rotating assembly is to have the crank reground.

and the actual top of the piston. In recent years, manufacturers have moved the piston rings closer to the top of the piston to minimize the area where unburned fuel can be trapped. This is done to help eliminate emissions and help fuel economy. In a performance engine, the same logic applies. The more efficient the combustion process, the more power an engine creates.

If you use a cast piston in a high-performance application, issues can develop quickly if detonation occurs. When spark knock (detonation) is encountered, the ECU removes timing and eliminates the detonation. If detonation occurs frequently, the piston is eventually destroyed. If you add aftermarket items such as a supercharger and do not tune the engine to work with it, the threat of detonation becomes more pronounced, and you need to replace the pistons sooner rather than later.

Cast or Forged

Several piston manufacturers build replacement pistons for the late-model Hemi engine. When upgrading to an aftermarket piston, forged is the only way to go. The difference between a cast piston and a forged piston is the manufacturing technique. Traditional cast pistons are considered sufficient in stock engines, and the casting process of making this type of piston is much less expensive than that of a forging. Cast pistons are made in a mold, where the mixture of aluminum, alloys, and silicone are poured into it to create the piston's shape.

Forged pistons are made from a single lump of steel that is stamped into shape with a die. Forged pistons are more durable and can be easily customized to fit any configuration. Some engine applications may require that a fly-cut be added on the piston face to assist in valve relief clearance, and this can easily be done when building a forged piston. The manufacturing techniques employed in the making of a forged piston help make it stronger, as there is more surface area concentrated into its shape. This does not necessarily mean that forged pistons are better than cast pistons. In fact, the technology used in the making of cast pistons is state of the art compared with the method of forging. The beneficial difference actually lies in the application.

The main characteristic that makes forged pistons better in high-performance applications is their strength and durability. The high silicon content of cast pistons makes them more brittle than a forged piston. This is the primary reason cast pistons require careful handling, as a mild shock applied to a cast piston may cause the material to break. If a mild shock can break it, imagine what detonation can do.

The added silicon in cast pistons gives the metal lubricity; it is mixed into the alloy to help limit heat expansion. This means that a cast piston does not expand as much as a forged piston under normal engine-running conditions. When forged pistons are used in an engine, more clearance must be allotted between the piston and the cylinder wall during assembly to allow for the expansion of the piston that occurs as the engine reaches operating temperature while running. The process of forging compresses the molecules inside the alloy, and this results in a denser surface area when compared to a cast piston. This denser material helps protect against the effects of detonation.

Although forged pistons are heavier than cast pistons, this weight is offset by the forged piston's ability to durably provide a higher compression ratio inside the engine. This increased durability allows the engine to reliably produce more power. Most turbocharged and high-performance car engines use forged pistons because they're more tolerant of the abuses of extreme heat, detonation, and pressures that are inherent in performance-oriented engines.

Although a stock engine can "make do" with a cast piston, forged pistons are decidedly more durable in terms of shatter resistance when exposed to extreme temperatures inside the combustion chamber. This doesn't mean that cast pistons are inadequate. In fact, they are more than adequate for most applications. You must analyze the different factors involved in your particular engine modifications to make the decision as to which type of piston to use.

Most builders agree that when building a high compression or supercharged engine, the use of forged pistons is highly recommended. Custom engine builders also prefer the wide variety of customizable designs that a forged piston provides. This allows them to match the shape of the piston with the kind of performance benefit they want to achieve. This also makes it easy to properly tune and enhance engine tolerance during testing and actual use.

Many companies offer pistons for Hemi-powered cars. The following are the most popular among Hemi car owners.

Mahle Motorsports

Mahle Motorsports' PowerPak pistons are available for both boosted

MODIFYING YOUR ENGINE

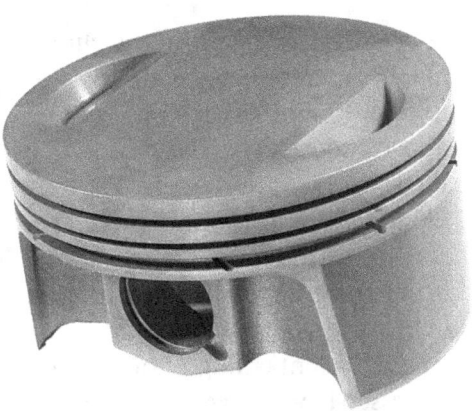

Mahle Motorsports' pistons are widely used in custom engine builds because of their durability and economical price. The pistons are coated so they resist scoring, wear, and noise. The PowerPak assemblies are made with high-quality steel pins, round wire locks, and low-drag file-fit rings. The retail price per set begins at about $750. (Photo Courtesy Mahle Motorsports)

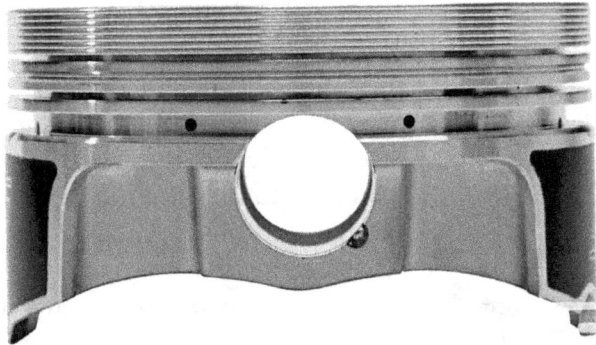

To add strength to their pistons, Wiseco has implemented a strutted-skirt design. This adds support/bracing to critical areas of the piston such as the skirt and wrist pin area. The pistons are designed to run at very tight tolerances, which eliminates noise (piston slap) and increases horsepower. The retail price of a complete set is about $700. (Photo Courtesy Wiseco Performance Products)

and normally aspirated applications. The pistons are first coated with a phosphate dry-film lubricant to eliminate micro-welding in the ring grooves and galling in the pin bores. The skirts are then coated with Mahle's proprietary Grafal skirt coating that reduces frictional drag, wear, and noise, because of its unique cushioning property. The assemblies are made with high-quality steel pins, round wire locks, and low-drag file-fit rings.

Wiseco Performance Products

Wiseco pistons are a 2618 alloy, and do not shatter like hypereutectic, cast, or 4032 alloy forged pistons. The strutted-skirt design is exceptionally strong and specially designed to run with as little as .004-inch clearance, with excellent skirt wear and minimal noise or rocking within the cylinder wall. They have radiused valve pockets for detonation resistance and increased airflow around the valves. They also use a 1.2-mm nitrided steel top ring, a 1.2-mm Napier second ring, and a nitrided 3-mm oil ring for reduced friction for more horsepower. They come with chrome-moly wrist pins and Spirolox locks (tool-steel pins are optional). They are coated with Wiseco's ArmorGlide skirt coating to reduce friction and noise.

Manley Performance Products

Manley's Platinum Series pistons are machined of high-strength 2618 materials, and each design is lightweight, yet durable enough to last a long time. Ring groove-to-skirt squareness ensures maximum horsepower. Round-wire wristpin locks, tool-steel wrist pins, and pressure-balance grooves are included with every set.

Diamond Racing

Diamond Racing pistons are specifically designed for 5.7- and 6.1-liter Hemis. Diamond uses a double-coated process for their pistons that combines a hard-coat anodizing on the piston top with Moly-coated skirts. According to Diamond, this is particularly useful in engines with power adders. The standard ring package features

Manley's Platinum Series pistons are specifically designed for use in 5.7-, 6.1-, and 6.4-liter Hemi engines. The high-strength alloy materials create a lightweight piston that is strong enough to last a long time, yet light enough to free some horsepower. A set retails for about $770. (Photo Courtesy Manley Performance Products)

Diamond Racing's pistons are specifically designed for the late-model Hemi engine. A hard-coat anodizing on the piston's top helps resist the heat generated by combustion, and Moly-coating on the piston's skirts help reduce friction. This is suited for engines with or without power adders. The retail price is about $675. (Photo Courtesy Diamond Racing)

1.5-, 1.5-, and 3.0-mm rings. The number-8 piston is clearanced for the reluctor wheel.

Connecting Rods

As with the cast (eutectic) piston, the powder-metal connecting rod used in factory Hemi applications has been designed to minimize weight and maintain strength. The powder metallurgy process also produces a more precision-cast part than regular forging. This reduces final-machining costs. Connecting rods are subjected to both compressive and tensile forces during the rotation of the crankshaft, so strength is a much-needed quality. During the compression stroke, the pressure inside the cylinder increases, pushing against the connecting rod. Depending on your engine's compression ratio, use of power adders, etc., that pressure can be intense and overcome a stock connecting rod's strength.

When combustion occurs, the connecting rod must endure a sudden and violent directional change as well as the pressure that is generated by the combustion process. The load on a connecting rod can be calculated with this formula:

Load = bore area x cylinder pressure

Where:
bore area = bore radius^2 x pi
pi = 3.14159

For example, a 4-inch bore has a surface area of 12.566 inches. If you achieve a cylinder pressure of 160 psi, the cumulative pressure on the rod at that point in the combustion is 2,011 psi (12.566 x 160).

Let's not forget that the spark plug fires just before the piston actually reaches top dead center (TDC). This means that the connecting rod is still on its way upward when the explosion hits the top of the piston. This further increases the force that the rod has to overcome.

This point in the combustion cycle also brings up the issue of pre-ignition and misfire. Cylinder pressure increases once the air/fuel mixture is ignited; if this ignition happens too early in the cycle it is called pre-ignition (detonation). Pre-ignition increases the load on the connecting rod earlier in the cycle, further straining it with compressive force. If the pre-ignition event is violent or frequent enough, the rod may be stressed beyond its limit. So, if you want to make sure that you have connecting rods that are able to survive the torture that you plan to inflict, maybe a new set of connecting rods is in order.

Forged or Billet

Forged connecting rods (much like forged pistons) are made with tooling dies, and extreme heat and pressure. The die is actually a "negative" of the connecting rod (it resembles a mold). During the forging process, a piece of metal is heated and then forced into the die using high pressure, often referred to as hammering. The formed metal is then removed from the die and takes the shape of a raw connecting rod, which then under-

You can choose from two types of steel when making a high-performance connecting rod. One is forged steel (shown) and the other is billet steel. Both have pros and cons and both make very strong connecting rods. (Photo Courtesy Modern Muscle Performance)

MODIFYING YOUR ENGINE

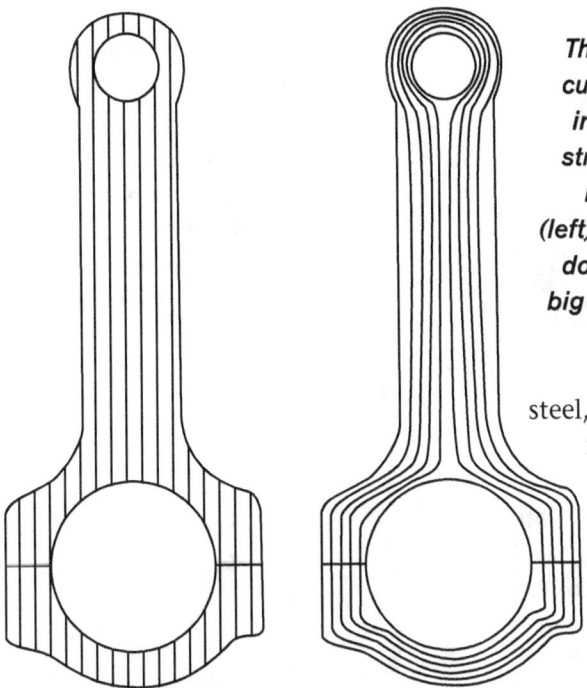

The alignment of the metal molecules that occurs during the forging process is a key factor in the strength of the forged connecting rod (right). Because a billet rod (left) is cut from flat steel, the grain doesn't align and flow around the big end of the rod as it does with a forged application (right).

goes final machining. This includes cutting and sizing the rod for the end cap, drilling holes for the rod bolts, and pressing in bushings for the wrist pins. A forged connecting rod can also be stress-relieved, heat-treated, and fine-tuned to achieve a specific weight.

The alignment of the metal's molecules that occurs during the forging process is a key factor in the strength of forged connecting rods. The forging process not only compresses the metal into the shape of the connecting rod, the heating and compressing also correctly aligns the grain structure of the metal, increasing its strength.

Billet connecting rods are built from a single piece of forged steel. The design is created using a computer program, and then each connecting rod is individually cut from the material using a water jet or other CNC-controlled machine. The downside of using billet rather than forging is the layout of the grain structure in the connecting rod. Because a billet rod is cut from flat steel, the grain doesn't align and flow around the big end of the rod as it does with a forged application. With a billet rod, the grain remains straight or vertical throughout the connecting rod.

Rod and Bolt Strength

Whether forged or billet, the materials that are used dictate connecting rod strength. When it comes to drag racing and street performance, engine builders have made steel the material of choice in most applications. The most common type of steel used for high-performance connecting rods is 4340 chrome-moly steel. All 4340 steel has a tensile strength of 145,000 psi; however, its hardness, ductility, and other properties vary based on the heat treating that it received. In addition, 4340 steel may also be referred to as aircraft-grade or aircraft-quality steel.

Quality rod bolts are also crucial to the survival of a connecting rod. As explained earlier, the combustion stroke not only puts compressive and tensile force stress on the connecting rod itself during rotation of the crankshaft, it also puts an inordinate amount of stress on the rod bolts. The inertial event from the sudden change in travel direction wants to yank the big end of the connecting rod apart.

Other Factors

Choosing the appropriate connecting rod for your application is just as important as selecting the best camshaft for a performance goal. It is also just as involved of a process, one that requires an understanding of your combination so you make a good decision. It is a good idea to check with the engine builder and manufacturer. You should know the engine's basics, such as stroke and displacement, and you should know operating RPM, projected horsepower, crankshaft material, and the intended or known compression ratio.

Many companies offer connecting rods for Hemi-powered cars. The following are the most popular among Hemi car owners.

Molnar Technologies

The H-beam connecting rods made by Molnar are made from 4340 billet material, are heat treated to increase tensile strength, and are then shot-peened to increase fatigue life.

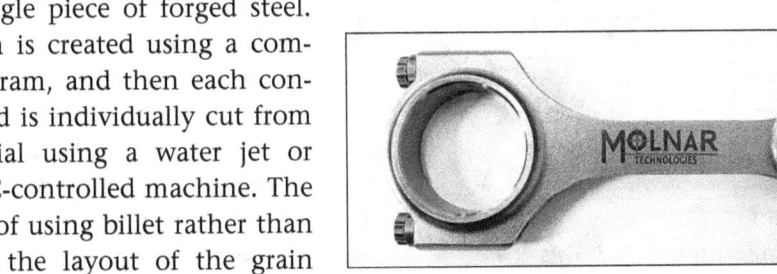

H-beam–style connecting rods from Molnar Technologies are heat treated and shot-peened to increase strength. It is important to choose the correct connecting rod when building your engine; choosing a rod not suited for an application results in catastrophic failure. The retail price for a set starts at $535. (Photo Courtesy Molnar Technologies)

CHAPTER 4

All rods come with a wear-resistant bronze bushing for long wrist-pin life and feature ARP fasteners. Finish sizes are held at +/- .0001 inch, which are the tightest tolerances you find in the industry.

K1 Technologies

Made of forged 4340 steel, K1's I-beam connecting rods are shot-peened for improved strength. They use only ARP fasteners, with the option of either 8740 or ARP 2000 material. The bore tolerances are held to +/- .0001 inch, and bronze bushings allow for a full-floating pin. Press-fit pins are available on some rod sizes. All K1 connecting rods are weight-matched into sets and then boxed.

Manley Performance Products

Manley connecting rods come in either an I- or H-beam configuration. Their H-beam connecting rods are manufactured from 4340 forgings, to the same standards approved by their OEM customers. They are weight-matched to +/- 1.5 grams and use ARP fasteners.

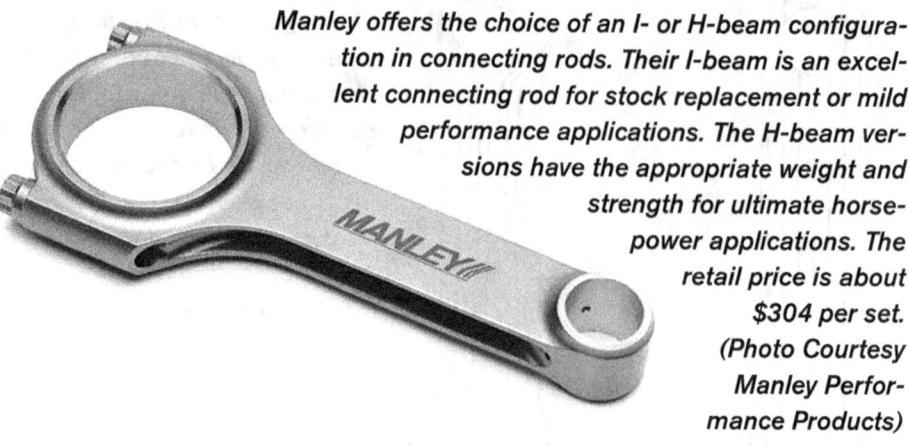

Manley offers the choice of an I- or H-beam configuration in connecting rods. Their I-beam is an excellent connecting rod for stock replacement or mild performance applications. The H-beam versions have the appropriate weight and strength for ultimate horsepower applications. The retail price is about $304 per set. (Photo Courtesy Manley Performance Products)

The Pro Series connecting rods are forged from aircraft-quality 4340 vacuum-degased material. Each Pro Series lightweight design combines the appropriate weight and strength for ultimate horsepower applications. Each rod is shot-peened after it is machined and Magnafluxed.

Crankshaft Dampener

When a Hemi crankshaft is made, it is initially either poured or pressed into shape (cast or forged). In addition, the crankshaft's material differentiates between the various grades of crankshafts.

A standard factory-production crankshaft is typically cast, has a tensile strength of roughly 65,000 to 80,000 psi, and is fairly brittle.

The cast crankshaft in your OEM application has to withstand the constant abuse that is incurred when your engine is running. The problem is, a cast crankshaft is fairly brittle. A forged-steel crankshaft is much more tolerant of this abuse and withstands more.

A forged crankshaft made from plain carbon steel, such as 1053 or 1045, has a tensile strength of roughly 110,000 psi. The tensile strength of a forged crankshaft might not seem like that much more than a good cast crankshaft, but tensile strength is only one part of the equation.

A forged-steel crankshaft is much more tolerant to flexing before failure occurs, so ductility is the forged crankshaft's major advantage over a cast iron one. Chrome-moly alloy steels (4130/4140) are commonly used for more serious performance crankshafts.

It's relatively easy to spot the difference between a cast crankshaft

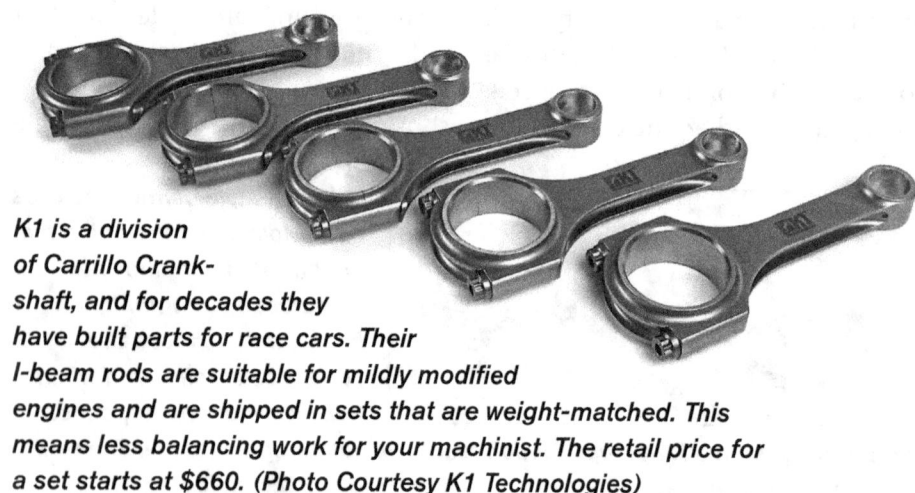

K1 is a division of Carrillo Crankshaft, and for decades they have built parts for race cars. Their I-beam rods are suitable for mildly modified engines and are shipped in sets that are weight-matched. This means less balancing work for your machinist. The retail price for a set starts at $660. (Photo Courtesy K1 Technologies)

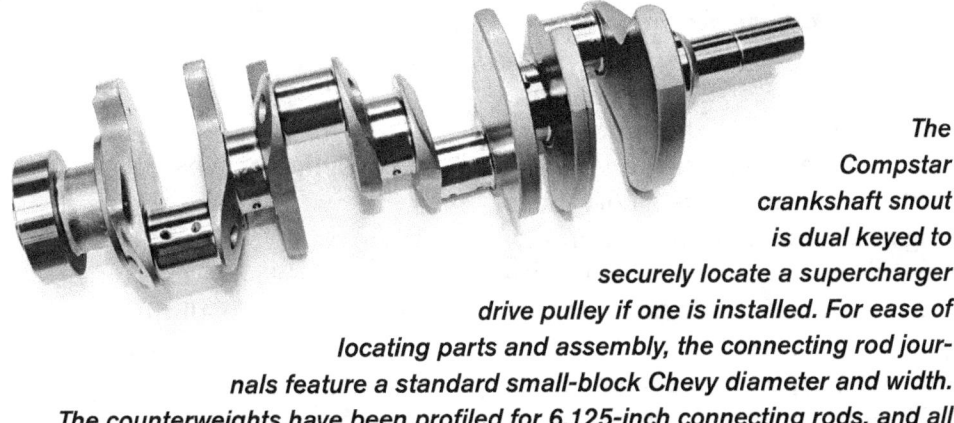

The Compstar crankshaft snout is dual keyed to securely locate a supercharger drive pulley if one is installed. For ease of locating parts and assembly, the connecting rod journals feature a standard small-block Chevy diameter and width. The counterweights have been profiled for 6.125-inch connecting rods, and all Compstar Hemi crankshafts are shipped with a billet timing wheel installed. The retail price is about $2,275. (Photo Courtesy Compstar Performance Products)

and a forged one. Cast units have a distinct parting line located on each of the counterweights; forged units are identified by a wide, raised die mark on the connecting rod throws.

Many companies offer crankshafts for Hemi-powered cars. The following are the most popular among Hemi car owners.

K1 Technologies

K1 Technologies' crankshafts are made of forged 4340 billet. The counterweight placements are designed for improved crankshaft performance. Each crankshaft is nitrided for improved bearing life and features a straight-hole oiling system for better lubrication. K1 crankshafts are available in stock, 4.050-inch, and 4.080-inch stroke.

Compstar Performance Products

Compstar (a division of Callies) has developed a crankshaft that is specifically designed for high-output applications. Not that your mildly built 5.7-, 6.1-, or 6.4-liter Hemi couldn't benefit from its use, but this is a hardcore part. Compstar crankshafts are manufactured from 4340 steel and are then machined to have a 4.050-inch stroke. When installed into a 6.1-liter Hemi block, this crankshaft achieves 426 ci, and with a 5.7-liter Hemi block, you get a nostalgic 392 ci. The crankshaft even helps improve crankcase ventilation and has a reduced weight, because the main journals are gun drilled.

Molnar Technologies

Molnar's 4340 forged crankshafts are heat treated to increase tensile strength, shot peened to increase fatigue life, nitrided for wear resistance, and mag-particle inspected to ensure against imperfections. Molnar crankshafts come in popular strokes from 3.593 to 4.080 inches.

Harmonic Balancer

The crankshaft twists and bends (flexes) relative to the loads that are placed on it by the connecting rods and pistons as the engine is running. Every time an engine's cylinder fires, torque is applied to the crankshaft through the piston and connecting rod. The crankshaft deflects under this torque, which initiates vibrations when the torque is released. At certain engine RPM, the torque that

Molnar crankshafts are available for many Hemi engine configurations, in both stock stroke (left) and increased stroker (right) versions. Molnar forged crankshafts are made from 4340-grade steel and are precision machined to exacting tolerances. Then these crankshafts are heat treated to increase tensile strength, shot peened to increase fatigue life, nitrided for wear resistance, and mag-particle inspected to protect against imperfections. The retail price starts at about $645. (Photos Courtesy Molnar Technologies)

is generated by the explosion in the cylinders is in sync with the vibrations that are present in the crankshaft. The result is resonance, and this resonance causes stress beyond what the crankshaft is capable of withstanding. Resonance can cause, at a minimum, bearing failure, and most definitely crankshaft failure.

To prevent this vibration, a harmonic balancer (dampener pulley) is attached to the front of the crankshaft. The dampener is composed of three parts: center hub, elastomer (an energy dissipating rubber), and outer ring. The outer ring connects the car's accessories via the serpentine belt and resists the acceleration of the vibration; the elastomer absorbs the vibrations.

Over time, the elastomer can deteriorate from age, temperature, or exposure to oil or chemicals, and unless rebuilt or replaced, this can cause the crankshaft to develop cracks, resulting in crankshaft failure.

Engines operate under varied conditions and at many RPM ranges. This operating range, coupled with the rate at which an engine accelerates, can have a considerable effect upon the harmonic dampener. Although rotating mass is an important consideration in engine design, when it comes to harmonic balancers, smaller and lighter doesn't mean better. The dampener you choose needs to be properly selected for the engine's displacement, actual horsepower developed, maximum RPM achieved, and the intended, actual usage of the engine.

In general, the correct dampener allows the engine to make more horsepower and live longer. Many companies offer harmonic balancers for Hemi-powered cars. The following is the most popular among Hemi car owners.

ATI Performance Products

The patented ATI Super Damper is the only crankshaft dampener that is designed exclusively for high-performance late-model Hemi engines. Whether for racing or driving on the street, ATI's harmonic balancers eliminate torsional crankshaft vibrations, exceed SFI 18.1 specs, and are even original equipment on 392 Mopar crate engines. The inner and outer shells are available in aluminum or steel and contain a steel inertia weight. This weight has six (two-ring design) or eight (three-ring design) computer-machined grooves to retain the proper durometer O-rings (dyno tested for each application).

Although an aftermarket dampener does not increase horsepower, it does allow the engine to safely make the most power it can. Plus,

The ATI Super Damper is an excellent choice for high-performance late-model Hemi engines. For your engine to deliver long reliable service, especially in high-performance applications, resonance needs to be eliminated. This dampener keeps vibrations to a minimum and should be considered an invaluable safety device. The retail price starts at about $428. (Photo Courtesy ATI Performance Products)

the added safety of a certified piece of equipment is more than worth the price.

Cylinder Heads

If you want your Hemi engine to make respectable power, you need a good set of heads. All three of the third-generation Hemi heads (2003–2008 Truck, Eagle, and Apache) benefit from decent intake flow numbers right from the factory. But, the exhaust port is an area that could use some attention. The intake flow on the stock 2003–2008 5.7 Hemi head is around 260 to 265 cfm at .550-inch lift. That is good for a stock head, but improvement can be had when talking performance. Exhaust flow, on the other hand, is roughly 290 to 340 cfm at .550-inch lift. Herein lies the performance challenge.

High intake flow can fill the cylinder, but after combustion, if the spent gases don't exit through the exhaust, you spoil the next charge of incoming air/fuel mixture with those spent gases. The late-model Hemi head is capable of a lot of flow, but again, there is room for improvement.

Head Porting

Porting the cylinder heads of your Hemi is the single most important thing that you can do to the heads to increase airflow and gain performance. Porting refers to the process of modifying the intake and exhaust ports, as well as the chamber (area around the valve faces) to improve the quality and quantity of the airflow that it can deliver. Your Hemi's cylinder heads (as manufactured) are usually not fully optimized for flow because of design and manufacturing constraints.

MODIFYING YOUR ENGINE

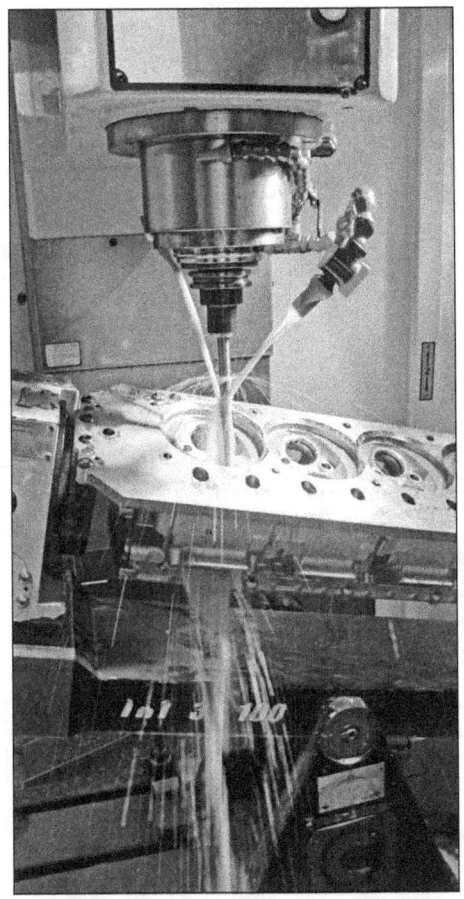

Porting your Hemi's cylinder heads is one of the best performance improvements you can make. Many feel that simply enlarging the ports increases power. But because port velocity has a huge effect on performance, the design of the port is much more important. What you actually want to do is to port the runner to a point that finds a gain in CFM without losing port velocity.

Porting the heads provides the additional attention that is required to bring the cylinder heads' flow up to peak efficiency. This process can even be applied to a daily driver to enhance its power output. The main objective of porting a cylinder head is to increase cylinder filling. The more air and fuel that are taken into the cylinder, the more power that engine produces.

For instance, every 10-cfm increase in air-intake flow can result in 5 more horsepower, but more airflow alone does not always deliver that extra power. You need to create a forcefulness of combustion in order to move the required large amounts of air quickly, and you need to ensure it happens at the right time in the engine's RPM for the use intended.

One of the most common mistakes when someone tries to port a Hemi's cylinder heads is to focus on increasing the size of the ports in an attempt to increase the amount of fuel and air moving into the cylinder. However, this larger port actually causes the airflow's speed to decrease, affecting the mixture's distribution around the cylinder and combustion chamber. This leads to the air and fuel being less atomized, especially at lower RPM, and can actually cause a reduction in mid-range power in many tuned engines. What you actually want is a gain in CFM without losing port velocity.

In a perfect world, all intake and exhaust ports would be almost straight. But because that is not possible, to achieve the best results, porting tries to make the port work as if it is straighter by widening the ports at specific points. By widening the port in certain areas, and leaving them untouched elsewhere, you can straighten the port, creating flow that is consistent across the entire port.

Focusing your port work on the area around the valveseat can exponentially benefit your Hemi engine. This porting could require narrowing or raising the port near the edge of the valve, and carefully designing and blending the valveseat angles with three or even five different angles. This requires special tools, and the idea is not only to direct as much air and fuel as possible around the chamber, but also to put it in the correct place within the cylinder, where the engine can achieve the best burn. A three- or five-angle valveseat pulls the flow outward, increasing the angle of entry. As much as 90 percent of effective porting takes place within an inch or so of the valveseat.

You can port the heads on your Hemi in different ways. One is to hand port the heads yourself. This requires removing the heads from the engine, and having a working knowledge of what works when actually grinding on the head's ports. If you're not comfortable with porting the heads yourself, you can remove them and have a reputable shop do it for you. Once the heads are at the shop, they may be ported by hand or by CNC porting.

Head Polishing

Many people think that enlarging the ports on a Hemi to as large as possible and then polishing them to a mirror finish is what porting is all about. This isn't always the case. Some ports on highly efficient race engines may be enlarged to their maximum possible size (in keeping with the highest level of aerodynamic efficiency), but those engines are highly developed for continuous use at very high RPM limits. Although larger ports flow more air and fuel at higher RPM, that same large port also sacrifices some torque at lower RPM, because port velocity is lost.

Remember, your engine does not see 6,000 rpm as often as it sees 2,500 rpm. Also, a mirror-like finish on the port walls does not actually provide the increase in flow that common thinking would suggest. On the contrary, the intake port's surface is usually and deliberately textured to

Stock Hemi Head Cylinder Flow

2003–2008 5.7 Hemi Flow Chart*

Lift (inch)	Intake (cfm)	Exhaust (cfm)
.100	70	38
.200	171	111
.300	244	169
.400	276	185
.500	290	189
.600	279	183
.650	284	184

5.7 Hemi Eagle Flow Chart*

Lift (inch)	Intake (cfm)	Exhaust (cfm)
.100	80	42
.200	181	112
.300	246	166
.400	310	190
.500	330	189
.600	336	187
.650	337	190

6.1 Hemi Flow Chart*

Lift (inch)	Intake (cfm)	Exhaust (cfm)
.100	83	41
.200	178	131
.300	246	187
.400	295	194
.500	316	195
.600	326	194
.650	326	195

6.4 Hemi Apache Flow Chart*

Lift (inch)	Intake (cfm)	Exhaust (cfm)
.200	180	131
.300	251	186
.400	316	215
.500	340	233
.600	343	240
.650	346	241
.700	345	241

*Tested on a Superflow flow bench at 28 inches of water.

a degree of uniform roughness to energize the boundary layer of air, which can noticeably alter the flow path and possibly even increase flow.

This is similar to the effect of dimples on a golf ball. Exhaust ports, on the other hand, may be smooth-finished, because there is (you hope) no actual wet fuel flow; smooth exhaust ports could be beneficial for minimizing carbon build-up.

Head Swapping

When the 6.1-liter Hemi first hit the market, enthusiasts soon realized that adding the 6.1-liter Hemi head and intake to a 5.7 Hemi resulted in a significant increase in power. But this change requires some basic changes to the car and engine. The chamber size of the 6.1-liter head is 72 cc, which is smaller than that of the 2003–2008 5.7-liter engines' 84 cc. If you only swap the heads, it boosts the compression ratio to roughly 11.0 to 11.25:1. Even with some serious custom tuning, this range is at the ragged edge of longevity of the stock pistons and connecting rods.

To decrease the compression ratio, you can use a thicker MLS gasket. You also need to use a 6.1-liter intake manifold, as the port dimensions for the 5.7- and the 6.1-liter Hemi are different. This swap also requires the use of 6.1-liter Hemi manifolds or headers, as the exhaust ports are also different.

If you want to add a set of Eagle cylinder heads to your 5.7-liter Hemi, you run into roughly the same concerns as with installing 6.1-liter Hemi heads and intake. Even with a .075-inch-thick head gasket, you are only able to lower the compression to 11.0:1. Again, when using stock 5.7 pistons and connecting rods, even with a good tune, it's on the edge. You also need D-port headers, a 6.1 or Eagle intake, and the later (2009–present) valvecovers.

Porting and swapping cylinder heads is a viable option, and if you contact the right people, you can secure a set of heads that are prepared for your application. When upgrading the heads, making sure that they are properly prepared is a big deal. Why pay for another set of stock heads? When performance enhanced heads are ported, the valveseats often receive a multi-angle valve job and the chambers and both the intake and exhaust ports are CNC ported.

CNC Porting

If you're planning to have the heads professionally ported, CNC porting is very precise because it is computer controlled. When using a CNC machine to port, the operator can calculate the required cross-sectional area and machine the port to that exact dimension every time (within less than .001 inch). CNC porting also maintains a consistent size throughout the length of the port. Therefore, each port in the head is identical, and every ported head is the same. This is a huge benefit over porting each head by hand.

Before CNC porting, the average street port was a basic cleanup (less time, lower cost). A professional port job was extremely time consuming (sometimes as long as three to four days) and much more expensive. Even with a professional job, you still had the inconsistencies of handwork. The CNC machine is consistent whether cutting .001 or .100 inch.

How long does it take to port a cylinder head with a CNC machine? The average cylinder head takes five to seven hours to do the actual porting. Although head design was based on net airflow for many years (and it still has importance), other factors must be taken into consideration. You must calculate the cylinder head requirements (power output, engine RPM range, bore, stroke, etc.) to get the desired cross-sectional area and flow within the port. ∎

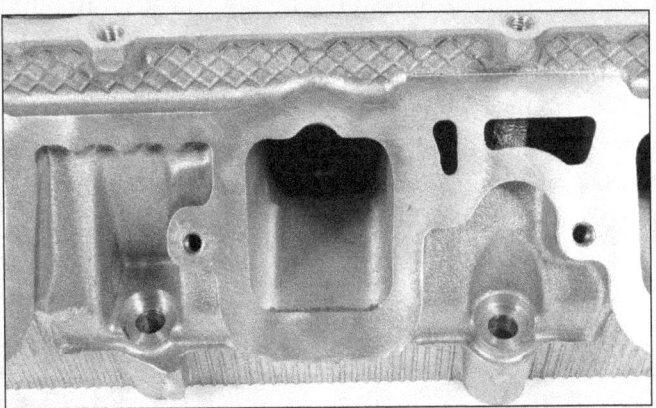

Although the intake flow on a stock Hemi head is very good, porting can make it better. Increasing the volume of airflow does not always deliver extra power. You need to increase the speed of the air entering the combustion chamber (port velocity).

From the factory, Hemi heads have decent intake flow numbers. But, the exhaust port is a bottleneck that needs attention. Getting more air into the engine is a good thing, but if you don't have an equal amount of air leaving the engine through the exhaust port, the results are minimal.

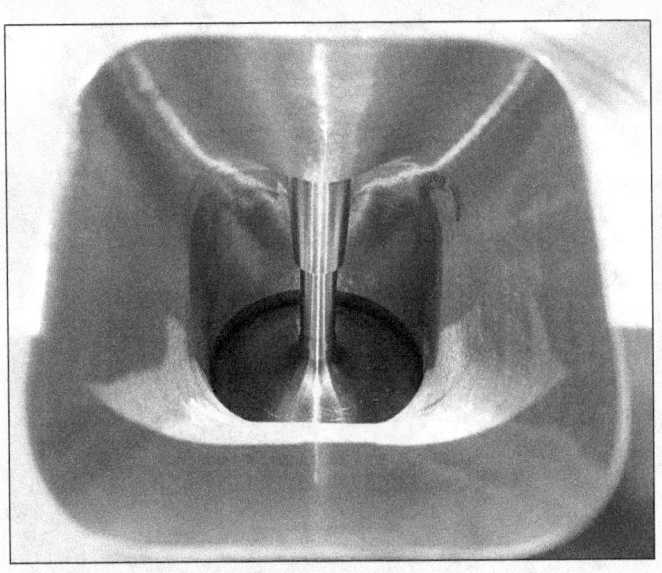

One of the main areas to focus on when porting cylinder heads is the area around the valveseat. Although porting this area requires special tools, a three- or five-angle valve job pulls the flow more evenly into the combustion chamber, increasing efficiency. As much as 90 percent of effective porting is accomplished within an inch or so of the valveseat.

CHAPTER 4

Head and Intake Swapping

Adapters are usually needed when swapping heads and/or intakes from one third-generation Hemi to another. Modern Muscle Performance in Martinsville, Virginia, is one supplier that makes intake adapter plates for swapping heads and/or intakes.

Camshaft

The job of the camshaft (sometimes called the bumpin' stick) in your Hemi engine is to operate the lifters, which in turn push the rocker arms, finally opening the valves. The camshaft is made of a cylindrical rod that runs the length of the engine, directly under the intake. It has a number of oblong lobes protruding from it that make the lifters go up and down (one for each valve).

The relationship between the rotation of the camshaft and the rotation of the crankshaft is of the utmost importance. Because the valves control the flow of the air and fuel mixture, they must be opened and closed at the proper time during the piston's stroke. For this reason, the camshaft in a late-model Hemi is connected to the crankshaft by a timing chain. The timing of the camshaft can be either advanced or slightly retarded when the engine is built, depending on the engine's needs. In 2009 and later Hemi engines, the VVT system is part of the camshaft and can do this as needed, without the driver even knowing it.

When looking at the camshaft specs of your Hemi engine, and deciding whether an upgrade is in

Before installing a camshaft with a larger lift and/or longer duration, all of the engine's parts, along with other aspects of the car, must be considered. Items such as the transmission/torque converter, rear-end gears, and usable engine RPM play a huge role in determining a suitable camshaft. Take a careful look at duration, lift, lobe separation angle, and centerline; they all have a huge effect on performance.

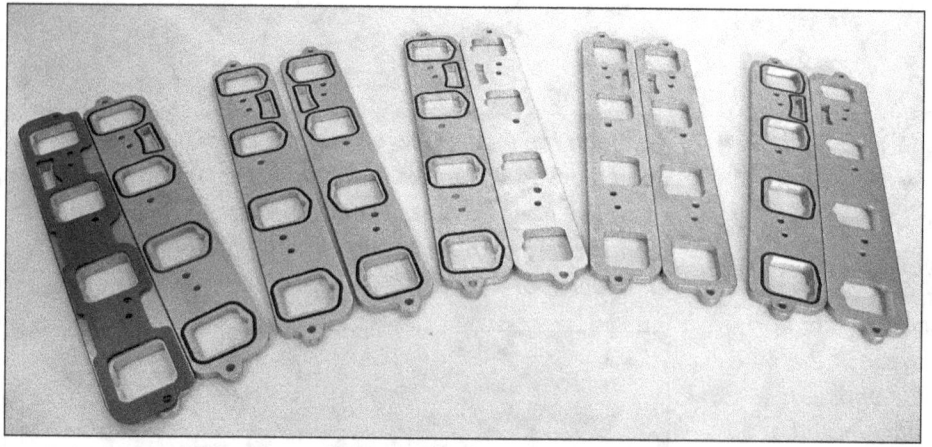

The cylinder head–to–intake ports are slightly different among the different heads, so these intake adapter plates might be necessary if you plan to swap heads and/or intakes on your third-generation Hemi. The retail price of the adapters is about $279.

The Apache head is available on 2011–present 6.4-liter engines. You can find this head on 2011 and later SRT Hemi Challengers, Chargers, and Jeeps with a 6.4-liter Hemi.

This head uses the same rockers and bolt pattern as the 6.1-liter cylinder head, but steps it up with 2.14-inch intake and 1.650-inch exhaust valves. The square intake ports are almost 2 x 2 inches and the flow is in the 340-cfm range. To fit the larger valves and improve the port, the valveguide is moved outside the port. For this reason, these heads only fit a 6.4 Hemi engine or one with 4.06-inch (or larger) bore, and require the use of custom pistons with the correct valve reliefs.

Camshaft Terminology

The following list explains the terminology used by camshaft manufacturers and what the numbers mean. It also describes how those numbers affect performance.

Duration

A camshaft's duration is the number of degrees of crankshaft rotation during which the valve is off the seat. In general, greater duration results in more horsepower. The RPM at which peak horsepower occurs is typically increased as duration increases, but this is at the expense of lower-RPM torque.

Engine builders can gauge a cam's profile aggressiveness by looking at the camshaft's duration at .020-, .050-, and .200-inch lift. The .020-inch number determines how responsive the engine is and how much low-end torque it can make. The .050-inch number is used to estimate where peak power occurs. The .200-inch number gives an estimate of the power potential.

A secondary effect of increased duration is an increase in overlap.

Overlap

Overlap is the number of crankshaft degrees at which both the intake and exhaust valves are off their seats. Overlap has a dramatic effect on idle quality, as the blow-through of the intake charge in the chamber (which occurs during overlap) reduces engine efficiency and is greatest during low-RPM operation.

In reality, increasing a camshaft's duration typically increases the overlap event, unless you spread the lobe centers between intake and exhaust valve lobe profiles.

Lift

The camshaft's lift is the actual amount of rise of the lifter, which moves the valve from its seat. The farther the valve moves from its seat, the more air that can be brought in or released from the cylinder. Increased lift does have some limitations. The amount of lift that can be achieved is limited by the proximity of the valve's face to the piston when the valve opens. Also, the dimensions and working parameters of the valvespring have a huge impact on the amount of lift. Higher valve lift can have the same effect as increased duration where valve overlap is less desirable.

Theoretically, a higher lift allows more airflow, but even by allowing more air to pass through the relatively larger opening, the length of the typical duration with a higher lift cam results in less airflow than with a cam having less lift but more duration (all else being equal). When referring to supercharged engines, higher lift could yield better results than longer duration, particularly on the intake side.

Lobe Separation Angle

The relationship between the centerlines of the intake and exhaust lobes is called the lobe separation angle (LSA). A 112-degree LSA means that the peak opening points of the intake and exhaust lobes are 112 degrees apart. This separation angle is ground into the camshaft and can't be changed.

LSA is another way of expressing camshaft overlap. When both valves are open at the same time, cylinder pressure drops. As an example, a camshaft with 106 degrees of LSA has more overlap and a rougher idle than one with 112 degrees. The smaller LSA usually makes more mid-range power.

Dual-Pattern Camshaft

A dual-pattern camshaft has different duration and/or lift specifications for the intake and exhaust lobes. Typically, the exhaust lobes have more duration than the intake lobes. This can be beneficial for engines like the late-model Hemi that has limited exhaust-port flow. ■

---

your future, there are a few things you need to consider. Choosing a camshaft involves a lot more than just considering the rest of the engine parts. The entire vehicle and the sum of its parts must also be taken into consideration.

Everything about the car's combination and intended use must be decided upon before choosing a camshaft. Once this is determined, the following things must be considered to get the correct camshaft: engine compression ratio, basic power range of the heads and intake, car's weight, transmission type (and torque converter stall-speed if automatic), rear gears, and tire size.

Camshafts have always been and continue to be the basis of discussion among engine builders and car enthusiasts alike. How much lift is needed and what are the proper duration, lobe centerlines, and separation angles? Many aspects and conditions must be considered. It requires years of experience and an in-depth understanding of how the engine works to become expert in choosing the best possible camshaft.

However, one thing is widely agreed upon: For the best performance and reliability, a roller camshaft is the way to go. For that reason, it's no surprise that from the factory, the camshaft inside your Hemi engine is of the hydraulic-roller type.

Flat Tappets or Rollers

Camshafts are available in two basic categories: flat tappet and roller. Flat-tappet cams were the only cams available in the muscle car era. The performance upgrade of the time was to use a lifter that had no spring, plunger, or oil inside (solid lifter). A flat-tappet lifter is, for the most part, flat on the bottom where it contacts the camshaft. A thin film of oil is the only thing preventing wear between the lifter and camshaft lobe. The flat-tappet camshaft was fine for the muscle car era. Today, virtually all pushrod-style engines use hydraulic-roller cams, and for a number of good reasons.

The sliding frictional force applied by the flat surface of the flat tappet is higher than the rolling frictional forces of a roller lifter. This means that a roller camshaft takes less horsepower to turn and generally does not wear out as quickly. An added benefit is that roller tappets do not require replacement when changing cams.

The roller's ability to open and close the valves more quickly encourages the design of more sophisticated camshaft profiles. If a cam profile has more area under the curve (the amount of power the car makes at lower RPM), it has the potential to make more peak power. Power under the curve is good because a car very seldom operates at the exact RPM that gives it peak horsepower or torque.

Roller profiles can be more "aggressive" and accelerate the tappet quicker than a flat-tappet camshaft profile. This benefits engine performance in two ways: More tappet lift can be achieved without the added duration that is normally needed to ramp up a flat tappet. The lift curve of a roller cam can be made "broader" without actually increasing lift.

Cam Swapping

Relatively speaking, swapping the camshaft in your Hemi doesn't require a lot of work to receive what could be the greatest gain in power that an engine can experience. The camshaft is one of the main determining factors in an engine's potential to make power, especially within a given RPM range.

Because the affected power band is different depending on the camshaft, one of the most important aspects to determine when selecting a camshaft is to have a realistic, specific RPM goal in mind before you begin. If you are changing the camshaft to get more low-end grunt, choose accordingly. On the other hand, gaining maximum high-RPM horsepower takes an entirely different set of camshaft dimensions. Lying to yourself about what you actually need and what you think you want is a huge mistake. It's has caused many car owners to park their rides and lose interest because the car was no longer enjoyable to drive.

Hemi engines respond well to more cam timing, but it is possible to over-cam an engine, especially one in a daily driver. The ideal situation for a camshaft swap on a daily driver is to ensure the cam upgrade improves the power output through the entire RPM range, not just at peak RPM. Big cams can provide a ton of extra power at the top of the RPM range, but these same cams often sacrifice low-RPM and mid-range torque for that high-RPM rush. The reality is that your Hemi spends much more of its life in the lower RPM range, even during spirited driving. Hemi owners should take that into account when considering the camshaft's specs for a swap.

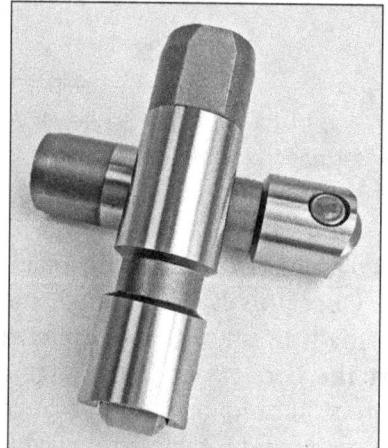

Inside your Hemi are the lifters that transfer the rotating motion of the camshaft to the lifting motion of the pushrods against the rocker arms. Because the Gen III Hemi does not have an adjustable rocker arm, hydraulic lifters must be used to maintain zero lash. If you currently have a Hemi with MDS and are installing a higher lift, higher duration camshaft you might need these lifters in order to remove the OEM MDS lifters.

Some feel that the MDS lifters cannot support the larger camshaft's higher-pressure springs and will collapse under the higher engine loads. That is why it is always a good idea to consult your camshaft manufacturer to learn what you need to do when upgrading the camshaft. (Photo Courtesy Fiat Chrysler Automobiles US LLC)

MODIFYING YOUR ENGINE

In 2009, the late-model Hemi acquired VVT. With VVT, the camshaft itself is advanced or retarded with respect to the crankshaft. The valve timing is advanced at lower RPM for more torque, and it can be retarded at higher RPM for more horsepower. The 2009 and later camshafts cannot be used in 2008 and earlier engines. (Photo Courtesy Comp Cams)

Variable Valve Timing

In 2009, the late-model Hemi took a big step up in complexity; it acquired VVT. With VVT, the camshaft itself is advanced or retarded with respect to the crankshaft. The valve timing is advanced at lower RPM for more torque, and it can be retarded at higher RPM for more horsepower. Yes, you have the best of both worlds.

The VVT definitely flattens the torque curve. Peak torque is increased a little, but more important is that the torque can come on much sooner. It is this added torque (more torque under a wider RPM band) that allowed the 2009 Charger axle ratio to drop from 2.87 to 2.65 without any loss of acceleration.

A camshaft phaser mounted to the front of the camshaft in conjunction with the timing gear changes the valve timing by changing the relationship between the camshaft and the timing chain. The phaser is actuated by engine oil pressure that is controlled by an oil control valve (OCV). The OCV consists of an electric solenoid and spool valve. The ECU actuates the OCV, which acts through a rotor, stator, and sprocket to change the relative position of the camshaft. Camshafts used in 2009 and later Hemi engines do not fit in previous-year engines.

Many companies offer camshafts for Hemi-powered cars. The following are the most popular among Hemi car owners.

Comp Cams

For pre-2009 Hemi engines, Comp Cams offers the Extreme Fuel Injection (XFI) and Tri-Power Extreme series of camshafts. If your Hemi is relatively stock, the Tri-Power Extreme is probably the right choice for you. This cam does not cause tuning issues, and it works well with other stock parts such as torque convertors and exhaust.

If you are building your Hemi to possess more than the stock power potential, the XFI camshaft points you in the right direction. The XFI features more aggressive and steeper-ramp lobes, allowing more power to be produced.

If you are building a 2009 and later Hemi, you need a 2009 and later specific camshaft.

Comp Cams' Hemi Phaser camshafts work with phaser limiters (locks) to fully use Chrysler's VVT technology. This allows the camshaft to pick up torque in the low RPM range, while maintaining power up high. These cams are engineered to handle 5.7- and 6.4-liter Hemi street/strip engines. Their unique, no-springs-required design maintains piston-to-valve clearance while enabling high-performance lobes using VVT. These camshafts are available in custom grinds and three different off-the-shelf grinds depending on engine type for improved performance over OEM options.

Comp Cams' Phaser Limiter Kits and Lock Kits limit the degree of maximum cam phasing to 14 crankshaft degrees (7 camshaft degrees) and are required for use.

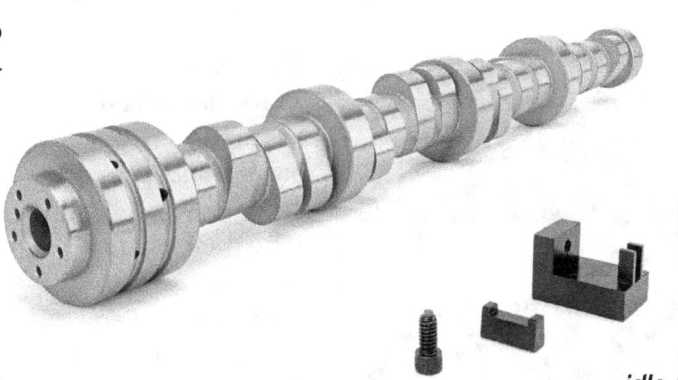

Comp Cams' Extreme Fuel Injection and Tri-Power Extreme series camshafts are for Hemi engines that are relatively stock. These cams retain a stock-sounding idle and work well with stock torque convertors and exhaust. You should choose the XFI camshaft for high-horsepower Hemis; it features a more muscle car–esque idle and is better suited for engines with multiple modifications. The retail price is approximately $500 (2008 and earlier), and $900 with VVT. (Photo Courtesy Comp Cams)

As with any camshaft upgrade, valvesprings must be changed as well. Swapping a camshaft in a 5.7-, 6.1-, or 6.4-liter Hemi is an extensive undertaking, and is probably not something that the average enthusiast can do in the driveway.

Crane Cams

Crane Cams has been at the forefront of camshaft development and design for a long time. When it comes to camshafts for the Gen III Hemi, Crane has once again stepped up to the plate and designed a camshaft for many applications. First are the HR208 and HR210 with excellent low-end and mid-range torque and horsepower. These cams create a smooth idle for daily usage, are MDS compatible, and do not require an additional performance tune.

The HR216 develops good mid-RPM torque and horsepower, a slightly choppy "muscle car" idle, and requires computer tuning or upgrade.

The HR222 delivers good upper-RPM horsepower, a choppy idle, and is considered a radical street camshaft. It also requires computer tuning and a valvespring upgrade.

Stroker Engines

One way to dramatically increase your Hemi's performance is to increase the actual stroke of the engine by installing a stroker kit. But what is a stroker kit, what are the advantages and disadvantages, and what is involved in building one?

A stroker engine is just an engine that has had the stroke of the crankshaft and connecting rods increased to be longer than was originally delivered from the factory. But why would you want to build a stroker engine? By increasing the stroke of the engine you can actually increase the size of the engine. For instance, kits are available to turn a 5.7-liter Hemi into a 392 (6.4 liters).

Making more power is not just about increasing the engine's cubic-inch displacement though. Camshaft specs, head flow, and a myriad of other parameters must also be taken into account. Without getting too detailed, you need to understand that not all components that work well with your 5.7-liter engine work best if you increase the stroke to a 6.4-liter engine. Everything must be taken into consideration, and increasing the engine's stroke is only one factor.

Cylinder Bore

Why not just increase the cylinder's bore diameter to increase the number of cubic inches? You might think that increasing the cylinder bore size has more of an effect on power than increasing the stroke when increasing the engine size. Theoretically this make sense, but the problem arises when enlarging cylinder bores; you can't physically make huge increases in the cylinder bore size. The constraints of the block simply do not allow it.

For example, most 5.7-liter Hemi blocks can only be bored about .030

If you have increased the displacement of your engine by changing the crankshaft, connecting rods, and pistons, you have built a stroker engine. Stroker engines are known for their high-torque capabilities at a low- to mid-RPM range. Stroker engines make a factory (cubic-inch) engine bigger. (Photo Courtesy Wiseco Performance Products)

The Crane Cams HR208 and HR210 camshafts increase low-end and mid-range torque and horsepower. If you want to add a little more performance in the mid-RPM area of the power band, the HR216 camshaft is your best choice. The HR222 is for the most increase in upper-RPM horsepower. The retail price is about $470 for each.

to .040 inch. Open the cylinders any more than that and the cylinder walls are thin enough so that durability could become an issue.

I know what you're thinking: "If I add a crankshaft with a longer stroke, won't that cause other problems, such as the pistons going too high and hitting the cylinder head?" If you only increase the stroke of the crankshaft, during crankshaft rotation it pushes the pistons too high and could pull the pistons down into the counterweight of the crankshaft. This is why the connecting rods must also be considered. By increasing the connecting rod length, you move the piston away from the counterweight. This longer connecting rod has the added benefit of making the connecting rod's ratio more acceptable.

Pistons

With a longer-stroke crankshaft and longer connecting rods, you still have the problem that the longer stroke is pushing the piston out of the block when you rotate the engine. Changing the pistons solves this. In stroker applications, the pistons' wrist-pin height is raised to help move the top of the piston back below the deck's surface. The pistons can be made shorter, but only to the point that leaves room for the rings above the wrist pin. The bottom of the piston must also clear the crankshaft throw when the piston is at bottom dead center (BDC). The dimension between the wrist pin and the top of the piston is the compression height of the piston. The location of the wrist pin is dictated by the stroke of the crankshaft and the connecting rod combination as well as by the actual piston design itself.

Some limitations are associated with moving the wrist pin and lengthening the connecting rod. Moving the wrist pin actually locates it within the oil-ring groove, and this is where the deck height of the block comes into play. The block's deck height is the distance from the centerline of the crankshaft's main journals to the deck surface where the head gasket goes.

For example, 5.7-, 6.1-, and 6.4-liter Hemis have a deck height of 9.250 inches. You must know the deck height of the engine so that you can position the wrist pin in the proper location for the piston to remain below the deck surface while the engine is running.

As I previously mentioned, an added benefit of a longer connecting rod is an improved rod ratio. A connecting rod's rod ratio is found by dividing the length of the connecting rod by the stroke of the crankshaft. A connecting rod's ratio affects the engine in several ways; a major one is side loading of the cylinder walls.

Side loading is the action of the stroke of the rotating assembly trying to push the piston out the side of the cylinder. Side loading is increased with lower rod ratios (shorter connecting rods), and a longer connecting rod actually decreases the angle at which the forces are pushing sideways.

Piston Dwell Time

An often-overlooked factor that contributes to the advantage of a stroker engine has to do with piston dwell time. This is the amount of time that the piston remains at the top and at the bottom of the stroke cycle while transitioning in either direction. An increase in stroke and rod length yields a longer piston dwell time. This longer dwell time allows a better flow of combustion and exhaust gases because the piston accelerates slower between the transitions.

This means that the intake charge has more time to enter the cylinder, and then the exhaust has more time to escape. This translates into more torque over a longer RPM range.

So what do you actually achieve by installing a stroker kit? You have more cubic inches, and more torque thanks to the greater leverage of the longer stroke. Torque, after all, is what gets your vehicle moving. This concept is obvious when you compare the torque ratings between a 5.7- and a 6.4-liter Hemi engine. Because displacement is just a factor of bore and stroke, by increasing the stroke of your current engine you can enjoy the satisfaction of more torque within the same package.

The increasing availability of aftermarket stroker kits has made the option extremely popular. If you want increased performance, a stroker kit is a wise alternative to building an engine that simply equals the factory displacement.

Stroker engines are nothing new, and in fact they are not even an aftermarket invention. If you look closely at factory engine offerings, you see that changes in displacement are often nothing more than a change in stroke. This was a cost-effective way for the factory to increase power for larger vehicles or future model upgrades, while reusing the same block and accessory components.

Clearance and Balance

As you may have guessed, certain issues must be addressed when assembling a stroker Hemi engine. First and foremost is the issue of clearances. Because of the increased stroke and connecting rod length changes, there have been instances of the connecting rod and crankshaft interfering with the bottom edge of the cylinder bore, pan rails, piston skirts, windage trays, and other areas inside the Hemi's block. Most kits have these clearances optimized to save you time, but it is always a good idea to preassemble the engine components and check for areas that might cause interference. As a rule, try to have a minimum of .030-inch clearance between any interference points.

Another consideration is rotating assembly balance. Typically, all stroker kits come properly balanced, but make sure to ask specifically if the kit you are purchasing is balanced. If you happen to find a kit that requires balancing, always perform the balancing with the harmonic balancer and flywheel that you intend to use.

Selecting a complete kit that provides the crankshaft, connecting rods, and pistons resolves many common compatibility and clearance issues. Buying a kit rather than the separate components provides predetermined combinations for your block and helps ensure safety. I urge you to gather opinions from fellow enthusiasts and engine builders, as stroker displacements remain fairly consistent among kit providers.

Many companies offer stroker kits for Hemi-powered cars. The following are the most popular among Hemi car owners.

Eagle Specialty Products

Eagle has stroker kits to turn a 5.7-liter Hemi into a 6.4-liter (392) monster, or if you have a 6.1-liter Hemi, you can have 6.7 liters (426 inches). Both crankshafts are made of 4340 steel and have a stroke of 4.050 inches. The 6.125-inch connecting rods come in either H- or I-beam configurations, and Mahle pistons finish the kit. It's tough to tell you what horsepower you can get from either kit, but the forged pieces mean that the sky is the limit.

K1 Technologies/Wiseco Performance Products

K1 and Wiseco have teamed up to deliver comprehensive stroker kits that are just what your Hemi needs. The kit comes with forged Wiseco pistons, ring packs, gas ports, skirt coatings, and offset pins. A variety of other features are available depending on your application. The K1 nitrided crankshaft is made of 4340 steel, core hardened and tempered to reduce stress and optimize tensile strength. You can choose from either forged or billet 4340 steel K1 connecting rods. The connecting rods are shot peened for improved fatigue life and are finished in the United States.

Compstar Performance Products

The professionals at Compstar (a division of Callies) can pair your crankshaft with the proper bottom-end components. Fully balanced and ready-to-assemble rotating assemblies from Callies not only save you time and money, they provide the peace of mind that your components are matched for compatibility, giving you a trouble-free project.

Built around a Compstar crankshaft and connecting rods, every Speed Pack is dynamically balanced with components that are weight matched. As a standard, Hemi Speed Packs use Mahle or Diamond pistons that employ 1.5-, 1.5-, and 3.0-mm, low-friction specialty rings. Each Speed Pack includes a crankshaft,

Stroker Combinations

5.7 Hemi
345 ci (stock)
392 ci (6.4 liter)

6.1 Hemi
372 ci (stock)
426 ci (7.0 liter)
440 ci (7.2 liter)

6.4 Hemi
392 ci (stock)
426 ci (7.0 liter)
434 ci (7.1 liter)

The K1 (shown) and Wiseco stroker kits are composed of quality components. Forged pistons and the nitrided steel crankshaft ensure a quality assembly. You can choose from either forged or billet connecting rods. The retail price of the kit starts at about $1,900. (Photo Courtesy Wiseco Performance Products)

MODIFYING YOUR ENGINE

connecting rods, pistons, wrist pins, rings, and bearings.

Valvetrain

The design of the Hemi head in your Challenger, Charger, Magnum, or 300C includes two rocker arm shafts per cylinder head. One shaft supports the rocker arms for the intake valves, and the other supports the rocker arms for the exhaust valves. This is because each cylinder has an intake and exhaust valve opposite each other within that cylinder. The stock rocker arms are easy to identify: The intakes have an "I" cast on the rocker arm, and the exhaust has no casting letter.

Three rocker shaft configurations were available from the factory. According to an engineer at Chrysler, the original design made use of metal spacers between the rocker arms to hold them in place during assembly. In early 2005, they started using C-clips to locate the rocker arms for assembly. In February 2007, Chrysler changed the assembly process and no longer needed to use the C-clip. So, when looking at different Gen III Hemi rocker arm assemblies, don't be surprised to see three versions. Also, you don't need to worry about which one to use when building an engine because they interchange.

Today you have many options for rocker arm upgrades. A good set

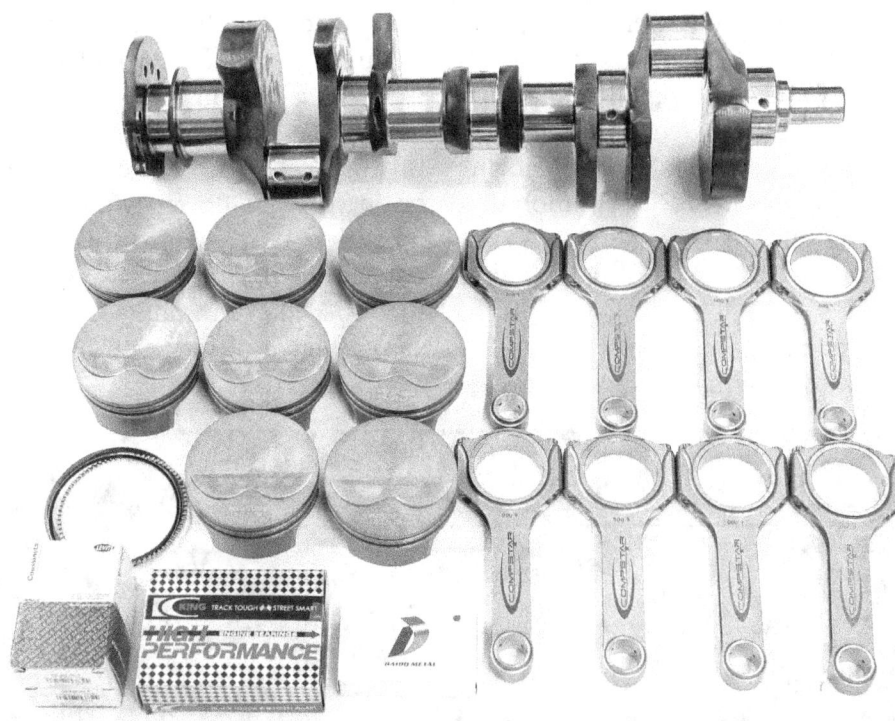

Built into every Speed Pack kit is either Mahle or Diamond pistons. Each Speed Pack includes the crankshaft, connecting rods, pistons, wrist pins, rings, and bearings. The retail price starts at about $2,200. (Photo Courtesy Callies Performance Products)

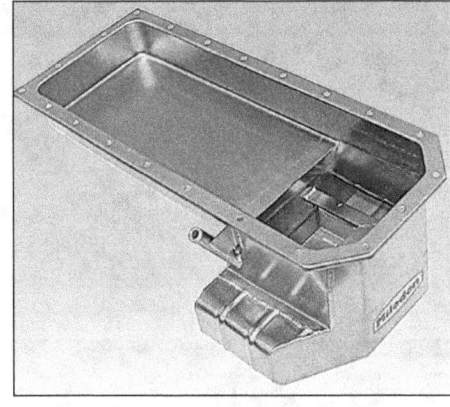

Aftermarket oil pans, such as this one from Milodon, are designed to provide optimum performance for a specific application. Milodon's street/strip oil pans ensure an ample supply of lubricant under rapid acceleration, while providing optimum oil supply to critical parts. Important features include oil control to allow good oil supply and maximum power, an increased sump capacity to ensure an ample supply of lubricant at lower oil temperatures, plus design considerations such as required ground and component clearance. (Photo Courtesy Milodon)

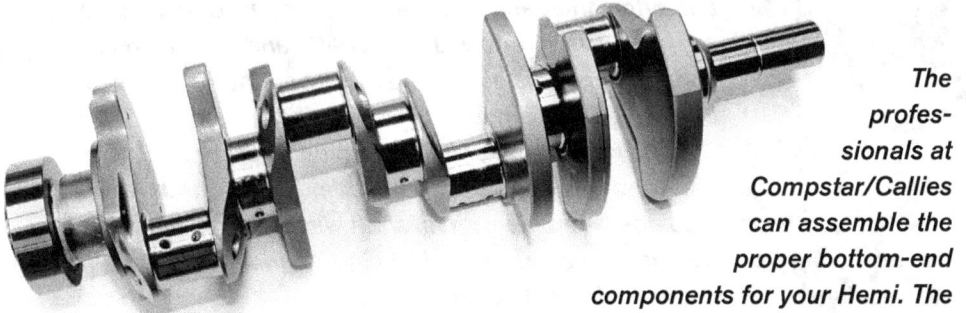

The professionals at Compstar/Callies can assemble the proper bottom-end components for your Hemi. The foundation of the assembly is a fully balanced kit with a Compstar crankshaft and connecting rods. (Photo Courtesy Callies Performance Products)

of replacement rocker arms should be chosen for their construction quality and engine application. From the factory, the Gen III Hemi rocker arms were sufficient for the engine when it was in stock condition. But if you change valvetrain parts (i.e., camshaft or valvesprings), the rocker arms should also be on your list of upgrades.

Most aftermarket rocker arms are constructed of billet aluminum and feature at least a roller tip. Many also use needle bearings at the fulcrum (where they meet the rocker shaft); this reduces friction and allows for an increase in horsepower-building potential. When contemplating an upgrade to the roller rockers, make sure that they fit under the stock valvecovers, unless you plan to use aftermarket covers.

When you increase the spring pressures of your valvesprings, it is highly recommended, that you also install aftermarket rocker shaft supports. These upgraded supports are designed to dramatically increase valvetrain stability over the stock supports. When choosing a rocker arm support, some require machine work for a proper installation and some are a direct bolt-on.

Windage around a crankshaft can definitely rob your Hemi of power. Oil in the engine coming into unnecessary contact with the moving parts inside the engine causes windage and results in power loss. This occurs when the oil is trying to run back into the oil pan (i.e., oil splashing against the counterweights of the crankshaft as it spins). Controlling windage allows an engine to make more power. Although a stock windage tray can be used, companies including Milodon also have windage trays that efficiently scavenge oil from the connecting rods and crankshaft.

Livernois Motorsports offers this rocker bar system for 5.7- and 6.1-liter Hemis. Their complete rocker bar system is designed to dramatically increase valvetrain stability for high-performance applications. This kit provides a significant bolt-on improvement over the stock rocker bar system and offers increased durability and reduced friction. For any serious upgrade with camshafts and higher-pressure springs, this kit is a must-have to keep the valvetrain stable in any high-performance Hemi engine.

The kit is made of billet aluminum rocker bar hold-downs that secure to the cylinder head with ARP bolts. It comes complete with all shaft washers and collars and has adjustable clamps for setting proper rocker-to-valve positioning. The shafts are 4130 chrome-moly steel and offer increased wall thickness. This greatly increases stiffness while decreasing deflection and flex.

Shafts are micro-finished to a very low RA (roughness average) to reduce friction between rocker arm and rocker bar. Then the shafts are DLC (diamond-like carbon) coated for the ultimate in friction reduction and durability. You can purchase this kit for about $1,700.

MODIFYING YOUR ENGINE

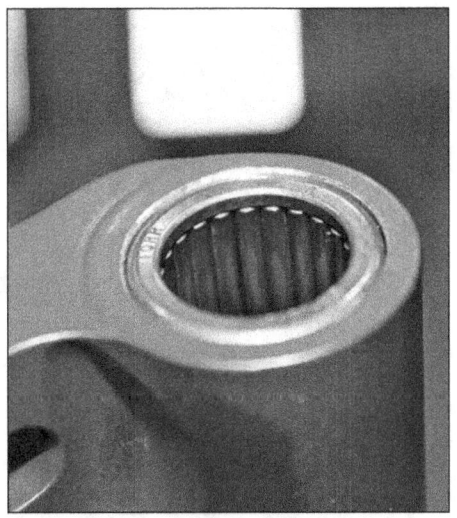

If you want to upgrade your rocker arms (and why wouldn't you if you're building a high-performance Hemi engine?), the 5.7- and 6.1-liter Hemi full roller rocker arm kit from Harland Sharp is just what you need. The rocker arms have 2024 billet bodies and use needle bearing fulcrums and roller tips. They mount on 5/8-inch-diameter shafts and receive oil the same way as the factory units. They come with billet steel spacers and hold-downs, and fit under the stock valvecovers. They have a factory 1.65:1 ratio, come in either adjustable or non-adjustable versions, and are anodized in the familiar Harland Sharp orange. They are available for about $1,700.

At the 2013 Performance Racing Industry (PRI) trade show, Hemi owners were pleased to see new T&D Machine rocker assemblies for the Apache head. If you want to increase the strength and durability of your Hemi valvetrain, but don't want to remove the head for machine work, you'll appreciate this assembly.

Both adjustable and non-adjustable versions are made from steel, and follow the factory-style shaft design. They're available with adjustable and non-adjustable rockers. The retail price is about $2,500 to $2,800.

CHAPTER 5

CUSTOM-BUILT ENGINE PACKAGES

With all this talk about increasing the performance of the engine in your Hemi-powered ride, you have yet another option: crate engines. A crate engine is a great option if you don't feel that a few bolt-on items will give you the increase in power that you need. Many enthusiasts are also concerned about modifying their car's original engine and risking a catastrophe, so this is a very popular option.

In the world of crate engines, a popular upgrade was once a crate engine from your local Dodge dealer. The crate engine came complete or almost complete (long-block), and was shipped to your dealer or shop, typically in wooden crates. A long-block is a partially assembled engine that consists of the assembled short-block, cylinder heads, camshaft, and valvetrain, but often does not include items such as valvecovers, intake, oil pan, the fuel system, electrical, and exhaust components. These items need to be removed from your original engine or another source.

Today, instead of going to your local dealer and ordering a crate engine, you can pick a performance shop, tell them what you want, and have them build whatever you can dream up. If you want to build a fire-breathing 6.4-liter engine, it's no problem. If you're looking for something a little more street friendly, just say the word. Buying a complete crate engine is a good option if you happen to find a car that needs just an engine, but crate engines are often purchased when buyers want a performance-oriented engine, and don't want to build and/or modify their existing engine. Crate engines come in a wide range of horsepower levels, and the sky (and your wallet) is the limit.

Buy or Rebuild

One thing is certain: Engine building costs increase every year, and most folks feel that as the cost to build a custom engine increases, a crate engine is the best way to go. Regardless of your position on whether or not a crate engine is cheaper or more expensive, buying a crate engine does mean you can immediately install it in your car. Sure, having the engine that's already in your car (or a spare engine) custom rebuilt to your new specs allows

Buying a ready-to-run engine like this one from Modern Muscle Performance in Martinsville, Virginia, eliminates the hassle of having to locate the parts needed to build an engine, and finding a shop to actually build it in a timely fashion.

132 DODGE CHALLENGER AND CHARGER: HOW TO BUILD AND MODIFY

you the comfort of designing the engine using components you feel work best for your given application, but to the general enthusiast, is that a necessity?

Many engine suppliers can build a Hemi engine and ship it to you or your shop, or they can take your existing engine and build it to your specifications, giving you a brand-new engine that is ready to go. Many of these shops have even made it very easy for you. You drop off your car and they remove, build, and reinstall your engine at their shop.

If you decide to rebuild the Hemi in your car yourself, that's not a bad thing. However, it is much more labor intensive than buying a crate engine. You have to remove the engine from your car, tear it down, and find out what you might need. Once it's torn down, how long are you going to be without a car to drive (if it's your only vehicle)?

If you are capable of doing the engine assembly work yourself, it might not be as costly as a crate engine, but keep in mind that you must have substantial base knowledge; you must know when you can reuse parts, what you should take to the machine shop, and again, how to

When choosing a crate engine, make sure the internals are strong enough for what you plan to do with the engine. A forged steel crankshaft is a good compromise of cost and strength. These crankshafts hold up to more demanding applications than a cast crankshaft. Many racers drill a 3/4-inch hole through the rod journals, parallel to the crankshaft's axis. This does, however, make the rod journal hollow and much lighter; some argue that the loss in strength isn't worth the performance benefits. For the ultimate in a crankshaft, billet steel is hard to beat. (Photo Courtesy Fiat Chrysler Automobiles US LLC)

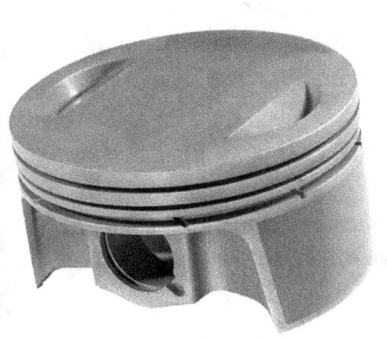

When it comes to the pistons used in your crate engine, make sure that the builder uses a high-quality version. Many forged pistons fit the bill. Simply using the correct alloy does not necessarily suffice when it comes to making a piston that withstands the operating characteristics of your engine. Good, solid design techniques include coatings applied to the piston's skirt area to reduce friction, and thermal barrier coating applied to the top of the piston to reflect heat into the combustion chamber.

Piston manufacturers have recently added another attribute to pistons called gas porting. This is the introduction of small holes that are drilled from the piston deck (a vertical gas port) or from the top ring land (a horizontal gas port) to the inside of the top ring groove. The purpose of a gas port is to apply combustion pressure directly to the top ring, forcing the ring face outward against the cylinder wall. (Photo Courtesy Fiat Chrysler Automobiles US LLC)

Many engine builders use a particular rotating assembly: crankshaft, connecting rods, pistons and wrist pins, piston rings, and sometimes even the rod and main bearings. Although many engine builders prefer to design their engines using specific components, the option of purchasing a rotating assembly "kit" offers a time savings, as well as potential cost savings for the builder. That's also a benefit for you: It saves you money. A pre-packaged rotating assembly provides a level of convenience by offering a system that has been pre-determined to suit a specific engine displacement and compression ratio goal. (Photo Courtesy Manley Performance Products)

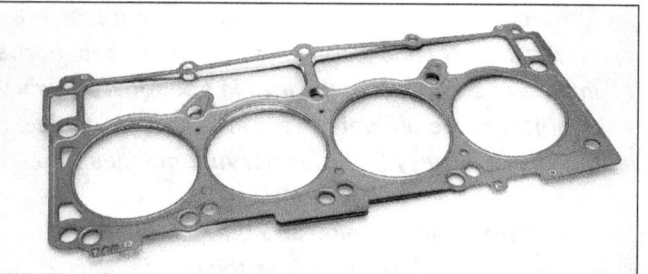

When choosing a camshaft, you really need to consider what you want your car to do. Most camshaft manufacturers have off-the-shelf grinds designed for specific applications. In order to choose the correct camshaft for a particular performance target, you need to define a couple of parameters: the RPM range where the engine should make the most power and the camshaft that matches the breathing characteristics of the cylinder heads, intake and exhaust manifolds, or headers.

On the other hand, if you're building a street performance engine for a daily driver with an automatic transmission and stock gearing, you want a camshaft that delivers good drivability with plenty of low- to mid-range torque and throttle response. The biggest mistake many enthusiasts make is to over-cam an engine. Using a camshaft that has too much valve lift, too much duration, and/or too much valve overlap for the application intended can have negative consequences.

Everybody likes to brag about big lift and duration numbers, but if the camshaft's specs don't match the engine's capabilities, you end up with an engine that underperforms and fails to meet your expectations. (Photo Courtesy Comp Cams)

From the factory the Hemi's heads were sealed using MLS head gaskets. An MLS gasket is constructed of three or more pieces of steel that are only attached together at a few points, typically by rivets. An MLS gasket is made of layers of steel with special treatment to the two outside layers of the gasket: A bead is rolled, or embossed, into the steel that goes around the cylinder bores, the water passages, and even the oil drain-back holes between the block and head. When the cylinder heads are bolted to the block, the gasket is compressed but the sealing beads aren't crushed flat. These beads provide the seal.

In the event that combustion pressure causes the head to lift off the block slightly, the beads are able to spring back a bit so that the seal is maintained between the block and heads.

Another feature of the MLS design is that it's easy to make the inner piece (or pieces) thicker or thinner, so that you can change the compressed thickness of the gasket without affecting the quality of the seal. MLS gaskets are available from companies such as Cometic, Felpro, and SCE.

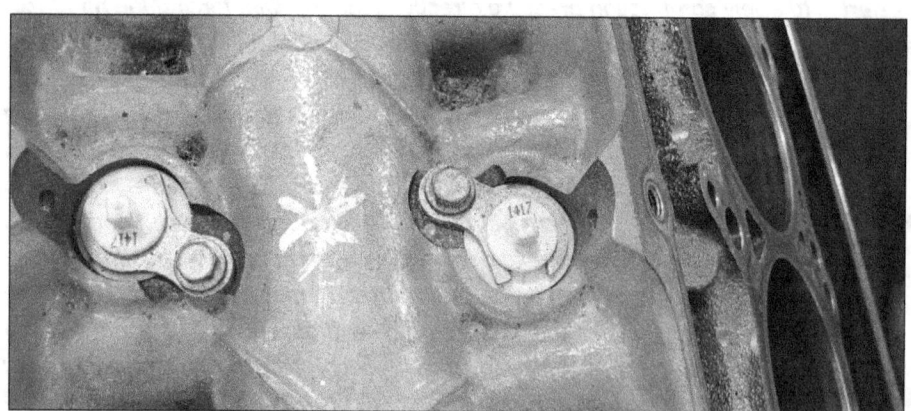

The Hemi block was originally designed with MDS that cuts out the operation of varying cylinders to improve fuel mileage. This means that the four holes in the lifter valley must have either the MDS solenoids (PN 53032152AC) or the plastic plugs (PN 53032221AA) that block off the MDS oil passages. Most modified crate engines come with the MDS disabled and the plugs installed.

CUSTOM-BUILT ENGINE PACKAGES

When it comes to connecting rods in your Hemi crate engine, you have two options. One is a cast rod, which is a little less expensive, and the other is a steel H-beam rod (shown) that costs a little more. The cast rod is alright to use in naturally aspirated engines making less than 550 hp, but if you plan on adding a supercharger or nitrous, or making more than 550 hp naturally aspirated, you really need to step up to the steel H-beam connecting rods.

Connecting rods and bolts are under an unbelievable amount of stress when an engine is running. For that reason, I recommend using the best connecting rods available for a particular application. Look at it this way: Using a stronger connecting rod than necessary is a good insurance policy against catastrophic failure. (Photo Courtesy Modern Muscle Performance)

When it comes to cylinder heads for your Hemi, you shouldn't have to worry about them; the engine builder already has that figured out. Just remember, swapping heads can be done, if you have the adapter plates, such as those from Modern Muscle in Virginia.

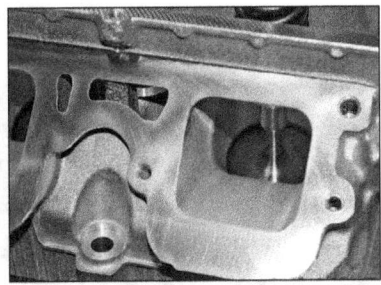

Although head choice is generally the engine builder's decision, you decide what kind of porting work is to be done, if any. Some builders offer a CNC-ported head, and that option is a lot less expensive than a hand-ported job.

assemble. If you are not sure that you want to get that deep into building the engine, it's safe to say that as a general rule, having a machine shop completely rebuild your engine probably costs more than a crate engine.

Cost Considerations

But why is a crate engine a less expensive alternative, and is it as good as a custom-built piece? The cost savings come into play because the companies selling crate Hemi engines have designed and built bulletproof combinations and streamlined the building process. Not only that, since they buy their parts in quantity, they can get a better price deal and pass the savings on to you.

Although a complete crate engine is not as cheap as an over-the-counter, do-it-yourself rebuilding kit, when compared to the cost of all aspects of a complete rebuild, they are very competitive.

Quality and Reliability Factors

Clearly, not all crate engines are created equal. Prices can vary, and so can the quality of the components that are used in their assembly. An engine is only as good as its foundation: engine block, crankshaft, connecting rods, and pistons. So pay attention to what is being used and do your research. When you're shopping for a crate Hemi engine, check out where the engine's power band is located. If you're building a street bruiser, having all your power at 6,000 rpm is a waste. Be honest, how often is your Hemi turning 6,000 rpm? In most cars, even those owned by performance enthusiasts, the engine spends most of its time between 2,000 and 4,000 rpm. For that reason, that is the power band that most people should consider.

Also, if you intend to add some type of forced induction, the final compression ratio needs to be considered. Numerous factors affect the maximum allowable compression ratio when supercharging an engine. Unfortunately, there is no cut-and-dried rule that applies to every application. When building the engine, the highest compression ratio that is feasible, and does not encounter detonation, should be used. If the compression ratio is too low, the engine will be sluggish during off-boost conditions.

DODGE CHALLENGER AND CHARGER: HOW TO BUILD AND MODIFY

CHAPTER 5

However, a compression ratio that is too high can lead to serious knock-related engine problems.

Unless you are planning to use some kind of sophisticated fuel and spark management (computer control), an effective static compression of 8:1 to approximately 9.5:1 is probably going to give you the best compromise for a reliable, street-driven boosted engine. This lower compression ratio also allows the use of more boost pressure. If you build an engine with a compression ratio of 10.0:1 or higher, to get the most out of it you need to run specialized ignition components and race fuel. That being said, the Hemi's factory compression ratio is above 10.0:1. Because of this, any kit that you buy to install on a stock engine will be limited to a boost of about 6 to 8 psi. Unless you enjoy working on your car more than driving it, you want to get an engine that's going to be reliable, and be that way for a long time. It's important to know what components are going into the engine, but it's just as important to know the reputation and experience level of the company that's building the engine. Buying a crate engine from a company with a lot of experience and a good reputation in building what you want is paramount. Finally, some crate engines come with a warranty and some don't. Some reputable crate engine retailers even offer a 3-year/36,000-mile warranty. It pays to check with a retailer and see what they offer.

Many companies offer crate engines for Hemi-powered cars. The following is one of the most popular among Hemi car owners.

Arrington Performance/ShopHemi.com

Arrington was originally established to build high-performance cars for professional NASCAR and NHRA race teams. Teams, such as Penske, Petty, and Ganassi, have been using Arrington engines for years. Arrington Performance/ShopHemi.com regularly introduces new and innovative products and services for late-model Hemi-powered cars. The company operates from a 105,000-square-foot facility that houses the finest race engine development, manufacturing, and testing program in the business as well as their cutting edge family of performance parts.

ShopHemi.com offers their 5.7-liter long-block as a fully customizable package. This long-block comes

---

Arrington 5.7-Liter VVT Block

Horsepower range: 400 to 550
Compression: 9.0:1 to 11.0:1 depending on application
Available combinations:
345 ci (5.7 liter): 3.917-inch bore x 3.580-inch stroke
366 ci (6.0 liter): 3.922-inch bore x 3.795-inch stroke
392 ci (6.4 liter): 3.922-inch bore x 4.080-inch stroke
410 ci (6.7 liter): 4.00-inch bore x 4.080-inch stroke

Block
Each block is hot tanked and sonic checked. The deck surfaces and bore centerlines are checked. The cylinders are CNC-honed with a torque plate, and then hand-clearanced for any stroker needs. The installation of billet main caps is available. ARP main studs are installed. The block is then painted your choice of color.

Rotating Assembly
Balanced Molnar or Manley forged crankshaft
H-beam connecting rods with ARP rod bolts
Mahle forged-aluminum pistons
Mahle piston rings (steel upgrade available)
Cleveite bearings

Phase VI Cylinder Heads
5-axis, CNC-ported
CNC valve job
1,511-psi springs
Viton valve seals
Springs capable of up to .645-inch lift

Arrington 5.7-liter VVT block. (Photo Courtesy Arrington Performance/ShopHemi.com)

CUSTOM-BUILT ENGINE PACKAGES

Arrington 6.1-Liter Block

Horsepower range: 450 to 630
Compression: 9.0:1 to 11.0:1 depending on application
Available combinations:
370 ci (6.1 liter): 4.055-inch bore x 3.580-inch stroke
392 ci (6.4 liter): 4.060-inch bore x 3.795-inch stroke
426 ci (7.0 liter): 4.080-inch bore x 4.080-inch stroke
440 ci (7.2 liter): 4.060-inch bore x 4.250-inch stroke

Block
Each block is hot tanked and sonic checked. The deck surfaces and bore centerlines are checked. The cylinders are CNC-honed with a torque plate, and then hand-clearanced for any stroker needs. The installation of billet main caps is available. ARP main studs are installed. The block is then painted your choice of color.

Rotating Assembly
Balanced Molnar or Manley forged crankshaft
H-beam connecting rods with ARP rod bolts
Mahle forged-aluminum pistons
Mahle piston rings (steel upgrade available)
Cleveite bearings

Phase VI Cylinder Heads
5-axis, CNC-ported
CNC valve job
1,511-psi springs
Viton valve seals
Springs capable of up to .645-inch lift

Arrington 6.1-liter block. (Photo Courtesy Arrington Performance/ShopHemi.com)

Arrington 6.4 Liter VVT Block

Horsepower range: 500 to 670
Compression: 9.0:1 to 11.0:1 depending on application
Available combinations:
392 ci (6.4 liter): 4.090-inch bore x 3.720-inch stroke
426 ci (7.0 liter): 4.095-inch bore x 4.050-inch stroke
448 ci (7.4 liter): 4.095-inch bore x 4.2500-inch stroke

Block
Each block is hot tanked and sonic checked. The deck surfaces and bore centerlines are checked. The cylinders are CNC-honed with a torque plate, and then hand-clearanced for any stroker needs. The installation of billet main caps is available. ARP main studs are installed. The block is then painted your choice of color.

Rotating Assembly
Balanced Molnar or Manley forged crankshaft
H-beam connecting rods with ARP rod bolts
Mahle forged-aluminum pistons
Mahle piston rings (steel upgrade available)
Cleveite bearings

Phase VI Cylinder Heads
5-axis, CNC-ported
CNC valve job
1,511-psi springs
Viton valve seals
Springs capable of up to .645-inch lift

Arrington Aftermarket Aluminum Block

Available combinations:
426 ci (7.0 liter): 4.125-inch bore x 4.050-inch stroke
449 ci (7.4 liter): 4.185-inch bore x 4.080-inch stroke
468 ci (7.7 liter): 4.185-inch bore x 4.250-inch stroke

Block
The deck surfaces and bore centerlines are checked. The cylinders are CNC-honed with a torque plate and then hand-clearanced for any stroker needs. The installation of billet main caps is available. ARP main studs are installed.

Rotating Assembly
Balanced Molnar or Manley forged crankshaft
H-beam connecting rods with ARP rod bolts
Mahle forged-aluminum pistons
Mahle piston rings (steel upgrade available)
Clevite bearings

Phase VI Cylinder Heads
5-axis, CNC-ported
CNC valve job
1,511-psi springs
Viton valve seals
Springs capable of up to .645-inch lift

Arrington aftermarket aluminum block. (Photo Courtesy Arrington Performance/ShopHemi.com)

with the rotating assembly parts found in their short-blocks but also includes top-end components, such as performance heads and camshaft. Each custom long-block is hand-built. Each engine is manufactured to match your needs and to complement all of your aftermarket parts.

Indy Cylinder Head

For more than three decades, Indy Cylinder Head has been supplying the Mopar aftermarket with high-quality engine parts and complete engines. Their years of racing experience have translated into maximum performance on the street. Through engineering and extensive testing they have been able to assemble the correct combinations of blocks, cylinder heads, manifolds, pistons, camshafts, and other engine components used to produce the ultimate in Hemi power.

Through extensive testing and engineering they have taken the 5.7-liter Hemi and upgraded it to 392 inches, and taken the 6.1-liter to 426 inches. In doing so, they offer raw horsepower with improved fuel economy and great performance.

Modern Muscle Performance Group

The professionals at Modern Muscle have more than 40 years of broad experience in CNC operation, supercharger installation, custom fabrication, restoration, technical help, and more. Simply put, they have the tools, knowledge, and experience to make your Hemi perform without wasting your time or money. If you have horsepower and torque on your mind, the amount of power Modern Muscle can get out of your ride is astonishing. Modern Muscle provides the very best in performance and performance parts for a Hemi with jaw-dropping results. Remember, you get turnkey help at Modern Muscle.

Each engine is available and designed specifically for either normally aspirated or boosted applications.

Indy 5.7 and 6.1 Hemi

Compression: 9.5:1
Available combinations:
392 ci (6.4 liter): 3.937-inch bore x 4.050-inch stroke
426 ci (7.0 liter): 4.090-inch bore x 4.050-inch stroke

Block
The deck surfaces and bore centerlines are checked. The cylinders are honed with a torque plate, and then any clearancing required is done for the stroker crankshaft. Billet main caps are installed. ARP head and main studs are installed.

Rotating Assembly
Internally balanced Compstar forged crankshaft
Compstar H-beam connecting rods with ARP rod bolts
Mahle forged-aluminum pistons
Clevite bearings

Cylinder Heads
6.1-liter heads are CNC-ported
Manley springs and retainers

Intake
6.1 Intake
CNC port matched
Polished inside and outside

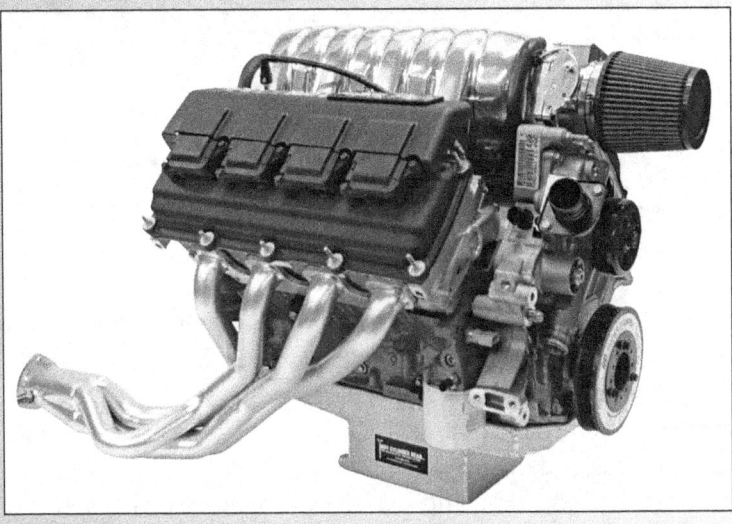

Indy 5.7 and 6.1 Hemi. (Photo Courtesy Indy Cylinder Head)

Modern Muscle 5.7- and 6.1-Liter Block

Compression: 9.0:1 to 11.0:1 depending on application
Available combinations:
370 ci (6.1 liter): 4.055-inch bore x 3.580-inch stroke
392 ci (6.4 liter): 4.060-inch bore x 3.795-inch stroke
426 ci (7.0 liter): 4.080-inch bore x 4.080-inch stroke
440 ci (7.2 liter): 4.060-inch bore x 4.250-inch stroke

Block
Every block that Modern Muscle starts with is checked for any cracks, bored if needed, and then honed with a torque plate. Finally, it is checked and receives any further machining if necessary to make it perfect.

Rotating Assembly
Balanced Molnar forged crankshaft
Molnar H-beam connecting rods with
    superior-quality rod bolts
Mahle 4032 or 2618 forged pistons (depending
    on application)
Cleveite H-series bearings (Calico coating
    available)

Cylinder Heads
5-axis CNC-ported
CNC valve job
Thitek aftermarket heads available
Aluminum block option also available

Modern Muscle 5.7- and 6.1-liter block. (Photo Courtesy Modern Muscle Performance Group)

CHAPTER 6

SUSPENSION, BRAKES AND CHASSIS

The chassis underneath the Charger, Challenger, Magnum, and 300C, is a product of engineering shared between Mercedes-Benz and Chrysler. The chassis delivers excellent ride comfort and control and has been a tremendous success with millions of cars in the field. The LX platform incorporates a Mercedes-Benz S-Class–similar double-wishbone front suspension and a rendition of the E-Class' five-link rear suspension. Previously, all Chrysler vehicles came from the factory with a "solid," or "live," axle. So this upgrade was a huge departure from what Chrysler was used to building.

A live axle is an axle assembly wherein the axles are encased in solid tubes that are welded to the center differential as one assembly. The axle assembly moves independently of the rest of the car, but the wheels are attached to the axle and move in uniform motion with the axle. An independent rear suspension is where each wheel can move independently. The center differential is rigidly mounted to the chassis and does not move with the wheels. The axles are not encased in tubes and are connected to the differential and wheels with CV joints. An IRS has less unsprung weight, which is the mass connected to the wheels, not the body of the car. Less unsprung weight makes for a better ride quality and improves handling over uneven surfaces.

Front Suspension

Your vehicle's front suspension is a short- and long-arm design with high-mounted upper A-arms (control arms), which place the upper ball joint at a level above the tires. This higher position of the upper control arm helps with suspension articulation, which helps keep the front tires at a more perpendicular angle to the road when cornering. The lower control arms consist of lateral lower links and tension struts that attach to the steering knuckle via separate ball joints. Gas-charged coil-over struts and an anti-roll bar attach to the lower control arms and complete the package.

Although the Hemi is very adept at making power, if you cannot get the power of your Challenger, Charger, Magnum, or 300 to hook to the pavement when going around a corner or launching from a red light, what good is it? Your Hemi car is blessed with an IRS. With this type of suspension, each rear wheel can move independently of the other.

All-wheel-drive models use forged upper control arms and single-piece cast-iron lower control arms that are packaged around the front-drive system.

The 2009 and up cars have a slightly different front suspension system as compared to the 2005–2008 models. The upper control arms on 2005–2008 fit on the newer models, but the caster increases from approximately 9 to 10 degrees positive to 15 to 16 degrees positive. This means that the caster cannot be brought into specification. The vehicle may still be drivable, but probably wears tires at a faster rate, and may also position the tire too far rearward in the wheel opening.

Rear Suspension

For the rear suspension, the five-link aluminum independent suspension uses coil springs, gas-charged shock absorbers, and (on Hemi-equipped vehicles) an anti-roll bar that attaches to the rear knuckles. Everything but the coil springs and shock absorbers are mounted directly to a steel subframe that attaches to the body with four large rubber isolators and bolts.

The use of a multi-link rear suspension allowed Chrysler the ability to incorporate both a good ride and very stable handling within the same package. In an LX/LC car, each rear suspension arm has a rubber bushing at each end. Consequently they react to loads along their own length in tension and compression, but not in bending.

Four-wheel disc brakes are used on all LX models, as are low-drag calipers. Hemi-powered vehicles (not SRT) use twin-piston aluminum calipers and 13.6-inch vented rotors up front, and single-piston aluminum calipers and 12.6-inch vented rotors in the rear. The aluminum units are gray anodized for corrosion resistance.

Tires

As good as these vehicles are, there have been some reports of relatively short tire life in what the car owner considers conservative use. Tire wear is directly related to two characteristics in the LX/LC chassis. One is a known high rate of bump steer. Contributing factors to premature tire wear from bump steer are worn, torn, or failed radius rod bushings. The second is high negative rear camber that occurs when the vehicle is carrying a load.

Bump steer is a toe-in and toe-out motion that is created as the suspension articulates over the road surface. The tires scrub off tread when subjected to this condition. You can simulate this grinding motion with your feet. Place your feet flat on the ground, twist them left and right until your toes point in, and then out. The resistance you feel is what causes tire wear as bump steer occurs. Raising or lowering the steering rack in relation to the wheel knuckle at rest corrects bump steer.

Camber is measured in degrees, both positive and negative. Incorrect camber can be the result of either a bad alignment, wearing parts, or by changing the ride height of your vehicle. Incorrect camber causes extreme tire wear by riding on the edge of the tires instead of the traction contact patch. Positive camber means that the top of the tire points away from the vehicle, and negative camber points the top of the wheel toward the vehicle.

Springs and Shocks

"But why does my car's chassis have a high negative camber under load?" The factory coil springs are usually the culprit when it comes to this condition. Even when new, the coil springs in a car produce 1 to 2 degrees of negative camber. Add any load to the rear of the car, and the condition is exacerbated.

Lowering the car and suspension tilts the wheels inward at the top as they follow a circular pivot path. Typically, a 2-inch drop can lead to –.75 degrees of camber. A 2-inch drop changes camber by –1.5 degrees, and a 3-inch drop can result in –2.0 or more degrees of change.

If your vehicle is equipped with Nivomat load-carrying rear shocks, you do not have to worry about a high negative-camber situation when the car is loaded with passengers or cargo. Nivomat is a self-contained hydraulic load-leveling system. As the load increases, the pressure inside the shock increases as oil is displaced from the reservoir to the inside of the unit, compressing the gas volume. This creates a progressive increase in spring rate and dampening, with little or no change in the ride quality.

The Nivomat system is like an ordinary monotube shock absorber with a hydraulic piston, tube, and accumulator, but there are two different configurations of the shock. The first looks like a conventional twin-tube air shock with a dust cover. What appears as a dust cover actually houses the high-pressure accumulator and low-pressure oil reservoir. The second configuration has its high-pressure accumulator at the top of the shock. This reduces the overall diameter of the shock and allows the shock to be installed in a more confined space; on your Hemi car with its independent rear suspension it can be mounted in a shaft-up or -down configuration as designed by the manufacturer.

What gives the Nivomat system its leveling capability is a pump mechanism and oil reservoir that can increase the accumulator pressure, and this increases the shock's lifting ability. It is used in combination with coil springs that are matched to the load capacity of the shock to reduce suspension travel while utilizing more of the piston and shaft travel of the shock.

This maintains the ride quality whether the vehicle is operated with a driver only, or to compensate for passengers and luggage. The big advantage to the Nivomat is that the shock absorber requires no plumbing, compressor, or height-sensing device to level the vehicle. The normal movement of the suspension over a regular road surface provides enough pumping action to level the vehicle. As long as the system is working, the shocks level the vehicle and keep the negative camber in check.

If the tube of your rear shocks is more than 59 mm in diameter, your car is Nivomat equipped. Most LX cars were delivered with standard-style rear shocks. It is possible for the rear camber's negative reading to increase 1½ to 2½ degrees with five passengers in the vehicle.

If your car experiences a high rate of negative camber and an alignment does not fix it, the problem could be one of two issues: worn coil springs or worn bushings in either the camber link, or possibly, the tension and compression links.

Noise Isolation

The rear suspension cradle in a Charger, Magnum, 300C, or Challenger is attached to the vehicle using four bolts passing through large rubber bushings. To make the passenger cabin quiet, these rubber bushings have gaps or voids in them to allow them to "absorb" and keep road and suspension noise from entering the cabin. Efforts to isolate these noises, unfortunately, reduce the durability of the components and the bushings either corrode or tear.

Step-Out

Subframe bushing failures exacerbate a known issue with virtually all LX/LC cars. The worn bushings allow the rear suspension cradle and assembly to move when experiencing a load condition, such as cornering or accelerating. This movement causes the rear end to want to "step out." This means that when the rear suspension cradle moves, the rear wheels become a second set of wheels that are now helping to steer the car. This is hard to notice under normal driving conditions, but if you do any type of spirited driving (autocross or drag racing), it can be highly pronounced.

The factory could have put solid mounts on the rear cradle and alleviate this condition, but Chrysler didn't because ride quality is paramount. Although solid mounts would eliminate the eminent bushing failure and improve the driving characteristics of the car, it would also transfer more road noise and place a greater load on the welds in the car's unibody construction. OEM bushings are dependent on an aluminum-to-rubber bond that holds the bushing's ferrule in place. If you see white oxidation on your subframe bushings, it may indicate the need for replacement.

Bushing Basics

An LX/LC car has more soften-the-ride suspension bushings than you can shake a stick at. What's even more surprising is how these bushings affect performance handling. It's because of the sharing with Mercedes-Benz that you have a sophisticated, affordable rear-wheel-drive luxury sedan from Chrysler. But, it's also because of these roots that you have some room for improvement when it comes to performance handling.

The Mercedes-Benz parts are designed to give a comfortable ride, which means they were made with a lot of "play" in them. The entire rear assembly/cradle, in stock trim, moves around considerably under acceleration.

Rubber Bushings

Rubber has been the industry standard for use in suspension bushings since the beginning of automotive design. However, the exact makeup of each component's rubber "blend" differs depending on where the parts are used in the suspension system. Some parts, such as anti-roll bar bushings, are rubber only, while others are reinforced with either an outer steel-sleeve only, or both inner and outer sleeves. This is the case with the control arm bushings in your Hemi car. The sleeves allow the suspension to "work," while the rubber tries to contain a large amount of flex from occurring when the suspension is under load.

Carmakers focus a lot of design effort on suspension and chassis bushings. This is because, in general, people riding in cars want a quiet and comfortable ride. So car manufacturers must eliminate as much noise, vibration, and harshness (NVH) from the car as possible while it is traveling on the road.

In the case of sleeved bushings, the rubber that is pressed in and around the inner and outer sleeves is required to absorb the flexing action of the control arm. This rubber is where your suspension flexibility happens. It is also where suspension failure first happens.

The constant loading and unloading of a rubber bushing causes it to lose its ability to rebound quickly, and could eventually lead to the rubber tearing loose from its inner and outer bushings. Because they are not designed to rotate the same as the surrounding suspension components, deflection occurs, which can damage the bushings prematurely.

A tremendous amount of vibration and noise occurs when your vehicle's wheels rotate. Imperfections in the road surface, potholes, and other obstructions are encountered while the tires are bouncing along on the rough pavement. As I mentioned earlier, the general public wants the ride to be comfortable and quiet, so soft bushings that isolate the body from the suspension and frame are used. The problem is, some owners want performance handling, and while those soft bushings are doing their job by deflecting and allowing the suspension arms and other parts to move around, this movement allows the wheels and tires to move an unwanted amount during cornering, acceleration, and braking.

Polyurethane Bushings

So, what's the fix for all this movement? Do you have to settle for a quiet and comfortable but "mushy" ride? Fortunately, you don't. Polyurethane bushings have been around for years and have many advantages over rubber bushings. Polyurethane is a blend of polymers that can be made in a variety of densities, generally referred to as the durometer of the bushing. A higher durometer simply means that the material (in this case, the bushing) is harder and less compliant.

Polyurethane (or urethane for short) is not the actual bushing, but rather the material used to make the bushing. Depending on the application, polyurethane can be as soft as a rubber band or as hard as plastic. Polyurethane also carries a higher load-bearing capacity, greater tear resistance, better compression resistance, greater abrasion resistance, and more tolerance to grease and oil than rubber.

Compliance is a bushing's ability to allow movement because of a force that is applied to it. In other words, it is complying with the force exerted against it. The bushing can also distort if it is subjected to the twisting motion that occurs during normal suspension movement. Generally, compliance and deflection are bad because they do not allow your car's suspension system to work at peak efficiency. Polyurethane bushings are designed to hold their shape while resisting compliance under load much better than rubber parts. This reduced bushing-deflection helps maintain more precise suspension geometry, resulting in improved handling.

Polyurethane bushings can have a graphite mixture inside it (graphite impregnated). The mixture makes the bushing self-lubricating and prevents it from squeaking as the suspension moves through its range of motion. This is beneficial because polyurethane bushings are compliant resistant; they do not "twist" like rubber bushings do. To allow the suspension to move properly, they pivot on an inner sleeve that is lubricated with grease.

Over the years, polyurethane bushings have gotten a bad rap because people say that all poly bushings squeak. The noise that they hear is actually high-frequency vibrations. True squeaking is usually caused by lack of lubrication, poor installation, use of an incorrect part, or polyurethane that may be too hard for the application.

Rubber or Polyurethane

The fact that rubber bushings allow the vehicle mounts to absorb vehicle vibrations and noise (which gives a soft ride) might create the notion that polyurethane makes the ride harsher. Some enthusiasts have noticed a slight increase in road noise and vibrations because of polyurethane bushings.

In most cases, polyurethane outperforms its rubber counterparts when used as a replacement for rubber bushings and mounts. Polyurethane lasts longer than rubber bushings and performs better by removing the sloppiness caused by worn or damaged rubber bushings.

In the end, if you are looking for a performance increase and an upgrade to your vehicle's suspension, polyurethane bushings are a great choice.

One thing to remember is that changing the bushings in your vehicle can be a fairly simple or a complex task that requires special tools and mechanical aptitude. For instance, to change the rear cradle bushings, you need to disassemble the rear section of the car. However, simply changing sway bar and/or shock bushings is easily accomplished in your driveway with simple hand tools.

Many companies offer bushings for Hemi-powered cars. The following are two of the most popular among Hemi car owners.

Pedders Suspension

If your vehicle has more than just a few miles on it, it's time to upgrade the bushings. The Pedders Bump-Steer Correction Kit is designed to reduce the tendency for toe-in and toe-out changes to within 3 mm. In addition, front lower-strut mounts, front/rear radius rod bushings, and lower control arm bushings help to provide consistent suspension geometry under cornering, acceleration, and braking. Pedders' bushings also allow a wider range of camber so that you can dial in the alignment to suit anything from everyday driving to aggressive road race conditions.

For the rear cradle, Pedders offers a rear camber-adjustable bushing, because the factory bushings don't allow any adjustment. Bushing adjustment is often required for cars that have been lowered, along with the full gamut of control arm and rear cradle bushings to minimize cradle deflection. According to Pedders, even under normal driving conditions the factory cradle moves from side to side, as well as fore and aft. This makes the car feel sloppy in corners, and once you feel a "Pedderised" car you know what you're missing. It also eliminates the differential-killing wheel hop.

Energy Suspension

Unlike factory rubber bushings, Energy Suspension's Hyper-Flex polyurethane components don't rot

Energy Suspension's Hyper-Flex components are designed to be free floating, and not put your suspension in a bind when encountering irregularities in the road's surface. You can purchase them in red or black; the company also offers complete bushing sets. The retail price is about $762 for a complete set. (Photo Courtesy Energy Suspension)

or deteriorate from exposure to oil, chemicals, or road salt. Hyper-Flex components are a free-floating non-binding design, and Energy Suspension track tests all of their products before taking them to market. Bushings are available in red or black; both offer the same basic chemical polyurethane formula, with graphite added to some of the black bushings for additional lubrication. They have bushings for the front suspension, rack and pinion, sway bars, differential and subframe.

You achieve greater stability, improved handling, and superior transfer of power to the rear wheels. Energy's components can take the abuse on the track and they are also suitable for everyday driving.

Frame Details

When it comes to your Charger, Challenger, 300C, or Magnum wagon, Dodge engineers needed to address stringent frontal-, side-, and rear-impact performance criteria. They used many advanced technologies to create a safe, strong, and quiet body structure.

Most of the platform is stamped from high-strength steel that creates a solid foundation. Strategic use of advanced materials inspires

Pedders' Bump-Steer Correction Kit reduces the tendency of bump steer, and their front lower-strut mounts, front/rear radius rod bushings, and lower control arm bushings provide consistent suspension geometry during all driving situations. If your car has been lowered, rear-camber adjustments are required. Pedders also offers a rear camber adjustable bushing because the factory bushings don't allow any adjustment. The retail price starts at about $580 for the LX street kit. (Photo Courtesy Pedders Suspension)

SUSPENSION, BRAKES AND CHASSIS

confidence during high-performance driving, contributes to the world-class ride, and provides exceptional occupant protection via a safety cage. Before the car is assembled, all of this steel needs to be welded together to make a complete body structure.

One of the most important structural elements of your vehicle is one that you can't see, the frame. The body of your Hemi-powered ride is a unibody construction. This means that the frame of the car is actually part of the body. The unibody frame and body structure provides greater structural integrity and impact absorption during a collision.

During construction, each piece of the car's body is spot-welded together; this allows a certain amount of body flex to occur. Although you want to virtually eliminate flex in performance applications, a certain amount is inherent in a car's construction. But because flex hurts performance, what can be done to fix it?

The way to approach body flex is to decide what you plan to do with your car. If you are simply driving to work every day, you may not need to do anything because you don't really have a problem. Chrysler designed and built the car to deliver years of trouble-free service, so enjoy the ride.

An employee installs components in a 2011 Dodge Challenger at Chrysler Group's Brampton Assembly Plant. The plant, located in Ontario, Canada, launched the all-new 2011 Chrysler 300 and Dodge Charger as well as the 2011 Dodge Challenger in January 2011. The 2011 Dodges combine advanced steels. With world-class torsional strength, the cars feature tighter and stiffer characteristics for an added sense of confidence and control during high-speed maneuvers. In addition, the rear structure of the 2011 Dodge Charger was strengthened to ensure enhanced front-to-rear stiffness continuity. (Photo Courtesy Fiat Chrysler Automobiles US LLC)

Project: Hotchkis Suspension Installation

I am sure that you don't want to compromise the ride quality of your car, but you do want to take a corner as if your car were on rails. A good, high-quality suspension kit is just what your car could use.

Although improving handling and reducing body roll typically induces a ride that feels "stiffer," the Hotchkis TVS kit does not make much of a change. You feel a more "firm" ride, but the first time you crank into a corner at a higher-than-usual speed, you have your ah-ha moment.

These suspension parts are theoretically "bolt-on," but the job can become complicated. The only specialty tool you need is a coil-spring/strut compressor to change the front springs. Although this install could be accomplished in a driveway with a jack and jack stands, having a two-post lift makes the job a lot easier. Finally, figure on spending at least 4 to 5 hours installing the new parts. When you're finished, don't forget to have the car realigned.

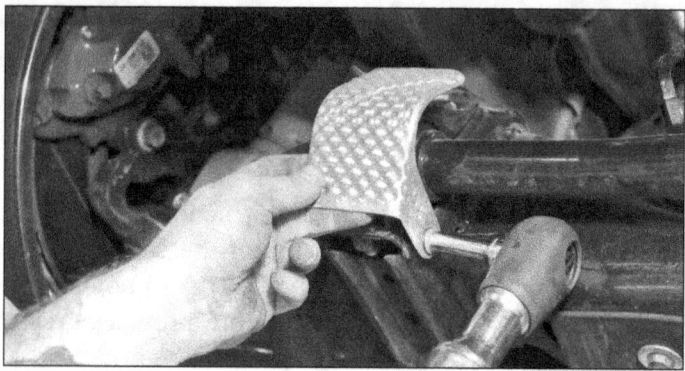

1 After raising the car off of the ground, make sure to pay attention to the stock sway bar orientation and position for future reference. Next, you need to remove the heat shields that cover the subframe mounts. Use a 10-mm wrench or a socket and ratchet.

2 With a 15-mm socket, remove the bolts/brackets that attach the front sway bar to the subframe. Once done, the sway bar should be hanging only by its end-links. Retain all removed hardware and brackets for reinstallation.

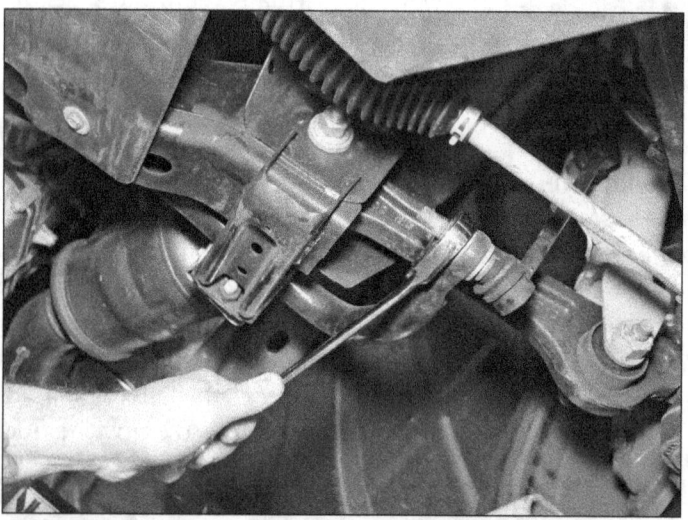

3 Next, disconnect the sway bar end links using both a 10- and a 21-mm wrench. Your stock sway bar should now easily come out.

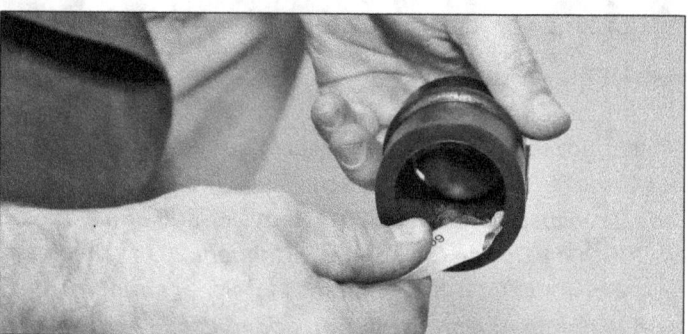

4 Before installing your new parts, apply a healthy amount of the provided grease to the new polyurethane bushings. Once greased, install the new bushings onto your new Hotchkis sway bar. Your kit comes with five packs of grease (two for the front, one for the rear, and two more for the front to be applied after approximately 6 to 12 months). The bushings should be re-greased every 6 to 12 months depending on your driving conditions.

5 Reinstall the new sway bar in just the opposite manner as removal. When it is in the car, attach the end-links to the sway bar. Do not tighten them at this time, as you need to be able to move the sway bar for final adjustment/install.

6 Next, lift the center of the sway bar and reconnect the subframe mounts back to the vehicle. You can now fully tighten all of the hardware (including the end-link bolts). You have just completed the front sway bar installation. Now on to the rear bar.

SUSPENSION, BRAKES AND CHASSIS

7 *Whether working with jack stands or a lift, make sure that the car can't roll when you lift the rear of it. When you are certain that the car will not roll, you can then lift the rear of the car high enough that the rear tires are off the ground. If working on the floor of a shop, support the rear of the vehicle with jack stands at the factory jack points, and remove the rear wheels.*

8 *With the rear tires removed, you can now get the shocks off of the car. Remove the rear shocks by removing the lower nut and bolt with an 18- and 15-mm wrench, and the two upper shock bolts going into the body with a 16-mm socket, ratchet, and extension.*

9 *If you pull back the plastic splash shield, you see there is a bracket that holds the rubber brake line in place (arrow). Remove the bolt that holds the brake line to the frame with a 10-mm wrench.*

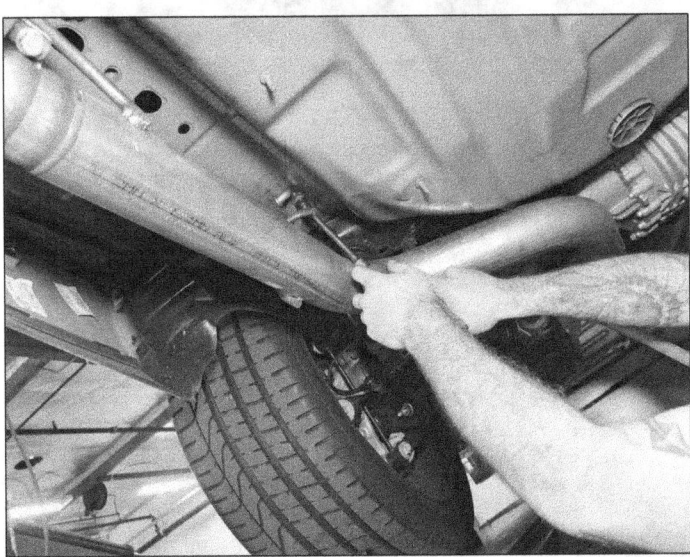

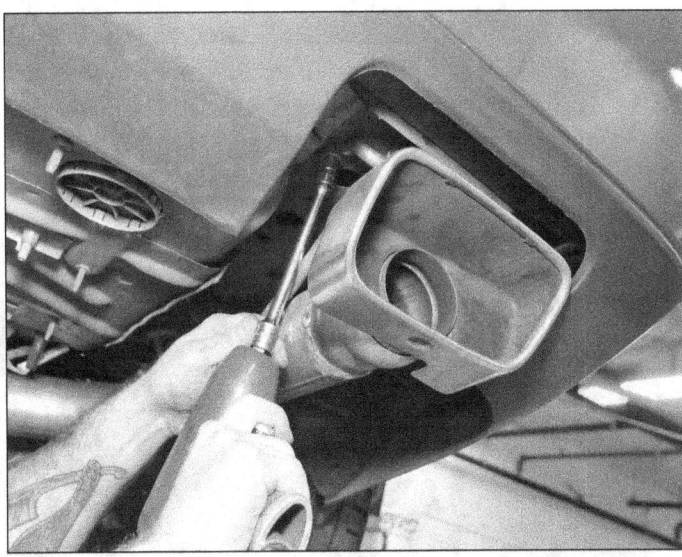

10 *You need to lower the exhaust to gain some clearance. First, unbolt the mid-brace by removing the four bolts using a 13-mm socket. Spray the rubber hangers with WD-40 and slide the rubber hanger off the exhaust support. Next, unbolt the remaining rear hangers using a 13-mm socket. Be careful, the exhaust drops down once these bolts are out.*

DODGE CHALLENGER AND CHARGER: HOW TO BUILD AND MODIFY

CHAPTER 6

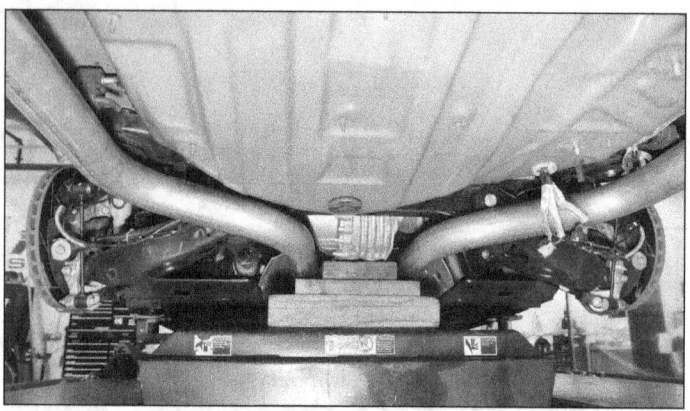

11 You need to support the differential housing. Use a jack for this, as you need to lower the differential in the next step. You can use a couple of pieces of wood or a rubber pad to cushion the contact point of the jack and housing. Remember, the jack stands should still be supporting the rear of the car.

12 Once the differential is supported, you can unbolt the four bolts that secure the rear cradle to the frame (two on each side) with an 18-mm socket. Now lower the jack that supports the differential about 4 or 5 inches. Make sure not lower it too much to avoid damaging the rear brake hard line.

13 With the rear cradle loosened from the car, the next step is to disconnect the sway bar end-links from the sway bar. This is accomplished by using a 15- and 16-mm wrench. Retain the bolts for reinstallation of the new sway bar.

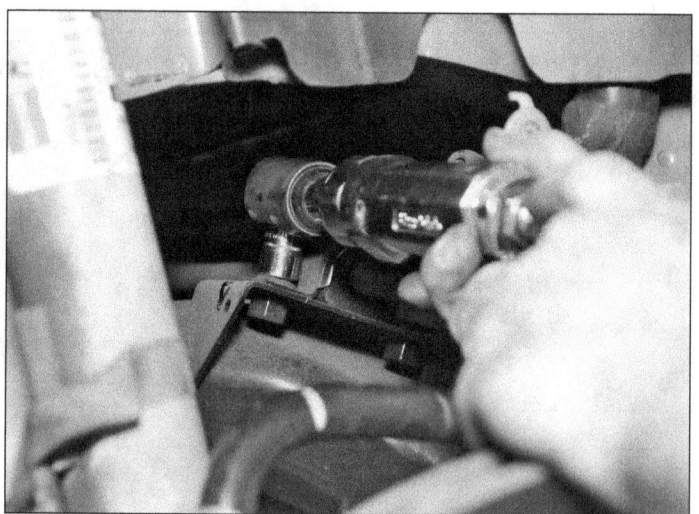

14 Using a 15-mm wrench, disconnect the four bolts that are securing the sway bar–to-subframe mounts. Again, keep these bolts for reinstallation. You can, however, get rid of the stock bushing brackets.

15 You should be able to slide the sway bar out from the side of the car. The only obstacle you might run into when removing the old sway bar is the brake lines. If so, carefully maneuver the bar around the brake lines.

148 DODGE CHALLENGER AND CHARGER: HOW TO BUILD AND MODIFY

SUSPENSION, BRAKES AND CHASSIS

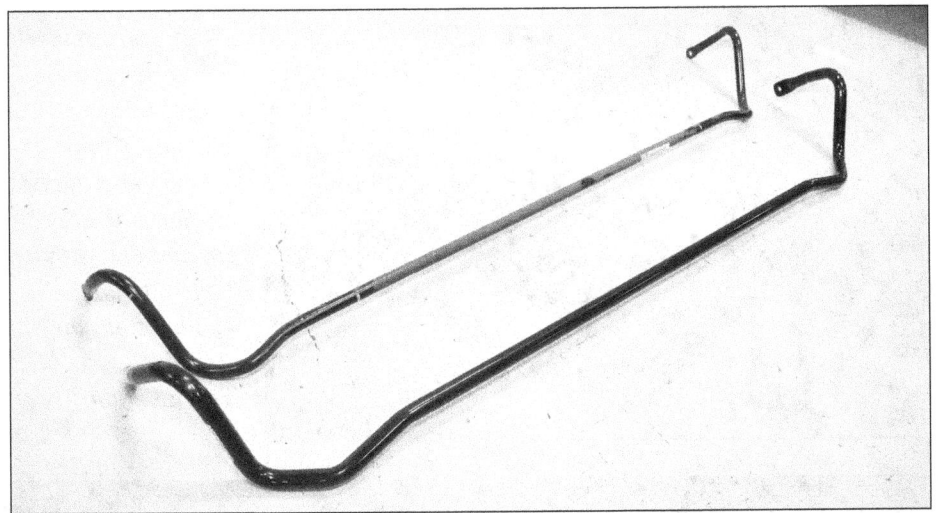

When you place the bars side by side, there is no comparison between the stock sway bar and your new Hotchkis sway bar.

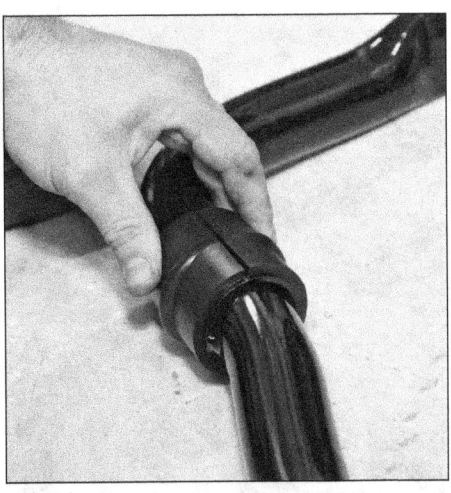

16 Before you install the bushings, lube them with the provided grease and then place them on the bar.

17 Now you can install the new Hotchkis sway bar into the factory sway bar location. This is done in the opposite manner as removal. Make sure that the bar is oriented as shown in the picture. Once in place, put the provided bushing mounts over the bushings, and make sure the grease zerk fittings are facing outward. Tighten the bracket bolts.

18 Finally, re-attach the sway bar end-links to the sway bar and tighten all hardware.

19 Once everything is back in place, you can raise the differential back into position. Do not raise it up against the body yet, as you need some "wiggle" room to maneuver and line up the cradle bolt holes. Start each bolt by hand to ensure proper threading. Once all four bolts are thread-started, fully tighten the cradle bolts.

CHAPTER 6

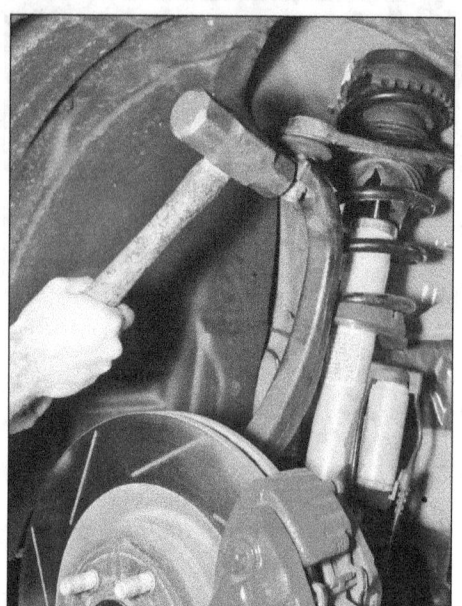

21 Loosen and remove the lower shock bolt with an 18-mm wrench, and the bolt holding the sway bar end link with a 21-mm wrench. Again, retain the bolts for reinstallation.

20 With the new sway bars installed, you can swap out the factory springs for the Hotchkis springs. Begin by loosening the upper control-arm ball joint bolt with an 18-mm wrench (do not remove yet). You can use a hammer to smack the control arm flat spot, and this should break the ball joint stud loose. Once loose, remove the ball joint nut. Do not let the steering knuckle hang by the brake line. Use a wire or string to hold the knuckle up. The hardware that you remove will be used for reinstallation.

22 You need to access the upper strut attaching nuts by opening the hood. The nuts are under a plastic cap. Once exposed, remove the three nuts that hold the shock to the vehicle with a 13-mm wrench or socket. Once again, retain this hardware for reinstallation.

24 For this part of the project, you need a spring/strut compressor. If you don't have one, you might be able to rent one from a local auto parts store, or have a shop handle this step for you. What you have to do is secure the spring/shock assembly in a spring compressor and remove the shaft nut (arrow). An 18-mm socket is needed.

23 Once the shock is out of the car, you can mark the shock top-hat and lower perch with a white marker or paint stick. This makes it easier to ensure that the proper orientation of the spring is confirmed for reinstallation.

DODGE CHALLENGER AND CHARGER: HOW TO BUILD AND MODIFY

SUSPENSION, BRAKES AND CHASSIS

25 Now you can remove the top hat, stock bump-stop, and stock spring. Sometimes the bump-stop is pressed into the top hat; if so, remove the stock bump-stop from the top hat boot.

26 Install the new Hotchkis polyurethane bump-stop into the top-hat boot assembly as shown here.

27 Place the new Hotchkis coil spring over the shock, and onto the bottom rubber bumper of the shock assembly. Make sure to orient the spring correctly; the smaller pigtail end is on the bottom.

28 Before compressing the spring and installing the hat and shaft nut, test fit the top hat onto the shock's shaft and see if your marks line up. If not, rotate the coil spring and rubber bumper until they align.

29 Once aligned, you can place the assembly in a strut compressor, and compress the coil spring and reinstall the shaft nut.

DODGE CHALLENGER AND CHARGER: HOW TO BUILD AND MODIFY

CHAPTER 6

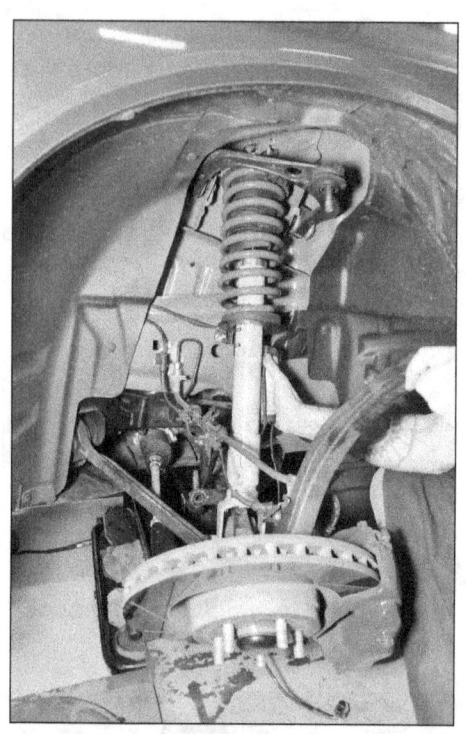

30 *Reinstall the strut assembly in the same manner as removal. When installing the lower shock bolt make sure the holes lines up with the shock clevis. Also make sure the threads start correctly by threading the bolts by hand. Once properly threaded, fully tighten the hardware.*

When installed, the Hotchkis system gives your vehicle the handling that it deserves. It also gives it the slightly lowered stance to completely change the overall "vibe" of the car. (Photo Courtesy Hotchkis Sport Suspension)

Racing Considerations

The form of racing you might try depends on the type of driving you want to do. Two good choices are road racing and drag racing.

Road Racing

Road racing is a general term that is used for most forms of auto racing held on paved, purpose-built racetracks (i.e., road courses), as opposed to oval tracks or off-road racing. Temporary facilities that are built on airport runways, large parking lots, and even closed public roads are sometimes included in the definition. Most of the time, these events consist of an Autocross event.

If you are planning to use your Challenger, Charger, Magnum, or 300C on a road course, or participate in an Autocross event, you need to know a few things about your car before you mash the go pedal.

Because these cars do not have a full frame, chassis flex is a real concern. Both the front and rear suspensions are housed in cradles that are independent of the body; just like every chassis ever designed, it has strengths and weaknesses. The LX suspension is a very good design, derived from a proven Mercedes-Benz architecture. As good as it is, though, it has been proven that during spirited driving situations, bump-steer, excessive bushing compliance, and a tall factory ride height combined with modest-rate coil springs and dampeners definitely limits the performance from the factory.

All these cars possess a wishbone–style upper control arm and a virtual pivot point in the lower front

The late-model Charger and Challenger can be road raced. They are fairly well balanced, and the IRS provides excellent traction while cornering. Some cars even come with the Road & Track package that gives you upgraded wheels and tires plus a performance steering and suspension package.

DODGE CHALLENGER AND CHARGER: HOW TO BUILD AND MODIFY

SUSPENSION, BRAKES AND CHASSIS

control arms. The front suspension is designed to maintain dynamic alignment geometry throughout all driving conditions. The lower control arm's virtual pivot design provides improved steering feel and control under most road conditions. The two arms don't actually intersect, but if you theoretically extend their axes to a point where they do finally intersect, you find a "virtual pivot point" that is ideal under a wide range of operating parameters.

The LX's rear suspension is limited by very compliant rubber bushings and coil springs with modest coil and dampening rates. This is evident in hard cornering.

When designing a race car, engineers try to keep the body/chassis as rigid (stiff) as possible. A car that doesn't flex allows the suspension to work properly and maintains stable geometry under load situations such as cornering, accelerating, and/or braking. When the body/chassis flexes, suspension settings can be adversely affected under different dynamic loads. When you try to make adjustments to a car that flexes, you end up chasing your tail because the chassis is working against you during each situation as the body/chassis flexes.

The point of optimal chassis torsional stiffness determines how effectively you can transfer the load from the front and rear axles while in a corner. With a stiff chassis, most of the "twist" of the axles, with respect to each other, happens in the suspension's deflection. That's a good thing because that deflection is well understood and is controlled by the shocks.

With a flexible chassis, the opposite occurs: The chassis flexes, and that flex limits how well the shocks can function. Some people run stiff springs and soft shocks because spring loads are position dependent whereas shock loads are compression dependent (dependent on how fast the suspension compresses) and therefore more difficult to assess. That is why you can do a better job of controlling the suspension if the chassis is stiff, and a better-controlled suspension means faster lap times.

When it comes to road racing and autocross, most owners want to take their street car and make it perform to the best of its ability. Autocrossing is a fun weekend activity that anyone can enjoy. But because you use your daily driver, you need to make a couple of compromises in the name of reliability and durability.

A full-on race car has no place on the street, but some race car tricks can be incorporated into your street car to stiffen the chassis.

Drag Racing

Drag racing is when two cars compete in a side-by-side competition to be first to cross the finish line. That finish line is most generally 1/4 mile away from the starting line. Drag racing has existed in both street racing and regulated motorsport forms since automobiles were developed. Unlike autocross racing, there is no cornering. The light goes green and you race straight to the finish line.

Most dragstrips participate in bracket racing. Bracket racing allows for a time handicap between the predicted elapsed time of the two cars. The effect of bracket racing rules is to place a premium on consistency (or performance) of the driver and car rather than on the car's power. This makes winning much less dependent on having a lot of money, and more dependent on a car's mechanicals and the driver's skill and ability to control the car. It also makes bracket racing popular with casual weekend racers. Some even drive their cars to the track, race them, and then drive them home. This format allows for a wide variety of cars.

If you plan to drag race your Charger, Challenger, Magnum, or

Mopar has a history steeped in drag racing, so when the company introduced the Drag Pak Challenger in 2008, they were out for blood. Cars such as this 2009 Drag Pak Challenger driven by Jeff Teuton started as a stock Challenger body-in-white with a composite lift-off hood, polycarbonate windows, manual rack-and-pinion steering, and lightweight brakes. Mopar also shortened the car's wheelbase to 116 inches and pushed the engine mounts rearward for better weight distribution. The car was available with either a late-model Hemi or an older LA-series small-block.

300, you first need to decide how far you want to go with your vehicle. Are you planning to make your car a daily driver that only sees the track occasionally, or are you going to build an all-out race car? Whatever your racing plans, one of the major hurdles that you need to overcome is the IRS.

When it comes to taking a car around corners, an IRS is tough to beat. Because the rear wheels are independent of each other, the movement of the body has no effect on the wheel contact with the road surface. This helps the car maintain a constant and smooth transition from a straightaway into a corner. Although it's a good thing for cornering, a drag racing car with each wheel "independent" of the other will have issues.

We all know that when a car launches, both wheels want to spin. With a live axle, the power is evenly distributed between the passenger-side and driver-side wheel. But, if an IRS is employed, the force exerted by the rear end can be diluted from one wheel to the other, as the car tries to "lift" each tire from the road surface independently. If you watch any LX, LY, or LC car launch at the racetrack, you'll very likely see the car "wheel hop" as it launches.

You can correct this condition. You can install aftermarket "no hop" bars, replace the factory rear control arms with aftermarket pieces, or if you plan to race consistently and use a lot of power, you might even want to consider installing a live solid axle.

Now that you have decided on your type of "competition," you might also want to perform some upgrades to your Hemi car to increase its performance on the track. If you're going to do that, you need to know what parts are available, and what is a benefit to your car.

Strut Bracing

A quick and easy upgrade for your vehicle is to install front and rear strut braces. A strut brace is a simple metal bar that is bolted to the top of the two strut/shock towers. This brace is used to horizontally support the suspension of the car. The strut towers are the mounting point for the top of the strut/shock absorber on the front of your vehicle, and they are directly connected to the car's chassis.

By using a brace to attach the driver-side and passenger-side strut towers together, you are adding to the rigidity of the chassis. This is typically more important for a car that corners under acceleration, such as during autocrossing.

Because the unibody design of a Hemi car is meant to distribute any force and resistance encountered across the entire chassis, the car inherently twists, and the strut towers want to flex and move depending on the directional force being applied. When this flex occurs at the front struts the car has a tendency to "fold" in on itself when cornering (a little exaggerated, but you get the point) and produce a certain amount of understeer.

A brace that links the towers keeps them parallel to each other, prevents movement of them, and helps plant your tires firmly on the road. The coil spring and shock absorbers on the front of the LC and LX chassis are combined into one suspension unit. This means that the entire vertical suspension load is transmitted to the top of the strut tower. Without the addition of a strut brace, the inner wheel-well inherently flexes with the strut towers relative to the chassis rails.

Choosing the correct tower brace comes down to two things: performance needs and, yes, aesthetics. If you want to race your Challenger, Charger, 300C, or even Magnum wagon around road courses, strut braces definitely add value because they tie together a number of other suspension modifications in addition to helping keep the car flat and grounded. Combine this with a set of performance struts and sticky tires, and you have a formula for cornering success every time.

Your Hemi car is built on a unibody design; therefore, it does not have a full-length frame underneath. This means that the body can inherently flex, and under spirited driving conditions, the car could feel "spongy," especially when cornering. One upgrade to combat this is to install front and rear strut braces to stiffen the chassis.

SUSPENSION, BRAKES AND CHASSIS

A rear strut-tower brace is also an option, and is installed between the rear shocks. A rear strut brace tends to reduce the amount of usable trunk space, but is installed in much the same way as a front brace.

Installation

Although under normal driving conditions the benefits of a front and rear strut-tower brace might not be very noticeable, once you get into performance driving you will wonder how you ever managed without them. The car feels much more stable, and with the tightened chassis your car is a lot more controllable, which is exactly how your car should feel.

But, buyer beware: Cheap braces simply attach at both strut towers. These offer some support, but not as much as a brace that attaches at multiple locations. Quality braces mount at several points: at both strut towers and at attachment points on the cowl/firewall.

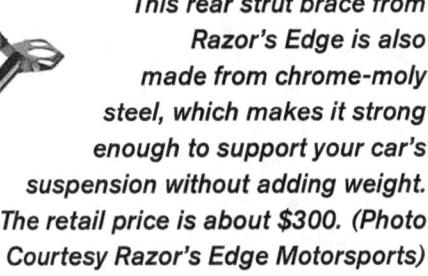

The install of a strut brace is fairly straightforward, and can be completed with simple hand tools in a couple of hours in your home garage or driveway.

Some front strut-tower braces interfere with engine covers (some trimming of the cover may be required) and twin-screw superchargers. If you already have a supercharger, make sure the brace fits before you buy it. If you already have the brace, and are looking at a supercharger, you might need to modify or replace the brace.

Many companies offer strut bracing for Hemi-powered cars. The following are the most popular among Hemi car owners.

This rear strut brace from Razor's Edge is also made from chrome-moly steel, which makes it strong enough to support your car's suspension without adding weight. The retail price is about $300. (Photo Courtesy Razor's Edge Motorsports)

Razor's Edge Motorsports

The strut brace from Razor's Edge Motorsports is made from tough 4130N chrome-moly alloy steel, which makes it strong enough to support a car's front end without adding weight. If you're looking for true race car performance and the best strength-to-weight ratio, this is the part for you. These strut bars are available for the front and rear, are an easy no-drill installation, and come with all hardware. Also included are replaceable wiper motor tabs for easy installation on all LX/LC cars from 2005 through 2013. Custom colors are available upon request.

Petty's Garage

The Petty's Garage strut-tower brace is engineered to install easily and reduce strut-tower flex. This brace greatly improves handling. The Petty brace is made from .049-inch-thick 4130 chrome-moly tubing and is hand bent and TIG welded by The King's race-seasoned fabricators.

Razor's Edge Motorsports' front strut braces are designed as a "bridge" to help support the front suspension of your car. They are made from chrome-moly steel and can be ordered in custom colors. This front brace controls the flex and increases cornering performance. The retail price is about $300.

CHAPTER 6

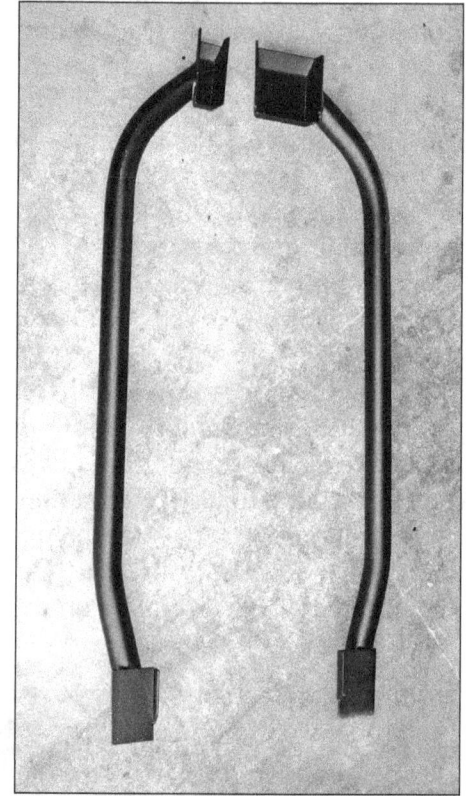

The name Petty is synonymous with racing, so when Petty's Garage came out with a strut tower for LX cars, their racing background helped produce a quality part. This brace is made from .049-inch-thick 4130 chrome-moly tubing, and this is hand-built. Install time is about a half day. The retail price is about $229.

Arrington Performance/ShopHemi.com offers a strut-tower brace that ties both strut towers together with a reinforcing connection against the firewall. This style of bar helps distribute the cornering force across the entire car, not just the strut towers. The company also offers strut braces designed to clear the engine cover, so no trimming is required. The retail price is about $500. (Photo Courtesy Arrington Performance/ShopHemi.com)

Subframe connectors are designed to stiffen the chassis of a car in two ways. First, they connect the front and rear subframe. Second, some can even support the floorpan at the rear seat mounts. Connecting the subframes together effectively reduces overall chassis flex. In other words, installing subframe connectors before the stress of hard launches and rigorous cornering takes its toll on your vehicle is a goof idea.

Petty personally approved its performance on LX- and LC-chassis cars.

Arrington Performance/ ShopHemi.com

Arrington Performance/ShopHemi.com offers strut tower braces for Challengers, Chargers, Chrysler 300Cs, and Magnums. The Arrington unit works by tying the two strut towers together and reinforcing the connection by bracing them against the firewall. When your vehicle takes a corner, the strut bar distributes the cornering load, which makes this an impressive and cost-effective performance-suspension upgrade. Arrington also carries strut braces that are designed to clear the engine cover, so no trimming is required.

Body Bridging

Because the LX- and LC-platform cars are built with a unibody construction, you can increase the body's rigidity in several ways. In addition to strut-tower braces, you can use subframe connectors. Connecting the front and rear subframes

---

DODGE CHALLENGER AND CHARGER: HOW TO BUILD AND MODIFY

SUSPENSION, BRAKES AND CHASSIS

is not new in the performance world. Racers have been doing it for years.

Even though most racers think of subframe connectors as a drag-race-oriented part, adding frame connectors is a great way to strengthen your car's body, and ultimately, improve handling and braking performance. "Bolt-in" frame connectors are touted to stiffen a car's body, and to some extent, they do. But, if you want the ultimate in support, weld-in connectors are a must.

When this modification is installed, handling is much improved; the ride quality and comfort are not sacrificed if the rest of the suspension components are left alone.

For those wanting to get every ounce of performance out of their car, adding subframe connectors and strut-tower braces is a great first step prior to adding other modifications. By strengthening/stiffening the chassis with these parts, the frame can better serve as a great platform for future upgrades, such as heavier springs, thicker sway bars, and stickier tires.

Many companies offer body bridging via subframe connectors for Hemi-powered cars. The following is one of the most popular among Hemi car owners.

Razor's Edge Motorsports

Razor's Edge Matrix frame connectors definitely improve a car's handling. These subframe connectors are designed to have no ground clearance issues. Made from 4130 chrome-moly material, this connector is specifically designed for the LX/LY chassis cars. It ties the inner and outer frame rails, and the rear lower control arm mount. The connectors are powder-coated for a long lasting finish. For maximum benefit they must be welded in.

These deliver far better chassis stiffness for all cars, whether you're a weekend warrior or have a serious car with high horsepower, sticky tires, and/or a competition-oriented suspension. They tuck in very close to the underside of the chassis and hang only as low as the side skirts of the car. Because it is recommended that they be welded in, special tools are required, and it takes the better part of a day to install.

Roll Bar or Roll Cage

Although you might think that a roll bar is a necessary item in dedicated race cars, you should also consider installing one in your Challenger, Charger, 300C, or Magnum. Even in stock form, some R/T and SRT-8 models are capable of speeds around 150 mph with only a simple tune. This is more than fast enough to be catastrophic in an accident.

Although new cars incorporate the latest construction techniques and passenger protection devices to enhance safety, if you happen to encounter a rollover accident, a roll bar gives additional protection to you and your passengers.

Also, many racetracks require at least a roll bar for any car quicker than 11.50-seconds in the quarter-mile.

That pipe also has another function: to strengthen and stiffen the body. And you know that a stiffened chassis creates a better performing car.

Roll bars are considered a basic four-point system. This includes a main hoop that runs from the driver's side of the floor (just behind the seat), up the side of the car, across the car against the roof, and then down the passenger's side of the car; a seat-belt harness bar (cross bar); and at least two rear bars going from the top of the main hoop toward the rear of the car. If you add two bars from the main hoop (at approximately shoulder height) to the front floor of the car, you have a six-point system.

Many people use the terms *roll bar* and *roll cage* interchangeably when describing a tubular structure inside of a car, but that is incorrect. A roll bar is good for dual-purpose street and track cars, and is a mandatory minimum when racing with convertible cars.

Roll cages begin with a roll bar, and add pillar bars, a windshield bar, a roof bar, a door bar, a dash bar, a harness bar, and two rear bars.

All bars and cages should fit tightly to the interior structure of the car. When someone says "four point," or "six point," they are referring to the number of welded "points" that the bar or cage uses to attach to the body of the car.

The most common type of material used in the fabrication of a roll bar or roll cage is one-piece DOM (drawn over mandrel) mild-steel tubing that is very strong. In some racing applications, the roll bar or roll cage is made with chrome-moly steel, which is much lighter than DOM tubing steel and is also even stronger, increasing the level of protection and the cost of materials.

In racing applications, roll bars are required to be certified by the racing sanctioning body. For drag racing, the roll bar must meet specific requirements for the speed and elapsed time that the vehicle is capable of operating. Whether you need a roll bar or a roll cage depends on what classes you plan to run at sanctioned events. To know what is legal for your car, check the rule book of the sanctioning body that regulates the event.

You can install a custom unit or a kit. Although not legal at most sanctioned events, you can even buy a roll bar that bolts-in to your car.

Weld-In Kits

A weld-in roll bar or roll cage kit usually costs about as much as a bolt-in kit, and comes with all of the required tubing. Although all of the bends have already been made, each piece of the tubing is generally left a little long so it can be cut to length. You can figure on spending at least another $500 to have this kind of cage welded into your car, but bear in mind that any changes or additions can quickly increase that cost.

Installing a weld-in bar or cage requires the removal of the interior, so as not to cause a fire from a welding spark. If you have the shop remove the interior, it can be expensive. If you do it yourself, be sure to set aside enough time, and remember how it all goes back in when the project is finished.

A custom-fit cage costs quite a bit more, typically in the $1,500 range. A good custom-fit cage can maximize both the safety and the rigidity of the car, because the bars are bent to fit snugly within the confines of the passenger compartment.

Many companies offer weld-in roll bar/roll cage kits for Hemi-powered cars. The following is one of the most popular among Hemi car owners.

Competition Engineering

This company has spent a lot of development time so it can offer the utmost in strength and fit without adding unnecessary weight. All tubing used in their kits exceeds the requirements of racing sanctioning bodies and is mandrel formed for uniform wall thickness. Every Competition Engineering kit has been designed to fit the specific application with only minor modifications to the interior necessary for installation.

Bolt-In Kits

Bolt-in kits are probably the most common roll cage found in cars that are raced at the amateur level. These cages are inexpensive, easy to find, and can usually be installed in a weekend with simple hand tools. Because many come painted and ready to go, they offer a quick and easy way to make your car look cool, and actually be a little safer.

One downside to bolt-in kits is that they are usually built with "loose" tolerances. This means that the gaps between the roof and the cage are generally larger than necessary. Bolt-in cages usually bolt to the horizontal surfaces of the car's floorpan because they're not welded to areas of structural support. As a result, a bolt-in cage can tear through the floor's thin sheet metal during a hard impact.

Bolt-in cage kits start at about $700. They are legal for most forms of club-level production-based road racing and some rally events.

Many companies offer bolt-in roll bar/roll cage kits for Hemi-powered cars. The following is one of the most popular among Hemi car owners.

RPM Rollbars

This company provides high-quality, high-performance roll bars for Challengers and Chargers. Backed by 25 years of experience, their roll bars are the only ones that are 100-percent welded yet completely removable. The RPM roll bar works with the factory seats and installs with very slight modifications to the vehicle's interior.

The bars are NHRA and SCCA legal to 10.0 quarter-mile estimated

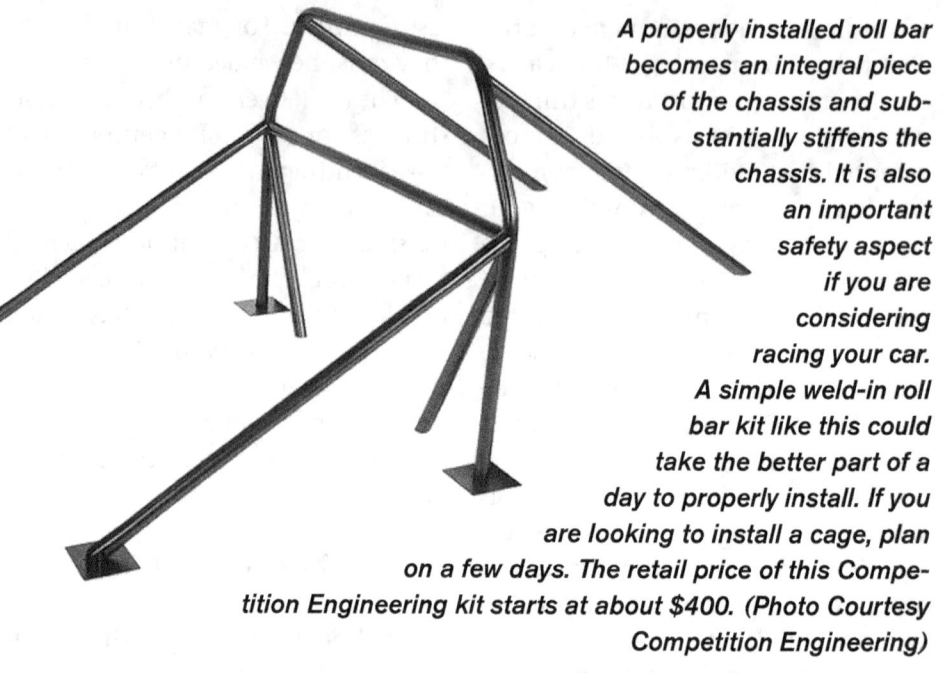

A properly installed roll bar becomes an integral piece of the chassis and substantially stiffens the chassis. It is also an important safety aspect if you are considering racing your car. A simple weld-in roll bar kit like this could take the better part of a day to properly install. If you are looking to install a cage, plan on a few days. The retail price of this Competition Engineering kit starts at about $400. (Photo Courtesy Competition Engineering)

SUSPENSION, BRAKES AND CHASSIS

If welding isn't an option, this RPM roll bar is designed to bolt in for a relatively easy installation. The bar is fully welded from the factory but can be installed and removed from your car whenever necessary. Not just for looks, the bar is NHRA and SCCA legal. The retail price is about $1,100.

times, and there are extension kits available to make them legal to 8.50 seconds. They come with NHRA/SCCA–legal door swing-outs and bolt-in seat-belt mounts. The bars are built using lightweight chrome-moly structural tubing, and the factory seat remains fully adjustable. Each kit comes with fully detailed instructions with pictures, and all hardware. The company guarantees that the bar will pass tech or they will buy it back!

Suspension Upgrades

From the factory, LX/LC cars are equipped with a strut suspension up front and a rear coil spring/shock suspension on the rear. This is a very reliable suspension system, and very amenable to upgrades.

Struts and Springs

The struts on the front are more than merely shock absorbers with a different name. Unlike an older muscle car that has a shock, a spring, and spring pockets, a strut integrates the different suspension parts into one compact assembly.

The strut actually serves multiple purposes. The coil spring that surrounds the shock absorber supports the weight of the car. The shock absorber is encased in the spring, and dampens the movement of the spring as it compresses and rebounds itself when the car is moving. The strut housing serves as a structural part of the suspension system, and connects the upper strut bearing (connected to the body at the tower) to the lower ball joint so that the entire assembly can then pivot when the steering wheel is turned.

The struts on your vehicle should be checked at least once a year, and it should usually be done in conjunction with a wheel alignment. Under normal conditions, the shock absorber portion wears out gradually, and you may not even notice the loss in ride quality, or even handling and control. However, signs that your car may have worn struts include bottoming out, excessive bouncing after

An employee at Chrysler Group's Brampton Assembly Plant moves a vehicle suspension onto the assembly line for placement in a new car. (Photo Courtesy Fiat Chrysler Automobiles US LLC)

DODGE CHALLENGER AND CHARGER: HOW TO BUILD AND MODIFY

CHAPTER 6

a bump, nose-diving when hitting the brakes, and excessive tire wear.

If your vehicle needs a strut service, it may also be a good time to think about changing the coil springs. Coil springs need to be removed when the struts are changed, and this way you would save on labor costs by doing it all at the same time. If you are changing, you might as well upgrade!

Many suspension parts can be upgraded easily and affordably. It is possible to make a big difference in handling and performance by upgrading just a few parts.

Sway Bars

If your vehicle seems to lean quite a bit when you corner, you might need new sway bars. The new, upgraded sway bar should be stiffer and thicker than the original stock bar. Because the bar is stiffer, it keeps the car flatter when turning during acceleration.

To put it simply, an anti-sway bar is a U-shaped metal bar that connects both of its ends to the wheels on opposite sides of the car; it also connects to the chassis somewhere in the middle. A properly designed sway bar should minimize body roll. The bar's resistance against body lean is its torsional stiffness, or resistance to twist. Less twisting of the bar results in less movement into jounce and rebound by the opposite ends of the suspension. This results in less body roll.

A sway bar's diameter has a dramatic effect on the torsional rigidity of the bar. The torsional (or twisting) motion of the bar is actually governed by the following equation:

$$\text{Twist} = (2 \times \text{torque} \times \text{length}) \div (\varpi \times \text{diameter}^4 \times \text{material modulus})$$

As the bar's diameter becomes larger, the amount of possible twist becomes smaller (torsional rigidity is a function of the diameter to the fourth power). This is why a very small increase in diameter makes a large increase in torsional rigidity.

In addition to the diameter of a bar, another important factor contributes to an anti-sway bar's torsional rigidity: the length of the moment arm (the amount of leverage between the vehicle and the bar).

Increasing the available amount of leverage makes the work easier. This is governed by the lever law: force x distance = torque. As distance (the length of the lever) increases, the resulting amount of torque also increases.

Because a sway bar is U-shaped, its ends serve as levers. As the distance from the straight part of the bar to the attachment at the end link becomes longer, the torque applied against the bar increases. This makes it easier for a given amount of energy to twist the sway bar. As this distance is reduced, torque is reduced, making it more difficult for a given amount of energy to twist the anti-sway bar.

Although adding an upgraded sway bar to a Hemi car is a good thing, many feel that sway bars should be the final tuning element for any vehicle. By using a larger bar, you will realize more benefits from a car that is better balanced, sprung, dampened, and bushed. For that reason, before you install upgraded sway bars you should consider subframe bushings, tension and compression bushings, castor adjustment, coils springs that are higher in spring rate and lower in ride height, and nitrogen-charged struts at all four wheels.

You must address these other aspects of your car before installing the sway bar. If you don't, the bar will still do its job, but the result will be substandard.

Another decision to make is whether to use a hollow or solid sway bar. Because a sway bar's torsional strength is a function of the bar's diameter, it stands to reason that with equal diameters, the benefit of a hollow bar is only weight. The material in the center of a solid sway bar has little bearing on the resistance of torsional force. You can increase the torsional rigidity of a hollow sway bar by employing a bar with a thicker wall.

Many companies offer sway bars for Hemi-powered cars. The following are the two most popular among Hemi car owners.

Eibach Springs

Eibach's Anti Roll Kit reduces the body roll of a Challenger, Charger, 300C, or Magnum with its increased design stiffness over stock sway bars. The result is increased handling and cornering grip in any performance-driving situation. Eibach bars are manufactured from cold-formed, high-strength aircraft-grade steel, and finished with a long-lasting powder coat finish. The front bar is 30 mm, and the rear bar is 16 mm. This is a non-adjustable kit.

The kit comes complete with greased urethane bushings for improved responsiveness and all mounting hardware and instructions for easy installation. Installation is fairly straightforward and can be completed in a few hours.

Hotchkis Sport Suspension

You can enhance the cornering performance of your Hemi car with a set of Hotchkis sway bars. The Sport sway bar package increases the front

SUSPENSION, BRAKES AND CHASSIS

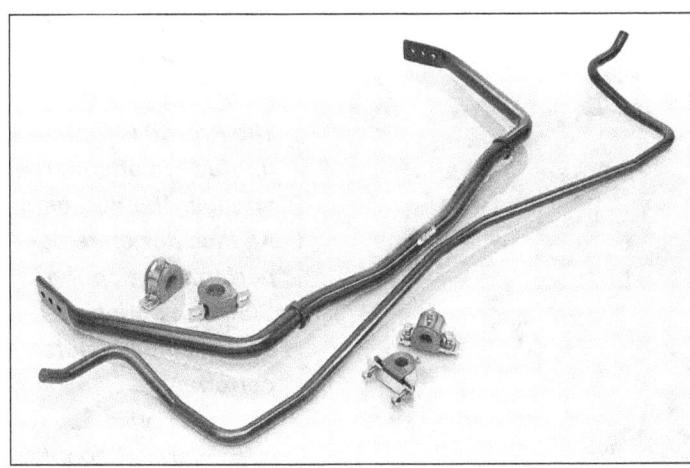

Eibach sway bars reduce body roll and make your car feel more stable when cornering. The bars are well constructed and designed for long life. The sway bars come as a kit with everything needed for the installation. The retail price is about $330. (Photo Courtesy Eibach Springs)

The Hotchkis Sport sway bar package increases the front and rear roll stiffness of your car, giving it well-balanced handling. With these sway bars, you can rotate the car on corner entry and steer with the throttle when necessary. The bars are powder-coated, and can be installed in a few hours with simple hand tools. The retail price is about $450. (Photo Courtesy Hotchkis Sport Suspension)

and rear roll stiffness, giving the car a crisp, quick turn-in response and balanced handling. These sway bars give the driver the ability to rotate the car on corner entry and steer with the throttle when necessary. Handling becomes comfortably neutral with added traction during cornering.

Hotchkis Sport sway bars feature a durable powder-coat finish, polyurethane bushings, and special grease-able rear brackets. The high-performance front bar diameter is 35 mm, and the stock is 30 mm. The HP rear bar is 19 mm and the stock bar is 15 mm.

Springs

Aftermarket springs cause the car's center of gravity to lower, which can be a great improvement for handling. Keep in mind that aftermarket springs may also be stiffer than stock springs, so the ride characteristics of your car are affected (it will typically be firmer/stiffer). Many enthusiasts feel that the opening between the fender and the tire of their car is too wide. So, quite frequently, the sole reason for upgrading and buying new springs is to reduce this gap and lower the car for a sleeker appearance.

The problem with this approach is that the spring rate of these "lowering" springs is often kept close to stock specification to allow their use with factory shocks and struts. These shorter springs reduce the amount of available suspension travel without the required increases in stiffness; this in turn increases the chances of the suspension bottoming out and destroying the shock absorbers or other parts. That is why buying springs should be a thorough process not based on vanity.

Because some spring manufacturers do not list individual spring rates, the best course of action is to find an off-the-shelf spring that actually improves handling. Choose a lowering spring that is as tall as possible, yet produces the desired result. Doing so reduces the chance of damage to the suspension.

To select the correct spring rate for your car you need to determine the exact corner-weight of the car (driver-side front, passenger-side front, driver-side rear, passenger-side rear) with the car at race weight (including the driver' weight as well as fuel, oil, etc.).

Spring rates are determined by the amount the spring compresses by the weight placed upon it. As an example, a spring with a 250-pound spring rate compresses 1 inch for every 250 pounds placed on it.

This sounds simple, but there's more to consider: The suspension geometry can influence how much the spring compresses. You have to compensate for the suspension's geometry when determining the correct spring rate for your car. Selecting the correct spring rate for your car can be very complicated. Luckily, many manufacturers have figured this out and have developed kits.

When choosing springs, be honest with yourself. If you do not plan to race your car very often, don't buy springs that are designed for racing. I am sure that almost everyone reading this book is building a nice street car, and you are looking for better than average handling. Let's say that you have a 2009 Charger with a 5.7-liter Hemi. Because you have a daily driver and are only looking for a better handling car with a close-to-factory ride, I would choose springs such as Hotchkis' "Sport" springs. These springs improve the handling characteristics of your car and improve stability in all driving conditions. The fact that they lower the car slightly more than 1 inch front and rear is a bonus.

When installing new coil springs, swapping the front springs requires special tools. If you happen to have the proper strut compression spring tool, the swap could be done in a couple of hours. If not, you can usually rent one from the local auto parts store, or you can figure on paying a few hundred dollars for a shop to do it. If you are capable of removing the entire strut assembly yourself, you could save some money: All the shop would have to do is change the springs on the assembly.

Many companies offer springs for Hemi-powered cars. The following are the most popular among Hemi car owners.

Eibach Springs

Eibach offers the Pro-Kit for frequently driven street Challenger, Charger, 300C, and Magnum cars. This spring system dramatically improves both a vehicle's performance and appearance. The Pro-Kit lowers a car's center of gravity, reducing squat during acceleration, body roll in corners, and excessive nose-dive when braking.

If you're looking for the ultimate in handling springs, Eibach Sportline springs are the extreme-performance springs. The Sportline kit was created for very aggressive street

Eibach offers two kits for upgrading the springs in your car. The Pro-Kit is for an upgrade in aftermarket springs. The Sportline Kit includes extreme-performance springs. Sportline springs achieve the ultimate performance handling. The retail price for each starts at about $260. (Photo Courtesy Eibach Springs)

drivers, those who crave a race-car attitude with maximum street performance. These springs achieve exceptional handling by aggressively lowering the car's center of gravity, and feature engineered progressive spring rates.

The Pro-Kit lowers the car approximately 1 inch up front, and 1½ inches in the rear; the Sportline lowers the car approximately 1¾ inches in the front and 2¼ inches in the rear.

Hotchkis Sport Suspension

Hotchkis coil springs offer a lowered stance and dramatically improved handling. With the aid of computer modeling and track testing data, Hotchkis was able to create the ultimate LX/LC spring. It improves handling and still delivers a comfortable ride. Hotchkis performance springs were developed as a complete front and rear balanced system. The kit includes four precision-wound springs. These springs typically lower the car approximately 1½ inches front and rear.

Hurst

Hurst is getting into the suspension game with the Stage One springs for the Challenger, Charger, 300C, and Magnum. The goal is to deliver a spring package that lowers the car, delivers a slight increase in spring rate, and keeps things simple and cost effective. In other words, these springs work with no changes to struts or shocks. The secret lies in their progressive rating.

Hotchkis springs not only lower your car, they also improve handling and deliver a comfortable ride. The Hotchkis springs were developed as a set and are sold as a set. Installing aftermarket springs in a car is an in-depth job; you might not be able to tackle the installation in your driveway. The retail price is about $370. (Photo Courtesy Hotchkis Sport Suspension)

SUSPENSION, BRAKES AND CHASSIS

Hurst tailored the initial spring rate to give you the overall reduction in ride height you desire (1 to 1½ inches) with a rate increase that firms things up for quicker handling. This is all done with a spring length that is very close to stock.

Suspension Kits

If you are looking for the ultimate in a suspension upgrade for your Hemi car, but don't feel comfortable buying the parts piecemeal, you're in luck. Plenty of suspension upgrade kits are available through the aftermarket; they provide all of the necessary parts and installation instructions in one package. Even though finding aftermarket suspension parts can be easy, selecting the proper parts that work well together can be far more difficult.

Plenty of high-performance suspension components are also available. To get the best performance from your vehicle, it is usually easier to buy a kit that has been engineered and designed for your car and for your intended purpose. These kits are fairly extensive and may require as much as a day and a half to install.

Hurst's Stage One springs lower the car, and with the progressive spring rate, they are a direct replacement spring that requires no other modifications. The retail price is about $280. (Photo Courtesy B&M Corporation)

Many companies offer suspension kits for Hemi-powered cars. The following are two of the most popular among Hemi car owners.

Hotchkis Sport Suspension

The Hotchkis Stage 1 TVS system for the Challenger, Charger, 300C, and Magnum offers a lowered stance, dramatically improved handling, and superior driver control. The engineers studied track testing data to develop a balanced handling system that is comfortable enough for everyday street use and well-balanced enough for the occasional track day or jaunt down your favorite twisty road. The system comprises high-rate sport coil springs that lower the car about 1½ inches, paired with front and rear sway bars.

All components are manufactured in the United States and come complete with hardware, greasable bushings, and a durable powder-coated finish. This bolt-on upgrade can transform your car into a canyon carver in no time.

Eibach Springs

The Eibach Pro-System Plus is a comprehensive kit that is the final step for total suspension dominance. This kit is designed specifically for a Hemi car. It offers the best-possible street performance without sacrificing ride quality. The kit is a combination of springs, bump-stops (secondary springs), dampeners, and sway bars. The kit is designed and tuned to operate as a complete performance suspension system.

The Pro-System improves turn-in response, increases cornering speed, and reduces body roll while retaining excellent ride quality. This is the

The Stage 1 TVS suspension system is a complete suspension package from Hotchkis. It improves the handling capabilities of your car and achieves a lowered stance for a cleaner look. The system is designed to deliver a comfortable ride and instill confidence in the driver while on a twisty road. The retail price is about $660. (Photo Courtesy Hotchkis Sport Suspension)

If you're looking for a comprehensive suspension package, the Eibach Pro-System Plus delivers exceptional street performance without sacrificing ride quality. This is a performance-focused suspension system aimed at the true driving enthusiast. This means that the car feels a little stiffer and more stable. The retail price is about $660. (Photo Courtesy Eibach Springs)

ultimate in a street-performance suspension system; a must for any true driving enthusiast.

Aftermarket Brake Upgrades

The 2006–2014 300C, R/T Charger, Challenger, and Magnum came standard with front brakes that used vented 13.6-inch rotors and dual-piston sliding calipers. The rear was fitted with 12.6-inch vented rotors and sliding single-piston calipers. SRT cars received 14.2-inch vented rotors in front with Brembo four-piston fixed calipers, and 13.8 vented rotors on the rear with Brembo four-piston fixed calipers.

The latest versions of the LX/LC platform (2009–present) have an interesting piece of programming written into the anti-lock brake system (ABS) that is designed to manage the gap between the brake rotor and the brake pad. The system is designed to produce the least amount of brake drag and the best possible initial pedal feel.

The way the system works is that after a stop, the controller tells the braking system to pull the pistons away from the rotor a small amount. On R/T and SRT models, if the system senses a high G-force maneuver that might cause the hub unit to flex and push the caliper piston back into the caliper, the system sends pressure to the caliper and pushes the brake pads back into the correct position. This is designed to prevent a long pedal travel for the next stop.

The 2006–2014 300C, R/T Charger, Challenger, and Magnum all came standard with front brakes that used vented 13.6-inch rotors and dual-piston sliding calipers. The rear was fitted with 12.6-inch vented rotors and sliding single-piston calipers. SRT cars (shown) received 14.2-inch vented rotors in front with Brembo four-piston fixed calipers, and 13.8 vented rotors on the rear with Brembo four-piston fixed calipers. In stock form, the braking system on a Hemi car is more than adequate, but upgrades are available.

The factory-installed brakes are more than adequate in a stock application. Heck, even when used in mildly aggressive situations, they are more than capable. But, they are designed for use in cars with standard engines that perform routine tasks, such as stopping while on the daily commute, getting groceries, and driving the kids to school.

So what happens if you subject the car to situations beyond the ordinary? Sooner or later, you experience a brake failure. If you have added performance items to enhance the power of your vehicle, why not take a look at the braking system?

Even in stock applications, the most common occurrence is brake fade. When brakes go beyond the normal operating temperature, you experience a loss in braking power. The stock brakes are generally adequate for a mildly driven street car, but if you use your car for high-performance

SUSPENSION, BRAKES AND CHASSIS

applications, the LX often needs better aftermarket brakes.

If you race your Hemi car, high-performance brakes are a must. Performance brake upgrades are designed to grip better and dissipate heat more efficiently than standard brakes. Although performance pads are a simple upgrade that greatly increase your car's stopping ability, the entire system needs to be considered. Many car owners might not realize that just replacing the factory-style rubber brake lines with braided stainless steel can also have a benefit.

Lines

Brake lines are a crucial part of a brake system. Like most cars, your Charger, Challenger, 300, or Magnum uses a hydraulic brake system. That means that the braking power is caused by fluid filling the brake caliper and pushing the caliper's piston outward, clamping the brake pads against the rotor. The brake lines have to carry that fluid from the master cylinder to the caliper, and they have to do it quickly. When your brake lines are not in good shape, braking power may be reduced, or the brakes may even fail in some situations.

Many performance vehicles use braided-steel brake lines for a couple of reasons. Some drivers appreciate that it's harder for stray objects, such as stones and other road debris, to puncture the braided line than the factory rubber line.

Another feature is that braided brake lines are not as susceptible to the bulging effect that occurs when pressure is placed inside them. During a braking situation, the rubber brake lines bulge (slightly) under pressure. When the line bulges, brake efficiency can be lost. Not only that, but the constant bulging eventually weakens the rubber line.

Rotors

Another great upgrade to the braking system of your Hemi car is to add cross-drilled and/or slotted brake rotors. Drilled and slotted rotors are readily available for LX cars. Drilled brake rotors provide necessary cooling to maintain performance. If the heat generated during braking can't escape, it leads to brake fade, which reduces stopping power.

The second reason to upgrade is brake-gas build up. Because of newer brake pad design and materials, however, that is not a common problem. The gas kept the pad from firmly contacting the rotor, which limited the car's stopping ability. One downside of using drilled rotors on your vehicle is that all of those holes tend to weaken the metal. For example, after repeated stressful driving/braking situations, rotors can develop cracks emanating outward from the holes.

Slotted brake rotors are designed to also move brake gas and heat away from the surface of the rotors. Think of the slots as irrigation ditches that move the gas and heat safely away from the rotor. As I mentioned earlier, drilled rotors have been known to crack around the holes, particularly under hard driving conditions. Because the slot/grooves don't actually penetrate the entire thickness of the rotor face, they tend to be a little more durable than a drilled brake rotor.

Pads

Brake pads contact and apply pressure and friction to the car's brake rotors. Although the role of brake pads as a braking component is pretty simple, the brake pads themselves are anything but simple. Because of the speed that a vehicle's wheels rotate, even while driving conservatively, and your car's weight, brake pads undergo extreme stress every time you slow down or come to a stop.

Organic brake pads, sometimes called non-asbestos organic brake pads, are made from natural materials, such as glass, rubber, and resins, that can withstand the high heat generated by braking. In fact, the high temperature actually helps to bind the materials in the pad. Kevlar is also an important component in the making of many other brake pads. The organic pads are also softer than Kevlar pads, which means they're often quieter.

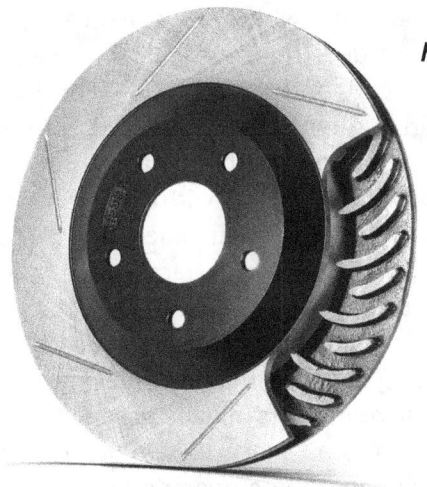

High-performance brake rotors are usually vented to allow more heat to dissipate away from the braking system and prevent brake fade. Although the slots in slotted brake rotors are carved into the face of the rotors, the vents run around the edge of the rotor. As the rotor spins, the heat escapes through these vents. Without the extra heat, there's less of a chance for brake fade, which makes the car perform better on the track. (Photo Courtesy Stop Tech High Performance Brake Systems)

The downside of organic brake pads is that, because they're softer, they typically wear faster. As they wear, they also create more dust (nontoxic), than other types of brake pads.

Because of these considerations, organic brake pads are a poor choice for high-performance cars that may need to stop quickly and/or often from high speeds. Organic and Kevlar brake pads are best suited for mildly driven street cars.

For high-performance applications, ceramic brake pads offer good braking performance, wear well over time, and are very lightweight. But, be ready to open your wallet, because they are expensive. Ceramic brake pads are made from ceramic fibers, a filler material, bonding agents, and they may even have small amounts of copper fibers within them as well. Because they're made of mostly ceramic material, these brake pads dissipate heat very well. This keeps their performance property strong, even after repeated hard stops.

Another great quality of ceramic brake pads is that they do not break down very much with repeated use. This means that they produce less dust than other types of brake pads. For those of you who really like to keep your wheels clean, what little dust they do produce is lighter in color and doesn't stick to the wheels.

Race cars can definitely benefit from using ceramic brake pads, but just about every other vehicle, including a street-driven Hemi, performs just fine when using another brake pad material. For most drivers, the extra performance of ceramic brake pads isn't worth the extra cost.

Most street cars are equipped with metallic brake pads. Made of iron, copper, steel, and graphite, these materials are mixed together and bonded to form the pad. They provide a good balance between performance and durability and are good at transferring the heat that is generated by friction with the brake rotors.

The downside of metallic brake pads is that they are heavier than organic and ceramic pads. If you are looking for every performance edge, this is a consideration. Being made of metal makes the pads very hard, and that is what makes them durable. But, because there isn't as much "give" in metallic brake pads, they tend to wear harder on the brake rotors than other types of brake pads.

Brake Upgrade Kits

Overall, the important thing to consider is the integrity of the braking system as a whole. The brake pads need to be in good condition; the brake rotors need to be in good shape, functional, and properly aligned within the caliper; and the brake lines need to be in good shape and secure. Any kind of damage to the vehicle's brake system can be extremely dangerous on the road.

In a nutshell, buying brake parts piecemeal is one way to upgrade the system, but finding a kit is probably the easiest way to do it. So how do you know which performance brake upgrade is right for you? As usual, it depends on the application. For street driving with the occasional spirited driving on curvy back roads, a smooth or slotted rotor with performance pads is more than adequate. For a track-driven car or race car, a more robust package is desirable. But be warned: Racing brake pads can "bite" so aggressively that they quickly wear out your rotors in daily driving.

A good place to seek advice on the appropriate upgrade package for your vehicle is to talk to the manufacturer. Just as when choosing engine parts, be honest with yourself about the intended usage of your car.

Braking performance depends in large part upon how much surface area the brake pads have to grab. Larger pads and brake discs make for shorter stopping distances. In addition, the increased surface area allows for greater heat dispersal. Excessive heat, as you know, is the enemy of stopping effectiveness.

For street use, some cars actually experience shorter stopping distances by adding a big brake kit, but might lose braking performance. The engineers that designed your car designed the brake system to accommodate the day-to-day changing weight and balance of the car (fuel load, passengers and cargo, etc.), suspension settings, and the stock tires. Changing any brake/tire/suspension component from stock changes how the brakes behave.

For example, a big brake kit on the front increases braking at the front tire, but this bias and weight shift doesn't let you take advantage of unrealized grip at the rear tires. This could result in longer stopping distances. All good brake kits increase braking torque without negatively affecting the bias. Good brake kits should be close to the stock pedal travel and be matched to the brake master cylinder.

Does this mean that big brake kits are a scam? Absolutely not! Every Challenger, Charger, 300, and Magnum has different limiting factors in braking. If you do nothing other than add a big brake kit you might shorten braking distances if the brakes were the limiting factor. Stickier tires, suspension changes, adjustments in the weight and

SUSPENSION, BRAKES AND CHASSIS

balance of the car, all change the behavior of the braking setup. Some cars have smaller rotors with undersized thermal capacity. As a car ages, or as you add upgraded parts, thus changing the factory setup, you might be able to take advantage of a big brake kit.

A big brake kit has greater rotor and pad mass to absorb the additional heat created by braking; it also has pad compounds that can handle high heat. Driver braking technique is also at play here.

So, would your car benefit from a big brake kit? It varies by car model, individual car setup, and your intended use, so the correct answer is, "It depends."

Before investing in a big brake upgrade kit or individual big brake parts, you must also be certain that your current wheel size is compatible with the kit. The kit or upgraded, upsized rotor in question usually indicates on its packaging the minimum wheel diameter that accepts the larger brake kit. The wheel size refers to the diameter of the rim only, not the diameter of the rim and tire combined.

If you're new to working on brakes, you may be wondering, "Can I do this myself?" The short answer is yes, with the proper tools.

Performance Brake Kits

Upgrading to a big brake kit has many benefits. However, if you increase acceleration and top speed, you need to improve brake performance so you maintain control under high-performance applications. The manufacturers engineer the kits to provide a higher performance brake experience for racing and performance street machines.

One of the first things you notice after installing an aftermarket brake kit is a decrease in the stopping distance. This is because there is a greater area of pad contact, allowing for better brake control. The calipers are usually a bridge design that allows for greater stopping control and decreased wear on your pads.

The wider pad area also allows for a broader range of stopping control because of the larger contact surface. Not only are the kits designed for optimal pad contact, but also greater heat disbursement and heat regulation. In essence, you gain stopping power and reduce the wear and tear on the brake pads themselves. The larger surface area is designed to ventilate heat away from the brake assembly as much as possible, extending the life of your pads. You want to ensure that when upgrading either the front or rear brakes, the brakes are properly calibrated to avoid unbalanced brake pressure on your vehicle.

It is really difficult to pick one brake kit over another; they all have features and benefits that are specifically tailored for certain driving situations. For instance, choosing a braking system designed for a race car might seem like a good option, but in actuality, that brake system can't survive the rigors of daily street driving. Brakes for racing are designed for very hard, very short-duration

Stop Tech's kits are available in different performance levels. The installation of a complete braking system is very involved and should only be done by an experienced mechanic. The installation can typically be done in a day. The retail price starts at about $2,900. (Photo Courtesy Stop Tech Brakes)

CHAPTER 6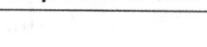

application. If you try to apply them to normal driving conditions (which is typically a steady pressure for longer periods), they fail.

If you want to upgrade to a larger rotor diameter you again need to decide what your driving conditions will be. You also need to know what size wheel is on your car. You have no reason to order a big brake kit if it will not fit inside the wheel that is on your car. Most big brake upgrade kits come with rotors that range from 12½ inches to 14¼ inches in diameter. That might not seem very large, but remember, the caliper is mounted outside the rotor and adds to the diameter at that location.

Let's say that you think you want a 14-inch rotor. In this instance, you would need a wheel with a diameter that is no smaller than 18 inches. Unfortunately, some stock wheels can be as small as 17 inches in diameter.

Many companies offer brake kits for Hemi-powered cars. The following are the most popular among Hemi car owners.

Stop Tech Brakes

Stop Tech brake kits are sold through dealers and distributors. Although their focus is on performance braking, just about all street cars can benefit from their braking knowledge. Their kits are available with a variety of performance-level options, and deciding on a kit is as easy as talking to an authorized dealer.

Wilwood Engineering

Wilwood offers big brake kits for the front and rear of your Challenger, Charger, 300C, or Magnum. It also offers a rear kit that replaces the factory disc brakes and uses the OEM parking brake assembly. High-capacity braking calipers, pads, and oversized rotors are matched to the OEM master cylinder output, ABS function, and individual vehicle bias requirements.

The enhanced brake performance, increased durability, and high-tech style complement big wheel, tire, and suspension upgrades on customized vehicles. If replacing the front and rear brakes, the job can be a little involved and use up most of a day, but can be accomplished with simple hand tools.

Hawk Performance

Hawk has simplified the process of upgrading your brakes to dramatically improve vehicle stopping distance without upgrading to expensive specialty calipers. A vehicle-specific, matched brake pad and rotor kit that comes in one box is now available. Cast from a proprietary formulation of premium alloys, their performance street rotor features a unique slot design specifically engineered to improve vehicle braking performance and driver comfort.

Quiet Slot rotors combine the look, feel, and durability of a performance rotor with the fitment and convenience of OEM design. This is a basic kit that can be installed in the driveway in a couple of hours with simple hand tools.

Performance Brake Pads

It's no secret that you want your vehicle's brake system to have smooth, repeatable braking under a wide range of temperature and road conditions. But who likes to constantly clean brake dust from their car's wheels?

First used as original equipment in 1985, ceramic friction materials have become recognized for their desirable blend of traits. Their composition allows the ceramic pads to handle high brake temperatures with less brake fade, and generate less dust and wear on both the pads and rotors. Ceramic compounds also provide quieter braking because they are able to dampen noise by generating a resonance frequency beyond the range of human hearing.

Another thing that makes ceramic materials a good choice is

Wilwood's rear brakes feature calipers, pads, and rotors that are designed to work seamlessly with the rest of the OEM braking system. They help increase braking performance, and the oversized rotors help fill larger-diameter aftermarket wheel applications. If replacing the front and rear brakes, the job can be a little involved and use up most of a day, but can be accomplished with simple hand tools by an experienced mechanic. The retail price starts at about $1,700. (Photo Courtesy Wilwood Engineering)

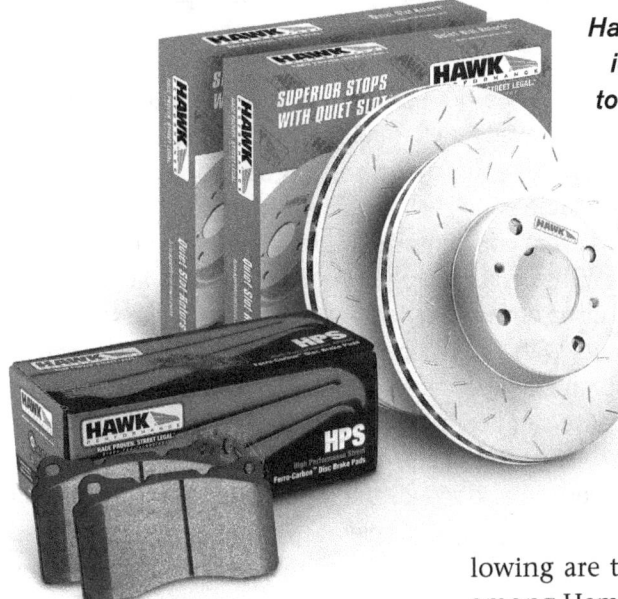

Hawk Performance offers a kit for upgrading your brakes to dramatically improve your vehicle's stopping capability without upgrading to expensive specialty calipers. The vehicle-specific, matched brake pad and rotor kit comes in one box. The performance drilled and slotted rotors combine the look, feel, and durability of a true performance rotor with the fitment and convenience of OEM design. The kit is also available with your choice of organic or ceramic pads. The retail price is about $370. (Photo Courtesy Hawk Performance)

the lack of brake dust. Although all brake pads produce dust as they wear, ceramic compounds produce a light-colored dust that is much less noticeable. Consequently, wheels and tires look cleaner longer.

Ceramic pads extend brake life more than most other semi-metallic and organic materials, and outlast other premium pad materials. Also, the cost of ceramic brake pads is just slightly higher than conventional premium pads.

Many companies offer brake pads for Hemi-powered cars. The following are two of the most popular among Hemi car owners.

Hawk Performance

Hawk's High Performance Street (HPS) disc-brake pads are renowned for increasing stopping power. The unique Ferro-Carbon formula was developed specifically for street performance, using aerospace and motorsports severe-duty friction technology.

The Hawk compound offers a higher coefficient of friction over stock brake pads, and can provide 20- to 40-percent more stopping power and a higher resistance to brake fade than most standard replacement pads. All Hawk HSP brake pads come with a limited lifetime warranty.

In addition to their HPS series of pads, they have a myriad of brake pads with different pad constructions to suit vehicles ranging from the everyday driver to an all-out race car.

Performance Friction

Performance Friction feels that the first step when upgrading brakes is to upgrade the brake pads from the organic or semi-metallic original equipment materials to a carbon metallic pad. These pads feature a material that doesn't compress when pressure is applied. They also have an improved initial bite and they typically reduce pedal travel by nearly 1/2 inch.

Performance Friction's street pads are made using the same process and technology as its race pads. The carbon metallic material delivers more stopping power than any other brake pad, and the unique friction material outperforms ceramic and semi-metallic pads with less noise and vibration. These are not run-of-the-mill brake pads.

Hawk Performance offers a brake pad that is a true upgrade from factory. Their HPS pads offer greater braking capability and a higher resistance to brake fade. If you are looking for a simple but effective way to shorten your stopping distance, this is it. The retail price starts at about $85. (Photo Courtesy Hawk Performance)

CHAPTER 6

Suspension Angles

The suspension angles that need to be considered and adjusted when aligning your car are camber, caster, toe, and thrust angle.

Camber

A suspension carries negative camber when the top of the tire tilts inward toward the center of the vehicle. Positive camber is when the top leans away from the center of the vehicle. Because a typical street suspension cannot completely compensate for the outer tire tipping outward when the vehicle leans in a corner, there is no magical, universal camber setting that allows a car's tires to remain vertical when traveling straight down the road and remain perpendicular to the road while cornering.

Driving styles can also influence camber angle. An enthusiastic driver who corners faster than a conservative driver gains more grip in a corner and longer tire life from a car that is aligned with more negative camber. However, with the aggressive negative camber, a reserved driver's lower cornering speeds cause the inside edges of the tires to wear faster than the outside edges.

What's the downside to negative camber? It leans both tires on a given axle toward the center of the vehicle. Each tire develops an equal and offsetting "camber thrust" force. This is the same principle that causes a motorcycle to turn when it leans even though the rider doesn't turn the handlebar.

With a high degree of negative camber, even when the vehicle is driven straight ahead, both tires try to steer the car inward. With a high negative camber, if the vehicle encounters a bump that only causes one tire to lose grip, the other tire's negative camber angle pushes the vehicle toward the side of the car that lost grip. On the rear of an LX/LC car, excessive camber can also reduce the available straight-line grip that is needed during rapid acceleration and sudden stops.

For street-driven vehicles, tire wear and handling requirements must be balanced to suit the driver's needs. The goal is to use just enough negative camber to provide good cornering performance while not having the load of the car wear on the inner edge of the tire when traveling in a straight line. Less negative camber reduces the car's cornering ability but results in more even, and slower tire wear.

If having a small amount of negative camber is good for a street car, what is good for performance driving? This is very subjective, and you need to be really honest with what you are trying to do. On a performance street car, I would start with the factory specifications. For autocross, track-day, and road-race cars, you can be a little more aggressive with camber, typically increasing by 1 degree. For a production road-race car or purpose-built autocross car, plus 2 degrees is acceptable.

If you align your car and add negative camber in an attempt to gain the maximum amount of grip when cornering, you experience premature tire wear during daily driving situations. As a rule, do not set the camber at more than 1 degree beyond the end of factory

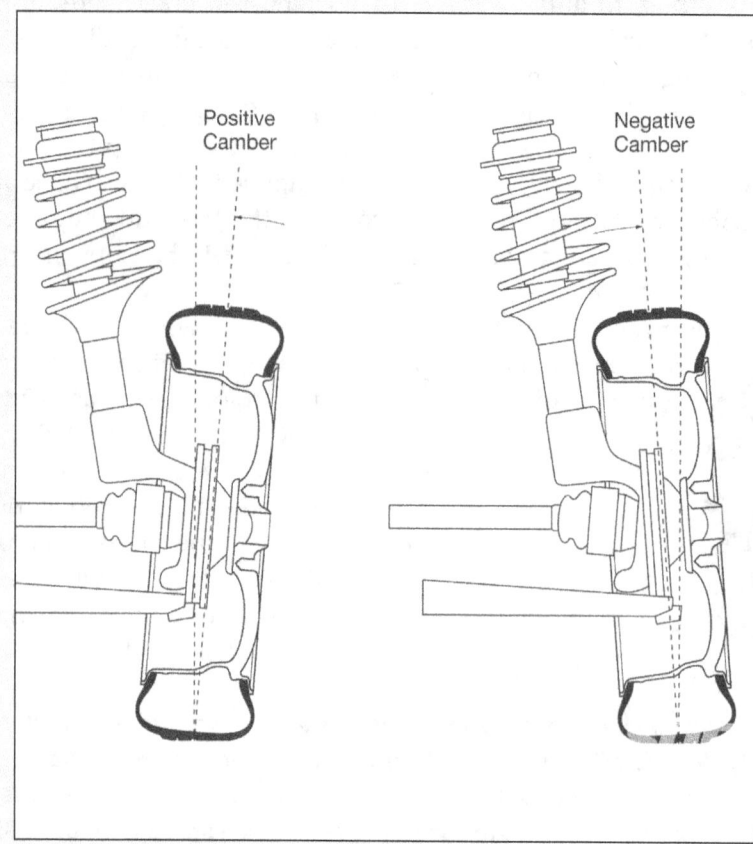

Camber angle is the difference between the wheels' vertical alignment, perpendicular to the road surface, as measured in degrees. If a wheel is perfectly perpendicular to the surface, its camber is zero degrees. Camber is described as negative when the top of the tire tilts inward toward the engine. If the top of the tire tilts away from the vehicle, you have positive camber. (Photo Courtesy Sean Gilchrest)

SUSPENSION, BRAKES AND CHASSIS

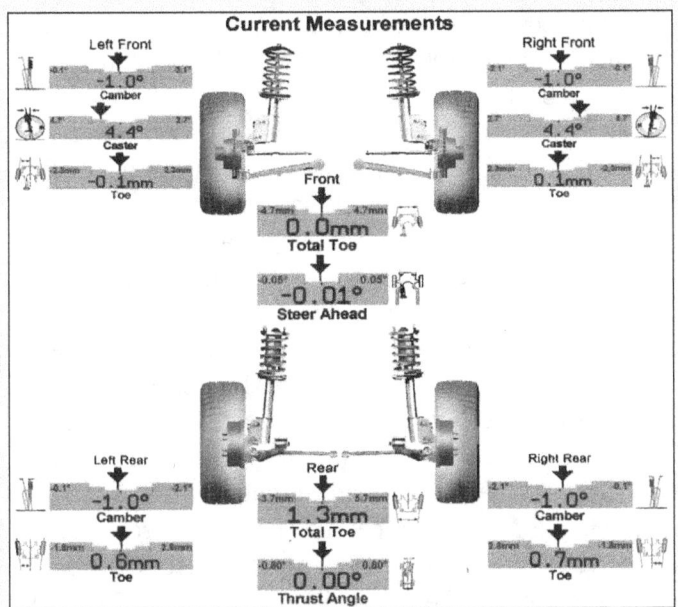

When you have the alignment on your car adjusted at the alignment shop, a technician typically provides a print out of the before and after specifications. When the alignment is within specification, all measurements should be shown in green.

specification. You might come across an example of someone running more than that. However, under normal driving conditions, the tires wear excessively fast and the contact patch is reduced when driving in a straight line. Hence, the more the negative setting, the less contact patch available for braking.

Caster

The pivot points on an LX/LC car are the upper and lower ball joints. Caster is expressed in degrees and measured by drawing an imaginary line running through the steering system's upper and lower pivot points (the upper and lower ball joints). Caster is positive if the top of the line is tilted toward the rear of the vehicle, and negative if the line tilts toward the front. A proper caster angle allows the vehicle to balance steering effort and provides high-speed stability and cornering effectiveness.

Increasing the amount of positive caster increases steering effort and the car's straight-line tracking ability, but also improves high-speed stability and cornering effectiveness. Positive caster also increases tire lean when cornering (such as having more negative camber) as the steering angle is increased.

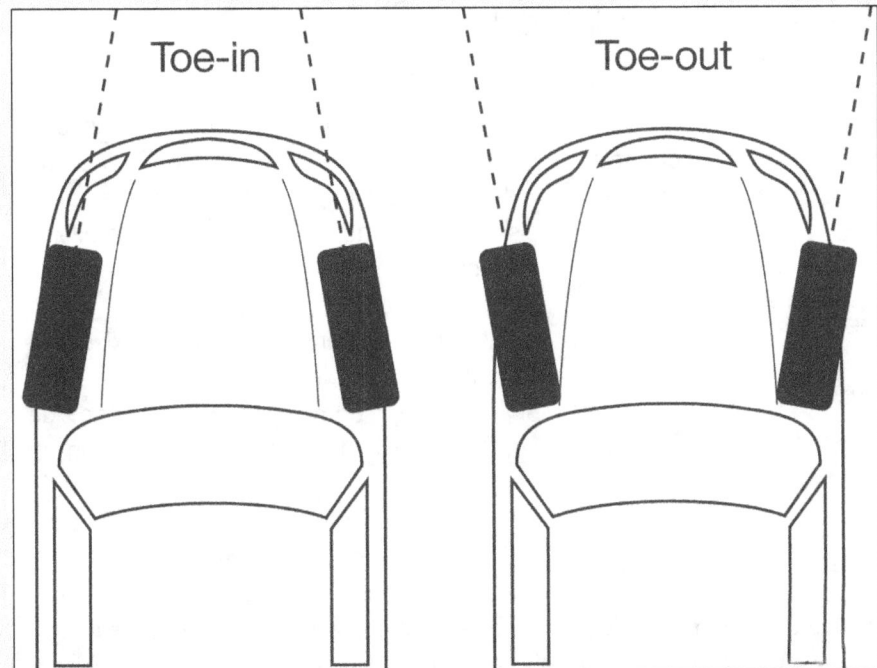

When the front wheels on a car are set so that their leading edges are pointed slightly toward each other (inward), the car is said to have toe-in. If the leading edges point away from each other, that is toe-out. The amount of toe can be expressed in degrees as the angle to which the wheels are out of parallel. Toe settings affect three major areas of performance: tire wear, straight-line stability, and corner entry handling characteristics. For minimum tire wear and power loss, the wheels on a given axle of a car should point directly ahead when the car is running in a straight line. Excessive toe-in or toe-out causes the tires to scrub, since they are always turned relative to the direction of travel. Too much toe-in causes accelerated wear at the outboard edges of the tires, whereas too much toe-out causes wear at the inboard edges. All cars are given a small amount of toe-in during alignment. This is because the force of the engine pushing the car forward causes the suspension to react in the opposite direction, causing the wheels to, in effect, straighten. (Photo Courtesy Sean Gilchrest)

DODGE CHALLENGER AND CHARGER: HOW TO BUILD AND MODIFY

Suspension Angles CONTINUED

Cross-Camber and Cross-Caster

Most alignments for street cars call for the front camber and caster settings to be slightly different between the passenger's side of the vehicle and the driver's side. These slight side-to-side differences are called cross-camber and cross-caster.

For vehicles set up to drive on the right side of the road, the driver's side of the car is given more negative camber (about 1/4 degree) and positive caster (again, about 1/4 degree) to help resist the influence of crowned roads that would cause it to drift downhill to the right shoulder. Because most roads are crowned, cross-camber and cross-caster are helpful for the majority of the time; however, they cause a vehicle to drift to the left on a perfectly flat road or a road that leans to the left.

Toe

The toe angle identifies the direction that the tires are pointing, as compared to the centerline of the vehicle when viewed from above. Toe is expressed in degrees or fractions of an inch. A car is positioned toe-in when imaginary lines running through the center of the tires intersect in front of the car, and toe-out when they face away from each other. The toe setting is used to help compensate for the suspension bushings flexibility (compliance), to reduce tire wear. Toe can also be used to adjust vehicle handling.

The rolling resistance of a tire causes a small amount of drag (friction) that results in a rearward force of the suspension arms against their bushings. Most rear-wheel-drive cars use some positive toe-in to compensate for this, enabling the tires to run parallel with one another at speed when the force is present.

Increased toe-in typically results in reduced oversteer, helps steady the car, and enhances high-speed stability. Increased toe-out typically results in reduced understeer and loosening-up the car, especially during initial turn-in at corners.

Before adjusting the toe outside the manufacturer's recommended settings to manipulate handling, be aware that toe settings influence wet-weather handling and tire wear as well.

Excessive toe settings bring drivability issues, especially when driving in heavy rain and on wet roads. This is because many highways have ruts that fill with water. Because excessive toe points each tire inward or outward, when the car encounters a puddle that causes one tire to lose grip, the other tire's toe setting pushes (excessive toe-in) or pulls (excessive toe-out) the car to the opposite side. This may make the vehicle feel unsettled and very nervous.

The car's toe setting is one of the most critical alignment settings relative to tire wear. A toe setting that is a little off can make a huge difference in tire wear. For instance, if the toe setting is just 1/16-inch off, each tire on that axle scrubs almost 7 feet sideways for every mile of travel. Incorrect toe robs you of tire life.

Thrust Angle

The thrust angle is an imaginary line drawn perpendicular to the rear axle's centerline. It compares the direction that the rear axle is aimed with the centerline of the car. It also confirms whether the rear axle is parallel to the front axle, and that the wheelbase on both sides of the car is the same.

A vehicle with independent rear axles may have incorrect toe-in or toe-out on both sides of the rear axle, or may have toe-in on one side and toe-out on the other. The suspension on each side of the vehicle must be adjusted individually until it has reached the appropriate toe setting for each side of the vehicle.

An incorrect thrust angle is often caused by an out-of-position axle or incorrect toe settings. So in addition to the handling quirks that are the result of incorrect toe settings, thrust angles can also cause the vehicle to handle differently when turning one direction or the other. ■

Alignment thrust angle is an imaginary line drawn through the car's centerline. It indicates the direction of the rear axle with regard to the centerline of the vehicle. It confirms whether the rear axle is parallel to the car's front wheels, and that the wheelbase on both sides of the vehicle measures the same.

SUSPENSION, BRAKES AND CHASSIS

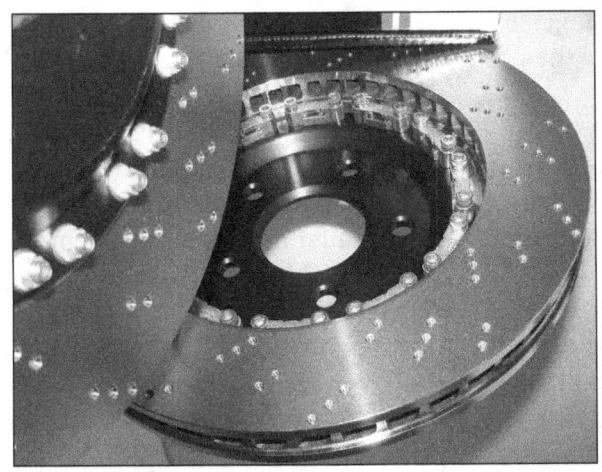

Performance Friction offers true high-performance one- or two-piece rotors for your Charger, Challenger, Magnum, or 300. Although your Hemi car came from the factory with a one-piece rotor, two-piece performance rotors offer substantial weight savings; as much as 10 pounds per rotor, depending on the specific application. The two-piece design allows the outer friction-ring to expand as it gets heated, without being constrained by the center section. This prevents rotor "coning" and subsequent tapered pad-wear and a spongy pedal feel. Because the center section and friction ring are fabricated from dissimilar materials, conductive heat transfer is reduced, lowering wheel bearing temperatures dramatically. Outer friction rings may be replaced when worn, while reusing the center hat, at substantial cost savings.

Wheel Alignment

Tires are an important part of your car. Can you travel anywhere without them? One aspect that I haven't covered yet that has a huge effect on performance and a tire's lifespan is wheel alignment. Improperly aligned wheels put extra stress on tires, and greatly increase the rate at which the tires wear out. As you drive down the road, the area of contact between the pavement and the tires produces friction. This friction puts a strain on the car's engine. If your car has improperly aligned wheels, it experiences an increase in friction, hurting performance and ultimately wearing tires prematurely. This extra friction also negatively impacts a car's gas mileage.

Although it's often referred to simply as a wheel alignment, the process of "aligning your wheels" is really a complex measurement of suspension angles with a variety of suspension components being adjusted.

An out-of-alignment condition can occur when a car's suspension and/or steering system isn't operating at the proper suspension angles. Worn parts (ball joints, bushings, etc.) often cause an out-of-alignment. It can also be caused by hitting a pothole or curb, or changing the car's ride height.

Three different types of alignments are possible: front-end, thrust angle, and four-wheel. During a front-end alignment, only the front wheels' angles are checked and adjusted. Front-end alignments are fine for some vehicles, especially those with a solid rear axle, but cars such as an LX/LC should never receive a front-end alignment only.

Cars with four-wheel independent suspensions (such as an LX/LC car) must get a four-wheel alignment. This procedure squares the car and includes measuring and adjusting the rear axle angles as well as the front. Not all cars are easily adjustable. Some require aftermarket kits to allow sufficient adjustment to compensate for accident damage or the change in alignment because of the installation of lowering springs. Such is the case with LX/LC cars. If the rear needs to be

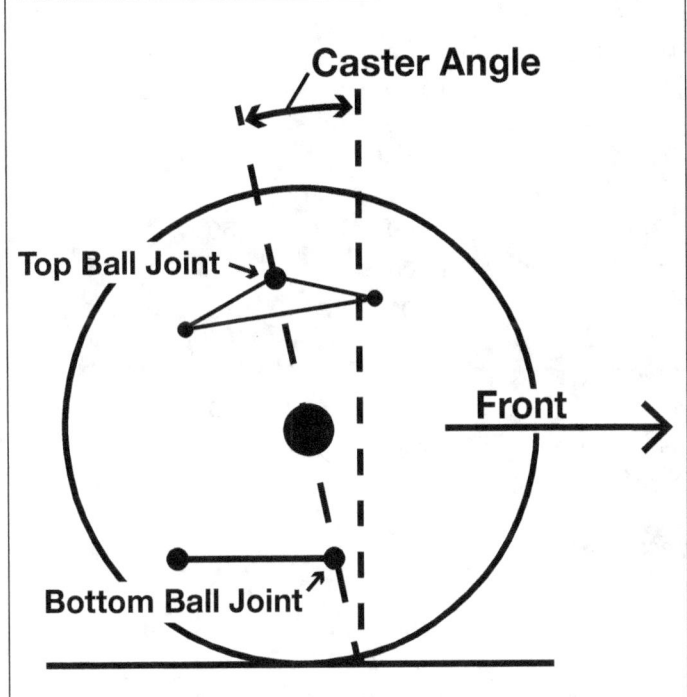

A main consideration when working on your suspension is to maintain proper wheel alignment when the installation of any aftermarket or replacement parts is accomplished. Proper wheel alignment is fundamental to making sure that your car's safety and its tire's tread life are held to an acceptable level.

adjusted, either offset bushings or aftermarket adjustable control arms must be added.

When aligning a vehicle that is used for autocross or track events, some racers sit in their car so that the driver's weight is in effect on the suspension angles.

Alignment Ranges

The car manufacturer's alignment specifications identify the preferred angle for camber, caster, and toe (with the preferred thrust angle always being zero). The manufacturer also provides an acceptable minimum and maximum angle for each specification. The minimum and maximum camber and caster specifications result in a range that remains within ±1 degree of the preferred angle.

If the alignment of your car can't be adjusted to within the acceptable range, replacing bent parts or an aftermarket alignment kit might be required. Fortunately, a kit is available for almost every popular vehicle thanks to the needs of body and frame shops doing crash repairs and driving enthusiasts tuning the suspensions on their cars.

If you are planning on driving hard through the corners and on freeway ramps, a performance alignment might be appropriate for your car. A performance alignment consists of using the car manufacturer's range of alignment specifications to maximize the tires' performance. A performance alignment calls for maximum negative camber, maximum positive caster, and the preferred toe settings. These alignment settings maximize performance while remaining within the vehicle manufacturer's recommendations.

If you are a competition driver who frequently runs autocross or road race events, you typically want the maximum negative camber, maximum positive caster, and the most aggressive toe settings available. If the rules permit, aftermarket camber plates and caster adjustments are good investments.

Alignment Parameters

Below are some alignment settings that could be used as a starting point to give you a ballpark setting for some general driving conditions. All of these specifications are listed in degrees.

Specification	Front	Rear
Original Equipment		
Camber	.75	.75
Caster	10.00	
Toe	.02	.10
Full Road Race		
Camber	1.00	1.50
Caster	11.00	
Toe	.02	.10
Drag Race		
Camber	.50	.50
Caster	10.00	
Toe	.02	.10
Aggressive Street		
Camber	.75	1.00
Caster	10.00	
Toe	.02	.10

SOURCE GUIDE

Advanced Flow Engineering
951-493-7100
afepower.com

Aermotive
913-647-7300
aeromotiveinc.com

Airaid
800-498-6951
airaid.com

Arrington Performance
866-844-1245
shopHemi.com

ATI Performance Products
877-298-5039
atiracing.com

BBK Performance
951-296-1771
bbkperformance.com

Baer Brakes
602-233-1411
baer.com

Callies Performance Products
419-435-2711
callies.com

Comp Cams
compcams.com

Competition Cams
800-999-0853
pcams.com

Competition Engineering
203-453-6571
competitionengineering.com

Compstar Performance Products
419-435-2711
callies.com

Corsa Performance
440-891-0999
corsaperformance.com

Crane Cams
866-388-5120
cranecams.com

DiabloSport
561-908-0040
diablosport.com

Diamond Racing
877-552-2112
diamondracing.net

Dynomax Performance Exhaust
734-384-7807
dynomax.com

Eagle Specialty Products
662-796-7373
eaglerod.com

Eibach Springs
800-507-2338
eibach.com

Edelbrock
310-781-2222
edelbrock.com

Energy Suspension
888-913-6374
energysuspension.com

Flowmaster
800-544-4761
flowmastermufflers.com

Harland Sharp
440-238-3260
harlandsharp.com

Hawk Performance
800-542-0972
hawkperformance.com

Hotchkis Sport Suspension
877-466-7655
hotchkis.net

HP Tuners
hptuners.com

Hurst
707-544-4761
hurst-shifters.com

Indy Cylinder Head
317-862-0224
317-862-3724
Indyheads.com

JBA Performance Exhaust
909-599-5955
jbaheaders.com

Just Suspension
800-872-1548
justsuspension.com

DODGE CHALLENGER AND CHARGER: HOW TO BUILD AND MODIFY

SOURCE GUIDE

K1 Technologies
440-497-3100
K1Technologies.com

K&N Engineering
800-858-3333
knfilters.com

Kenne Bell
909-941-6646
kennebell.net

Kook's Custom Headers
866-586-KOOK
kooksheaders.com

Legmaker Intakes
888-773-5649
speedlogixstore.com

Livernois Motorsports
313-561-5500
livernoismotorsports.com

Magnaflow Performance
800-959-9226
Magnaflow.com

Mahle Clevite
mahleclevite.com

Manley Performance Products
800-526-1362
manleyperformance.com

Milodon
805-577-5950
milodon.com

Modern Muscle Performance Group
276-663-1555
modernmuscleperformance.com

Molnar Technologies
616-940-4640
molnartechnologies.com

Mopar
mopar.com

MV Performance
770-725-7862

Nitrous Outlet
866-648-7637
nitrousoutlet.com

Nitrous Oxide Systems
714-546-0592
nosnitrous.com

Pedders Suspension
pedders.com.au

Performance Distributors
901-396-5782
performancedistributors.com

Performance Friction
800-521-8874
pfcbrakes.com

Petty's Garage
336-495-6653
pettysgarage.com

Procharger
913-338-2886
procharger.com

Ram Clutches
803-788-6034
ramclutches.com

Razor's Edge Motorsports
954-788-2348
razorsedgemotorsports.com

RPM Rollbars
877-201-8910
rpmrollbar.com

SCT Performance
407-774-2447
sctflash.com

ShopHemi.com
866-844-1245
shopHemi.com

SLP Performance
855-757-7373
slponline.com

Stack Performance
stackperformance.com

Strange Engineering
847-663-1701
strangeengineering.net

Stop Tech Brakes
310-933-1150
stoptech.com

Tube Technologies Inc.
951-371-4878
ttiexhaust.com

Wilwood Engineering
805-388-1188
wilwood.com

Wiseco Performance Products
800-321-1364
wiseco.com

Vortech Engineering
805-247-0226
vortechsuperchargers.com

Zex
888-817-1008
zex.com

www.ingramcontent.com/pod-product-compliance
Lightning Source LLC
Chambersburg PA
CBHW081446070526
44586CB00019B/2257